Postmodernism and Gandhi

Postmodernism and Gandhi

Upasana Pandey

RAWAT PUBLICATIONS
Jaipur • New Delhi • Bangalore • Hyderabad • Guwahati

ISBN 81-316-0372-5

Published by
Prem Rawat for **Rawat Publications**
Satyam Apts, Sector 3, Jawahar Nagar, Jaipur 302 004 (India)
Phone: 0141 265 1748 / 7006 Fax: 0141 265 1748
E-mail: info@rawatbooks.com
Website: www.rawatbooks.com

New Delhi Office
4858/24, Ansari Road, Daryaganj, New Delhi 110 002
Phone: 011 2326 3290

Also at *Bangalore, Hyderabad* and *Guwahati*

Typeset by Rawat Computers, Jaipur
Printed at Chaman Enterprises, New Delhi

To
didi...
Aradhana Pandey

Contents

Preface

The concept of 'postmodernism' emerged during 1970s and reached at its peak in the eighties and nineties. It has influenced almost every aspect of our thought and methodology. As the word itself indicates, postmodernism is the aftermath development of modernity, a reaction as well as a reconstruction. Postmodernity challenged all the basic premises of modernism. In fact, the essence of modernism lies in a rational transformation of social, economic and political order of a society. While the rational transformation of social order implies a movement in the direction of a rational scrutiny of traditional practices, the rational transformation of economic order involves technological advancement. Similarly, rational transformation of political order signifies continual diffusion of political power to wider groups of society and ultimately to the people in general. It means modernity stands for rationalism, i.e., rational enquiry of beliefs or practices – both past and present. However, postmodernists argue that rationality paves the way for a very limited understanding – most of our learning is through experiences and experiences are more related to our emotions. They claim that things must come from the mind.

Modernity stands for universalism, or uniformity of action also, which means to link the whole society with the commitment to rule of evidences. On the contrary, postmodernists say that there cannot be any universality as all knowledge is culture-specific and context-specific. Universal and ethical truths, if they exist at all, cannot be specified. Any conclusion arrived at on the basis of blind universals, would completely misunderstand the relevance of others' life world and their mode of living. Further, any claim to essentiality is a denial of all our indigenous and local knowledge within which the people of the developing nations operate and survive.

This is the reason that all the postmodernist thinkers assert some kind of particularity in their assertions. For example, David Harvey talks about spiritual and moral basis of action, Jacques Derrida puts emphasis on deconstruction, Michel Foucault talks about madness of civilization and fragmentation of power and Kenneth Thompson of cultural pluralism. In the similar way, Jean-Francois Lyotard presents his Theory of Language Game. All of them with one voice have suggested that it is impossible to develop any meta-narrative, meta-theory and meta-language.

Since Gandhi also presented his critique of modernity in his own way, many thinkers treat him as a postmodernist thinker. In order to determine whether Gandhi is a postmodernist or not, one will have to examine and review all of his thoughts thoroughly. The present book is being brought out to fulfil this objective.

The first chapter aims at defining modernism and postmodernism, both the context and the content. It also discusses the consequences as well as divergence. For this purpose the chapter is divided into two parts. While the first part discusses modernism – its origin, meaning, definitions and characteristics, and its critical evaluation, in the second part a full-length discussion is presented about postmodernism – its origin, meaning, definitions, and characteristics, and its critical evaluation.

The Gandhian philosophy comes only in the second chapter. It aims at discussing Gandhi's critique of modernism. According to Gandhi, modern civilization was grounded in a fatally flowed theory of man: how, unlike ancient civilization, which was soul- and spirit-centred, the modern civilization was body-centred and in that sense 'materialistic', and how such a flawed theory was the ontological basis of the human sense of particularity. Hence, Gandhi concluded that modern man had neither the inclination nor the ability to slow down the tempo of his life, relax, compose himself, reflect on his pattern of life and nurture the inner springs of energy. He lived outside himself and exhausted himself physically and spiritually.

In the third chapter an attempt has been made to highlight contemporary debate on Gandhian philosophy as premodern, modern and postmodern. Those who have treated him as premodernist claim so because he has rejected science, technology and mechanistic cosmology. Some treat him as a modernist because he considers individual as one of the supreme considerations and exhorts that "if individual ceases to count, what is left of society". They argue that this was the fundamental belief of Gandhi, which he held with other political thinkers of Enlightenment. Ronald J. Terchek, along with Thomas Pantham, Dannis Dalton, Richard B. Gregg and Manmohan Choudhary, claims that complete moral autonomy, even if it means civil disobedience, was Gandhi's goal and, if this is so, then, he is fully a modernist thinker.

There are also others who treat Gandhi as a postmodernist because he believed in a decentralized political and economic order with village communities at the centre. For example, Susanne and Lloyd Rudolph find the postmodern Gandhi in the contesting discourse of the counter-culture voices against modernism that he found in Tolstoy, Ruskin and Thoreau. According to Rudolphs, the use of 'contesting discourse' allowed Gandhi to give truth a 'contextual and experimental form'.

This debate can only be solved when we analyse Gandhi's own views and discuss them threadbare. Thus, the fourth chapter aims at analysing the fundamental values of Gandhian thoughts – the values on which his whole socio-political philosophy rested. The chapter is divided into two parts. Part I discusses at length how far Gandhi's truth is the ultimate reality and in the absolute sense God; how he did not indulge in any metaphysical speculation like a theologian; how he simply claimed what your soul says is truth; and how he maintained that it can be realized only through trial and error.

To attain the truth, *ahimsa* (non-violence) is the only means, according to Gandhi. Non-violence not only implies the absence to violence but in its positive sense it also connotes active or pure love. Non-violence is the law of species as violence is the law of brutes. Thus, for Gandhi, non-violence is not an individual virtue but a course of spiritual and political conduct – both for individual and for the community. To understand the real or ultimate meaning of the term 'non-violence', it is essential to know the basic characteristics of a *Satyagrahi*. Thus, this part also deals with the qualities of a *Satyagrahi*.

Part II of the chapter discusses the new world order, which makes Gandhi's philosophy a unique one. Different aspects of Gandhian philosophy, like his views on politics, economy, religion, education and the status of women, are discussed here at length.

The last chapter is a critical evaluation of findings. It establishes that the Gandhian philosophy cannot be exactly labelled as premodern, modern or postmodern. In fact, Gandhi was looking for a comprehensive and balanced approach. To define a society with its single determinants would be a partial attempt. In ancient times we tried to do so with the help of religion; in modern era we did the same exercise with the help of reason and now in this postmodern era we are doing it with the help of language discourses. However, a balanced and comprehensive approach is yet to be explored. It is possible if religion, reason and morality all will lay their active, vibrant and comprehensive role in their own sphere of action. A unique blend of both these philosophies, i.e., postmodernism and Gandhi, may pave the way for a new horizon.

I hope the work will develop interest and inquisitiveness among its readers and will compel Gandhian scholars to re-read Gandhi's philosophy to fulfil expectations of the contemporary world-order. A fresh look into a discipline is always required as it helps to satisfy anxiety of new generations into the subject.

July 28, 2010

Upasana Pandey
Rajghat, Varanasi

1

Defining Modernism and Postmodernism

By nature man is a thinking being. Everyday he creates a new thought and try to build a social set-up accordingly. To criticize the old thought and to propound a new one, conducive to the present world order, has been an in-built nature of a man's personality. It is this aspect of his personality which has resulted in the development of new ideologies and consequently a new era. Modernism and postmodernism may be cited here as a result of man's curious nature.

In fact, modernism is a revolutionary change, which implies a process of rational reorganization of society, without any regard for tradition being irrational or non-rational. Tradition connotes routine acceptance of a body of beliefs and action patterns from the past just out of sheer reverence for the wisdom of the past. The constituents of tradition are givenness, a past, recurrence, filiations and uncritical acceptance. More important than anything else to a traditional society is its proclivity to accept the heritage from the past without critical scrutiny, almost in a deferential spirit. As against this, a modern society is characterized by a "disquiet positivist spirit" – a spirit of rational scrutiny of every belief, or practices – both past and present. In this sense, while tradition is a mode of uncritical acceptance of the past, modernity is a mode of rational scrutiny and restructuring.

Therefore, modernization connotes a change from traditional to modern societies which are characterized by the predominance of such non-traditional values as secularity, universalism, role specificity and individuality. It is such a reason-based scientific society where there is no regard for the non-rational or uncritical acceptance of the traditional norms and values. It is a society which is created and controlled by an abstract individual. In such an individualistic and rationalistic society all those traditional norms and practices have been rejected which are not aimed at enhancing and advancing individual's life. Thus, a modern society can be characterized by the features like rationalism, universalism and individualism. All these ideologies have the same objective to make individual's present physical life more progressive, conducive as well as prosperous. In short, it may be stated that modernization is a rational transformation of the social order, which is created by men for their own self.

But, the inherent curious and critical capacity of modernists was not satisfied here. Very soon there emerged a new ideology by criticizing all these basic features of modernism. If modernism had its faith in rationalism, the new philosophy, called as postmodernism, has its foundation on intuitions as well as emotions. Representatives of this new philosophy argue that reason is not the only means to know the truth. Postmodernism seems to have its faith in fragmentation, differences and discontinuity. Postmodernists criticize any notion regarding meta-languages, meta-narratives or meta-theories. There is emphasis to develop the perspective of local rather than universal, of sphere rather than depth, and of deconstruction rather than construction. They argue that defining truth only in rational context by ignoring all historical and cultural contexts is not acceptable. It would be like accepting dominance and imperialism of rationality.

Similarly, while modernism is defending universalism, postmodernism has its faith in local culture and local knowledge. Postmodernist thinkers raise their point against meta-narratives. They believe that generally it is not possible to define the whole universe within certain fixed framework; instead, a true knowledge of a subject must necessarily be local.

Further, postmodernist thinkers reject the basic notion of modernist philosophy that human being can be categorized under the category of essentialism. Accordingly, an individual's identity or a subject's nature is totally dependent on local elements and whenever there came a change in time and space, it will automatically be changed. Thus, discourses must be studied in local context.

When and how modernity was emerged? What were its basic features? What were its assumptions through which all the streams of knowledge get effected? How modernisms pave the way for postmodernism? How thinkers criticize the basic tenets of modernism to develop a new ideology of postmodernism? This chapter discusses all these points at length.

I
Modernism

Origin

Originated from the Latin word '*modernus*', modern means "of present, recent times".[1] *Encyclopedia of Social Sciences* defines the term 'modernism', as under:

> Modernism may be described as the attitude of mind which tends to subordinate the traditional to the novel and to adjust the established and customary to the exigencies of the recent and innovating.[2]

Similarly, *A Dictionary of Political Thought* says: "... the self that comes from living 'now' ... Etymologically, the term is connected with 'mode,' and hence fashion, it occurs with its modern sense."[3]

According to *International Encyclopedia of Social and Behavioral Sciences*, "the term 'modern' (Latin *modernus*) has been in use since the fifth century AD to distinguish 'new' or 'current' from the 'old' or 'antique' (Latin *antiques*), especially as a means of describing and legitimizing new institutions, new legal rules, or new scholarly assumptions".[4]

Thus, origin of the term 'modernism' show that the term 'modern' derives from the Latin *modo*, which simply means "of today" or what is current, as distinguished from earlier times.[5] Etymologically, it may be cited that 'modernism' connotes of contemporary, of recent, thought of the recent origin or of contemporary time is modern.

Meaning and Definitions

Modernity (or for that matter, modernism) is defined differently by different thinkers. Firstly, there is a group of those thinkers who define the term as an antonym to tradition. These thinkers believed that contrary to the tradition characterized by givenness, a past, recurrence and uncritical acceptance, modern society is a rational or scientific society, which is created or invented by man for his own self. Mike Featherstone, while defining the term 'modernity', says:

> Modernity is generally held to have come into being with the Renaissance and was defined in relation to Antiquity, as in the debate between the ancients and the moderns ... Modernity is contrasted to the traditional order and implies the progressive economic and administrative rationalization and differentiation of the social world processes which brought into being the modern capitalist-industrial state and which were often viewed from a distinctly anti-modern perspective.[6]

Thus, originated from the Renaissance and Reformation movements, modernity separated ancient from present. The essence of modernization thus lies in a rational transformation of the social order, which implies a movement in the direction of rational scrutiny of traditional practices. Similarly, rational transformation of the economic order involves technological advancement and rational transformation of the political order signifies continual diffusion of political power to wider groups of society and ultimately to the people in general. In fact, modernization connotes a transformation from traditional to modern societies, which are characterized by the predominance of such non-traditional values as secularity, universalism, role specificity and individuality. It is understandable that modernism is conceived as an antonym of traditionalism in the ideal-typical sense of tradition.

In the words of Edward Shills:

> ... tradition connotes routine acceptance of a body of belief and action patterns from the past just out of sheer reverence for the wisdom of past. Thus defined, the constituents of tradition are: givenness, a past, recurrence, filiations and uncritical acceptance. More important than anything else to a traditional society is its proclivity to accept the heritage from the past without critical scrutiny, almost in a deferential spirit. As against this, a modern society is characterized by a 'disquiet positivist spirit', that is, a spirit of rational scrutiny of every belief or practices both past and present. Thus interpreted, modernization implies a process of rational reorganization of a society, without any regard for such aspects of tradition as are irrational or non-rational. It is in this sense of tradition as a mode of 'uncritical acceptance' of the past and modernity as a mode of 'rational scrutiny and retouching' that modernization can be defined as an antonym of traditionalism.[7]

The above statement connotes that if 'ancient' stands for uncritical following of norms and customs, 'modernity' stands for their rational evolution. According to Shills, this is the rationality which separates modernity from tradition. Hence, traditional societies are those where rules and regulations are followed because of their givenness, whereas in modern societies each and every norm is followed only through rational inspection and scrutiny.

One of the main sources of the modernists' approach to the critique of traditional society is found in their enthusiasm for science, and the notions of progress and reason for which it seemed to provide a guarantee.[8] Thus, modern society is the scientific society which is invented by man himself. Therefore, scholars have defined modern society as a industrial society. Krishna Kumar says:

> Modern society is industrial society. To modernize is to industrialize. It might be possible to give some other meaning to modernity, but to do so would be perverse and misleading. Historically, the rise of modern society is intrinsically connected to the rise of industrial society. All the features that we associated with modernity can be shown to be related to the set of changes that, no more than century's age, brought into being the industrial type of society. What this immediately suggests is that the terms industrialism and industrial society cover far more than the economic and technological components that make-up their core. Industrialism is a whole way of life. It encompasses economic, social, political and cultural changes. It is by undergoing such a comprehensive transformation through industrialization that societies become modern.[9]

The above statement defines modernity as an industrial society. Industrialization is the basic feature of a modern society because it has its impact on social, economic and political aspects of man's life. Consequently, we can see the changes in the respective fields.

> Modernity may also mean ecoism by which we mean the domination of all social life by economic activities, economic goods, economic criteria of achievement. Modern society is primarily concerned with money as a common measure and means of exchange. It pushes into the background alternative possible pre-occupations with family and kinship, which pervade early, primitive societies, or politics and welfare, which are typical for traditional agrarian societies (e.g., in the Middle Ages).[10]

It means modernity stands for the rational and scientific development which is affecting other related fields and thus an individual's life is getting affected.

Mark Solomon explains modernity as a process which converts an agrarian society into an industrial society. In his words:

> ... modernization ... is a process by which agrarian societies become wealthy industrial nations.[11]

This obviously implies a dichotomy of agrarian and industrial societies with its focus on industrialization as a generic source of modernization. In its usually accepted sense, industrialization is defined as a process by which the working population of a society increasingly gets engaged in production and service sectors of non-agricultural occupations. The acceptance of a mechanized productive system is believed to generate large-scale changes in the structure of pre-industrial societies. This belief has given rise to the 'convergence' hypothesis, which implies that all industrial societies tend to converge to an identical social system. Accordingly, modernization signifies structural change from pre-industrial to industrial society.[12]

Another school of thinkers believes that modernity is a triumph of the individual. John Naisbitt and Patrica Aburdence belong to this category. They define modernity in the following manner:

> ... triumph of the individual as the central among the 'mega trends' characterizing the modern epoch. They mean by that the final ascendancy of the human individual – instead of community, tribe, group, nation – to the central role in the society. As individual is emancipated from irreplaceable, imposed group bonds, free to move among social collectivities, choosing his/her membership at will, self-determined and responsible for his/her own actions, success as well as failures.[13]

In the traditional society individuals were bound to follow some irrational practices but the modern age evolved by man through his capacity to think and capacity to have control over all happenings around him. Here, emphasis is placed more and more on the present life than on the past or future. Thus, it may be said that modernity is an ideology, which gives more importance to an individual's present, rather than unrecoverable past and invisible future.

Further, structuralist thinkers define modernity as a structurally organized society. They are of the opinion that in modern society all the work is defined in a very structured manner. There is not any confusion about the duties to be performed. Each and every member of the modern society knows his area of work whereas in the ancient society a single man was responsible for all the work to be done. Hence, this school of thinkers sees modernization as a process of structural differentiation, functional specialization and higher-order integration.

According to Talcott Parsons:

> It [modernization] refers to a change from relatively undifferentiated to increasingly differentiated social forms attended by ever more complex specialization and functional interdependence. In terms of role system it envisions a shift from ascribed, functionally diffused and particularistic roles to specific achievement oriented and universal roles.[14]

As regards organizational developments, Parsons identifies the following four 'evolutionary universals' as fundamental to the structure of a modern society: bureaucratic organizations, money and markets, a universalistic legal system, and democratic association in both government and private forms. These developments, are believed to lead the "increasing generalized adaptive capacity of societies", which in turn, is regarded as a measure of modernization.

Ralf Dahrendorf, while defining modernity in the similar context, says:

> Modernity as differentiation at work place ... It is most significant in the sphere of labour, where there appear a great number of specialized, narrowly defined occupations and professions, requiring diverse skills, competences and training. But it is also pronounced in the sphere of consumption, where the staggering variety of options or 'life-chances' faces every potential consumer. Both raise tremendously the scope of choices, in education, occupational carrier and life-style.[15]

In this way, started from the economic field, modernity has its impact not only on market, commerce and business but also on society, education, culture and even family construction. A new kind of lifestyle has developed where traditional norms and practices have lost their existence or they are replaced by modern rational scientific norms, which are universal in nature. That is why, Stuart Hall, David Held and Tony McGrew define modernity as a cluster of institutions:

> Modernity can be characterized by a cluster of institutions, each with its own pattern of change and development. Among these we would include: the nation-state and an international system of states; a dynamic and expansionist capitalist economic order based on private property, industrialism, the growth of large-scale administrative and bureaucratic system of social organization and regulation; the dominance of secular, materialist, rationalist and individualist cultural values; and the formal separation of the 'private' from the 'public'.[16]

It sounds that modernization is a multifaceted process. As defined in rationalistic terms, the concept of modernization means a process of directed social change, which implies deliberation, projection and a vision of direction. The question of direction is of utmost importance to the image of the modernization. And, it is here that rationality assumes significance as a source value of modernity.

Modernization is, therefore, a double-edged concept, implying a retrospective as well as a perspective reference. Viewed in a retrospective way, it refers to a type of social change, which originated during the industrial revolution of England (1760–1830), and in the political evolution of France (1789–1794). As a perspective term, modernization denotes a process of directed change through which the Third World countries seek to catch up with the so-called modern nations. Accordingly, there are two possible connotations of modernization: one, that the term is reserved to denote the changes which some of the European nations underwent in the last few centuries under the impact of scientific, technological and political revolutions; and two, to extricate the term from its European historical moorings and apply it as an analytical tool to change rest of the world.

If there is a common feature in the various definitions of modernization, it is the explicit or implicit recognition of the centrality of rationality in the process of modernization. Along with rationality, universality and individuality entail other values, which comprise modernity. Accordingly, modernization may be defined as a process of structural transformation along with rational line and universal norms, irrespective to any reference of any model because individual is the creator as well as the controller of this modern society.

Basic Characteristics of Modernism

Rationalism

Rationalism is the fundamental feature of modernism. Rationalism means the thinking which is based on reason. Those ideologies which can be supported or rejected on the basis of reason will create generic value of modernity. In fact, "the essence of modernity ... lies in a rational transformation of the social order; it implies a movement in the direction of a rational scrutiny of traditional practices".[17]

Throughout the Middle Ages, all the branches of knowledge, viz., metaphysics, logic, ethics, politics and economics, were held together in one coherent whole through the meditation of the "queen of the sciences", Theology. In the thirteenth century, the realms of nature and grace, the knowledge yielded by natural reason and revelation, were conceived as complementary. But, in the fifteenth and the sixteenth centuries, the authority of Church, the guardian of theology, was challenged by nationalistic and intellectual forces with which it was unable to cope successfully. The massive, coherent structure raised by St. Thomas Aquinas had already been attacked within the church by men like Duns Scotus and William of Occam, and the Church itself lacked the moral authority necessary to harmonize the new intellectual forces with the old. With the repudiation of the authority of the Church and the disintegration of scholasticism, the medieval edifice of thought collapsed – the keystone of the arch, theology, discredited. This revolt against authority, which characterized the period of the Renaissance, necessitated the search for some substitute method of arriving at knowledge and the intellectual activity of the fifteenth, sixteenth and seventeenth centuries.

But if the Church and its system were repudiated, what could take its place? If man's thought and purposes were no longer to take their start from the only tradition available, where could they begin? And, the only possible answer was "with him". The biggest question of this transitionary period was, "if a man was not going to start as a member of a system, accepting that system and his own place in it, then from where he must start?" In the search of all these questions, man entered into a new age, which was called as modern age.[18]

French philosopher Rene Descartes (1596–1650) is called the "father of rationalism". With Descartes the philosophical tradition of realism, which dominated philosophical speculation from Thale to William of Occam, was first seriously challenged. For, until the fifteenth and sixteenth centuries, it was nowhere seriously disputed that knowledge is knowledge of real objects. It is not the external world of real objects which is the starting point of modern philosophical speculation but the individual mind or experience. Although there are numerous suggestions of changed perspective before Descartes, it is with Descartes that the proclamation of the autonomy of human reason becomes explicit.[19] The characteristic feature of modern philosophy is the emphasis which it places upon the individual as the ultimate source or medium of authority. Repudiating all traditional authority, modern philosophy proclaims the autonomy of human reason.[20] In fact, the essence of modernity lies in a rational transformation of the social order, which implies a movement in the direction of a rational security of traditional practices.[21]

Descartes described in his *Discourses on Method* (1931) how he determined to reject all traditional principles and doctrines and to rely solely upon his own reason to discover the truth. He writes:

> I did not wish to set about the find rejection of any single opinion which might formally have crept into my beliefs without having been introduced there by means of Reason, until I had first of all employed sufficient time in planning out the task which I had undertaken, and in seeking the true Method of arriving at a knowledge of all the things of which my mind was capable.[22]

Not a true skeptic, Descartes employed doubt as a methodological device. His "doubting", therefore, had an element of artificiality about it. He employed it as an "Archimedean fulcrum". He further elaborates:

> While we thus reject all that of which we can possibly doubt, and feign that it is false, it is easy to suppose that there is no God, nor heaven, nor bodies, and that we possess neither hands, nor indeed any body; but we cannot in the same way conceive that we who doubt these things are not; for there is a contradiction in conceiving that what thinks does not at the same time as it thinks, exist. And hence this conclusion, I think therefore I am, is the first and most certain of all that occurs to one who philosophizes in an orderly way.[23]

Descartes fundamental axiom was: "I think therefore I am". Having rejected everything except this one axiom, he then sought to erect an entire philosophy upon this one certain truth. He regarded intuition and deduction as the most certain routes to knowledge. Descartes employed three arguments for the existence of God, one of which was that God must exist to create the thinker and sustain him in his existence. He then argued that God would not deceive the thinking beings whom He had created and that as consequence there must be some real world revealed to us through our perceptions. Otherwise, our sense-perceptions would be mere illusions. But how are we to distinguish that which is an illusion from that which is real? And, Descartes declares that it is only that which can be apprehended "clearly and distinctly" which is to be regarded as real. As regards material things only extension and motion, he further argues, are clear and distinct; such qualities as colour and smell are not essential features of material things for they are not, he declares, clear and distinct. They belong not to the things themselves but are a part of the subjective experience of the person perceiving them.

Body and mind are conceived by Descartes as two separate and distinct things. The essential feature of mind is thought or consciousness, the mind is a kind of "thinking substance". The body is an "extended substance" and independent of the mind. The interconnection between body and soul which the Christian tradition emphasized is thus explicitly denied. But if the mind is independent of the body and the body of the mind, how, then, do the two manage to work together. And Descartes' only answer is that God so constituted the world that they do. God is thus brought in at the last moment to retrieve his system from collapse but without any rational explanation of how this is so. Mind is reduced to a kind of immaterial spirit and man has become, as Santayana has rather aptly expressed it, "the clumsy conjunction of automation with a ghost".

Modern philosophy has highly influenced by Descartes' conception of rationality. It can be seen in the writings of Niccolo Machiavelli (1469–1527), who is regarded as the first political philosopher of the modern age that he borrowed this rationality by Descartes and applied it to political thought. He separated politics from religion and ethics. Machiavelli writes:

> Religion has become a mere tool in the hands of the political rulers. It is not the foundation of man's social life but a powerful weapon in all political struggles. This weapon must prove its strength in action ... Religion is only good if it produces good order, and good order is generally attended with good fortune and success in any undertaking. Here the final step has been taken. Religion no longer bears any relation to a transcendent order of things and it has lost all its spiritual values. The process of secularization has come to its close, for the secular state exists not only *de facto* but also *de jure*, it has found its definite theoretical legitimization.[24]

Machiavelli discarded politics from ethics the same way as every rational scientific tool must divorce itself from ethics. The focus of attention had shifted from God to man and greater emphasis, as a consequence, was put upon temporal security than upon eternal salvation. The distinction between a 'higher' and a 'lower' world tended to be obliterated as attempts were made to explain all phenomena 'naturally'. Concerned with politics as it "is" rather than with politics as it "ought to be", Machiavelli laid the foundation for a modern political science and anticipated the attempts of the nineteenth century's positivists to found a natural science of politics. He was not as much immoral as he was non-moral. It is in this sense that *The Prince* is to be understood, i.e., as a technical treatise on the means of gaining and keeping power. Machiavelli is less concerned with the uses to which power is to be put, with the ends in the terms of which power is to be sought, than he is with the technical means of acquiring and keeping it. In *The Prince*, especially, he is concerned primarily with that which is politically expedient, the morality of the policy or action being a matter of indifference. In a chapter concerning "In What Manner Princes Should Keep Their Faith", Machaivelli writes:

> Where the very safety of the country depends upon the resolution to be taken, no consideration of justice or injustice, humanity or cruelty, nor of glory or of shame, should be allowed to prevail. But putting all other considerations aside, the only question should be, What course will save the life and liberty of the country?[25]

For a state neither religion nor ethics is required. The prince of a state is supreme and administration of a state is controlled by him only. Prince's rationality is the basis of the administration. That is why, Machiavelli demands:

> A prince then should know how to employ the nature of man, and that of the beasts as well ... It being necessary then for a prince to know well how to employ the nature of the beasts, he should be able to assume both that of fox and that of the lion; for whilst the latter cannot escape the traps laid for him, the former cannot defend himself against the wolves. A prince should be a fox, to know the traps and snares; and a lion, to be able to frighten the wolves, for those who simply hold to the nature of the lion do not understand their business.[26]

Hence, with Machiavelli, politics gets a kind of separation from all its previous metaphysical and ethical roots and the state is declared to be an autonomous entity. The implications of that autonomy did not emerge clearly until our own day but with the destruction of the natural rights theory, which for several centuries obscured the dangers latent in this autonomy, "there was no longer any great intellectual or moral power to check and counter balance Machiavellism". For Machiavelli the only values that really matter are those of greatness, power and fame. In this sense, Machiavelli is truly modern. Here are laid the foundations of *Realpolitiko* or "power politics". Such a conception is made possible only by divorcing politics from its foundation in metaphysics and ethics. Politics conceived as a self-sufficient end itself is the distinctive contribution of Machiavelli to modern political thought.

Reformists have also made their valuable contribution to the development of the modern political philosophy. Martin Luther and John Calvin can easily be cited here. "The spirituality of Church was almost lost in secular and temporal ambitions and the Church appeared to be much more concerned about the increase of its revenues that it did about the salvation of individual souls."[27] The sale of indulgences by licensed vendors and the widespread popular belief that such indulgences removed the guilt of sin were the immediate target of Luther's criticism but his reforms went much deeper. In his attack upon the veneration of relics, the adoration of images, the practice of making pilgrimages to holy places and formal, ritualistic practices there was an attempt to purge the Church of pagan, superstitious practices and to bring people back to a conception of Christian piety that such practices obscured. In an effort to emphasize the total dependence of man upon God, Luther preached the doctrine of salvation by faith alone. He thought that man by his own effort or works can never merit salvation; salvation is by the grace of God alone. Man is totally depraved. He writes:

> There are two kinds of believing, first, a believing about God which means that I believe that what is said of God is true. This faith is rather a form of knowledge than a faith. There is, secondly, a believing in God which means that I put my trust in Him, give myself up to thinking that I can have dealings with Him, and believe without any doubt that He will be and do to me according to the things said to Him. Such faith, which throws itself upon God, whether in life or in death, alone makes a Christian man.[28]

Luther was very much clear that justification is a personal experience requiring neither priesthood nor Church for its meditation. He argued that all believers are worthy to appear before God, to pray for others, to teach each other mutually the things that are of God.[29] It not only emphasized the direct responsibility of each individual for his own salvation but also the fact that through prayer and reading of scriptures the individual might have direct access to God without relying upon any intercession in his behalf by a special priesthood.

In fact, the reformers believed that if the scriptures were made available to the people in the vernacular, they could hear God speaking to them directly and personally. They seemed to believe that the scriptures were more or less self-evident in meaning and it has been said with some justification that the Protestant Reformers sought to replace an infallible Church with an infallible Book. Yet, what the Reformers were most anxious to teach was that the world of God is a personal rather than a dogmatic revelation. Too much concern with theological and philosophical problems, they believed, obscured the fact that salvation depends upon personal trust in a personal saviour.

The question still remained as to how the Scriptures were recognized, by what authority established as Scriptures? Having denied both the authority of the Church and the authority of reason, the reformers were forced into the position of claiming that the Scriptures were 'self-authenticated'. Thus, Calvin writes:

> Let it be considered, then, as an undeniable truth that they who have been inwardly taught of the Spirit feel an entire acquiescence in the Scripture, and that it is self-authenticated, carrying with its own evidence, and ought not to be made the object of demonstration and arguments from reason; but that it obtains the credit which it deserves with us by the testimony of the Spirit.[30]

Henceforth, there is no ecclesiastical, authoritative, moral law, the Church does not shoulder the responsibility for the individual; the only rule for conduct is the impulse of the individual conscience. For the first time, with the Reformation, there appeared this conception of grace that saves a man without changing him, of a justice that redeems for self-inflicted wounds but does heal them.[31]

Thus, reformers emphasized that the sacredness of every man's vocation or 'calling' pointing out that it was not by leading a life of detachment from the world that one best service to one's fellow men through the conscientious pursuits of whatever vocation God happened to call him. There is no longer any room for the conception of 'Super nature' at all; the whole idea of graded system, leading from nature up to super nature, from secular morality to that which is spiritual and supernatural had faded away. Instead, we find the notion that human nature is very depraved and that redemption consists not in perfecting nature but in restoring it to its pristine condition.

Getting influenced by these notions of reformists' movement of the medieval age, thinkers of the next generation have concentrated their studies on human nature. Thomas Hobbes, in his famous work *Leviathan* wrote sixteen chapters on human nature. He defined human nature from negative perspective. He said that whatever exists was matter and whatever changing is motion. Underlying everything is matter in motion. It was this underlying assumption upon which he sought to erect a doctrine of man and a theory of state. [32]

As an imperialist, Hobbes argues that there is no conception in man's mind, which has not at first, totally, or by parts, been begotten upon the organs of sense. The tests are derived from that original. Anticipating modern behaviouralistic psychology, he argued that it is physical stimuli 'pressing' upon our sensory organs, which give rise to material impression in some automatic fashion. All the different phenomena of sensation can ultimately be explained in terms of the fundamental laws of motion, i.e., in terms of physics or of a kind of psychology. Hobbes, in his introduction to the *Leviathan*, says:

> Nature, the art whereby God hath made and governs the world, is by the *art* of man, as in many other things, so in this also imitated, that it can make an artificial animal. For seeing life is but a motion of limbs, the beginning whereof is in some principal part within; why may we not say, that all *automata* (engines that move themselves by springs and wheels as doth a watch) have an artificial life? For what is the *heart*, but a *spring*; and the nerves, but so many strings; and *joints*, but so many *wheels*, giving motion to the whole body, such as was intended by the artificer? *Art* goes yet further, imitating that rational and most excellent work of nature, man. For by art is, created that great Leviathan, called a Commonwealth, or State, in Latin Civitas, which is but an artificial man; though of grater stature and strength than the natural, for whose protection and defense it was intended ... .[33]

It was on these naturalistic grounds that Hobbes proceeded to justify the institution of absolute monarchy instead of defending its 'divine authority'. But, his defence of absolutism did neither please the royalists, nor the opponents of absolutism. Besides, it demands for natural rights of men because, they have the mind, the reason to divide what is right or wrong. Because of this rational presence in man, he entered into a contract or agreement that resulted in the existence of state or commonwealth.

It follows from Hobbes' conception of sovereignty that the Church is and of logical necessity must be subordinate to the state. A Church, he defines, as "a company of men professing Christian religion, united in the person of one sovereign, at whose command they ought to assemble, and without whose authority they ought not to assemble". And, he adds, "because in all commonwealths, that assembly, which is without warrant from the civil sovereign, is unlawful; that Church also, which is assembled in any commonwealth that hath forbidden them to assembly, is an unlawful assembly". There can be no such thing as universal church "because there is no power on earth, to which all other commonwealths are subject ... *Temporal* and *spiritual* government, are but two words brought into the world to make men see double, and mistake their *lawful* sovereign". The "chief pastor" among all pastors within a commonwealth cannot be anyone else than "the civil sovereign".[34] There is no inconsistency between the obedience to God and obedience to the civil sovereign, Hobbes declared, because if the sovereign is a Christian, he will allow men to believe that Jesus is the Christ (the only article of religion, Hobbes says, necessary for salvation) and he will require obedience to all the civil laws; in which also are contained all the laws of nature, that is all the laws of God: for besides the laws of nature and the laws of the Church, which are part of the civil law (for the Church that can make laws is the commonwealth), there be no other laws divine.

Since Hobbes denies the authority of God and of reason, the only way out of his predicament is the substitution of an *artificial authority* created by individual acts of will and embodied in an absolute sovereign will. Although Hobbes uses this theory to defend absolute monarchy, it is essentially the same solution to the problem of authority posed by individualism which is adopted by liberalism. Hobbes, however, already anticipates the conclusions which liberalism must ultimately reach in theory, once it has abandoned its Christian conscience, and which, in fact, it does reach in the twentieth century.

Liberalism was a product of the climate of opinion that emerged at the time of the Renaissance and the Reformation. As the political expression of the new individualism, it was a political declaration of faith in the autonomy of the human reason and the essential goodness of man. Both a mode of thought and a way of life, it reflected the political, social, religious and economic aspirations of the rising commercial class. Individual freedom was its major premise as well as its goal. The Renaissance produced the concept of autonomous individual or the 'masterless man'. No longer was the God the focal point of thought and life, but man. No longer was it a question of discovering that which was in conformity to God's will but rather that which was in conformity to human reason.

Thus, liberalism may be defined as the embodiment of this new individualism and accordingly, it espouses individual freedom as its goal. Freedom from what? Freedom from every authority that is capable of acting capriciously or arbitrarily. Freedom to develop all his potential as a human being endowed with reason. In fact, liberalism was the embodiment of the demand for freedom in every sphere of life – intellectual, social, religious, political and economic.

John Locke (1632–1704), the father of liberalism, was of the opinion that man is not only a social animal but also a rational being. "Locke's view of Christianity entirely ignores the aspects of the faith which have in other days been most prominent. A rationalist to the core, he does not even contemplate as possible an appeal to any authority but that of ordinary reason. The truth of Christianity was to be proved like the truth of any historical or philosophical theory. It was simply a question of evidence, and especially of the overwhelming evidence of the Christian miracles. The fact, indeed, that those miracles were brought in confirmation of a perfect system of morality, made it possible to accept them. But, the excellence of that system appeared not from its transcending the limits of human knowledge, but from its entire coincidence with the teaching of the unassisted intellect."[35]

Locke believed that human mind at birth is a *tabula rasa;* it is like a white sheet of paper on which nothing has been written. From experience alone, the mind derives its content. The sources of our ideas are sensation and reflection. Sense data are partly revelation of external things in their mathematical relations and partly sensations which these evoke within us. The first, he calls, primary qualities and identifies them with the "essential qualities of matter" and the sensations he calls "secondary or derived qualities". The primary qualities, such as extension, solidity, position in time and motion, are always present when matter is present, whereas the secondary qualities, such as the sensation of colour, odour and sound "are in truth nothing in the objects themselves, but powers to produce various sensations in us" and depend upon the primary qualities. From this Locke draws the conclusion the "the ideas of primary qualities of bodies are resemblances of them, and their patterns do really exist in the bodies themselves, but the ideas produce in us by these secondary qualities have no resemblance of them at all. There is nothing like our ideas, existing in the bodies themselves. They are, in the bodies we denominate from them, only a power to produce those sensations in us: and what is sweet, blue or warm in idea is but the certain bulk, figure and motion of the insensible parts, in the bodies themselves, which we call so."[36] It follows from this that "the mind ... hath no other immediate object but its own ideas" and that knowledge is "nothing but the perception of the connation or and agreement of disagreement and repugnancy of any of our ideas. Knowledge is simply the perfection of the agreement of two ideas.

Thus, with Locke, there emerged the conception in the realm of thought that knowledge is the consequence of experience contrary to the traditional perception that only the so-called superior classes (Pope, priests) of a society are entitled to attain knowledge. In this way, Locke contributed a lot in developing the modern concept of rationalism.

Similarly, Hugo Grotious (1583–1645) also believed that authority in a natural law is derived not from revelation but from human nature itself. "The principles of that law", he thought, "were such that they are in themselves manifest and clear, almost as evident as are those things which we perceive by the external senses. Accordingly, the source of law is man's innate or instinctive desire for social order. To this sphere of law belong the abstaining from that which is another's, the restoration to another of anything of his which we may have, together with any gain which we may have received from it; the obligation to fulfil promises, the making good of a loss incurred through our fault, and the inflicting of penalties upon men according to their desert".[37] Grotious added that man is not only a social animal but also a rational being who "within the limitations of human intelligence" is able to judge between agreeable and harmful alternatives without yielding unduly to fear, "the allurement of immediate pleasure", or to "rash impulse".[38]

Men are driven by their social instinct to associate with one another and by their intelligence and recognition of their mutual dependence to band together by *agreement* into a political community. The basis of civil society is a contract. And "since it is a rule of law of nature to abide by pacts (for it was necessary that among men there be some method of obligating themselves one to another, and no other natural method can be imagined), out of this source the bodies of municipal law have arisen. The mother of the law of nature is the social nature of man but "the mother of municipal law is that obligation which arises from mutual consent; and since this obligation derives its force from the law of nature, nature may be considered, so to say, the great-grand-mother of municipal law". Similarly, pacts made by mutual consent between states are the foundation of the law of nations, the ultimate source of which is nature itself. Municipal law and international law are conceived to be at once the product of individual wills, consent, and the embodiment of natural justice. Obligation to obey the municipal law derives both from the force of the wills that have consented to it as well as from the recognition by individual conscience of its inherent rightness.

The importance of Grotious' conception of natural law was methodological. What Grotious endeavoured to do, and in the eyes of his contemporaries with success, was to provide a *new method* of arriving at this content – a method that did not depend upon revelation but was, in seventeenth century's terms, *scientific*. The law of nature, Grotious defined, as "dictate of right reason", which points out that an act according as it is or is not in conformity with rational nature, has in it a quality of moral baseness or moral necessity; and that, in consequence, such an act is either forbidden or enjoined by the author of nature or God.[39] Hence, it is clear although Grotius' appeal was theoretically and ostensibly an appeal to 'sound reason' much of what he had to say was acceptable as 'sound reason' because it appealed not only to the reason in men but also to their Christian conscience. Moreover, not only did Grotius secularize the conception of natural law but he also developed a conception of natural rights, which was to have a profound influence upon all subsequent political thoughts.

Being influenced by all these, there came a revolutionary change in the perception of different branches of knowledge at the beginning of the eighteenth century. Thus, the eighteenth century has long been characterized as the "Age of Enlightenment". In an essay on the meaning of Enlightenment, published in 1784, the German philosopher Immanuel Kant writes: Enlightenment is the liberation of man from self-imposed tutelage. Tutelage is the incapacity of using one's own understanding except under the direction of another. This tutelage is self-imposed when its cause lies not in the lack of understanding but in a lack of resolution and courage .... Dare to use your own understanding. That is the motto of Enlightenment.

To be enlightened, Kant writes at another place, is to think for one's own self and to think for one's self means "to seek the highest touchstone of truth in one's self, i.e., one's own reason". In fact, the basic idea underlying all the tendencies of Enlightenment was the conviction that human understanding is capable, by its own power and without any recourse to supernatural assistance, of comprehending the system of the world and that this new way of understanding the world will lead to a new way of mastering it.[40]

Although it proclaimed itself to be uniquely an Age of Reason it was a particular kind of reason that it exalted. Reason, of course, was not unknown in former centuries nor was the appeal to its authority unique with the eighteenth century. Life in accordance with reason was an ancient ideal long before discovered by the Greeks and passed on as part of their heritage to Western civilization. Nor had reason, as some erroneously suppose, been repudiated by Christianity. The Christian religion teaches that it is through faith in Jesus Christ as the embodiment of the reason that governs the universe, that human reason directed in love to God can be trusted to lead men to the truth. Christianity does not repudiate reason but subordinates it to the revelation of God's nature in Jesus Christ, thus securing its integrity and giving it direction.

Since a life in accordance with reason was an ideal shared by the ancient Greeks and the Christians, and since the appeal to its authority was not unique with the eighteenth century, that century might be more correctly characterized as the Age of Scientific Rationalism, than as the Age of Reason. For the reason to which appeal was made as the ultimate authority, was a reason 'freed' from the revelation of God in Christ but bound by the truths of Nature as revealed by the methods of scientific empiricism. It was not that the eighteenth century substituted reason for faith as some suppose, but that it exchanged, one kind of faith for another, a faith in the methods of scientific empiricism for those of theology.

To be 'enlightened' was to be freed from God's revelation in Christ, to dispense with "the revelation through Holly Writ and Holly Church". However, the eighteenth century did not begin by repudiating the tenets of orthodox Christianity but by converting them into a 'reasonable' religion acceptable to minds enlightened by the new science.

In short, the Enlightenment was the creation of a new framework of ideas about man, society and nature, which challenged the existing conceptions rooted in a traditional world view, dominated by Christianity. The key domain in which the Enlightenment intellectuals challenged the clergy, who comprised the main group involved in supporting the existing conception of the world, concerned the traditional view of nature, man and society, which was sustained by the Church's authority and its monopoly over the information media of the time. These new ideas were accompanied by and influenced in their turn many cultural innovations in writing, printing, painting, music, sculpture, architecture and gardening, as well as in other arts. Technological innovations in agriculture and manufacture, as well as in ways of making war, also frame the social theories of the Enlightenment. In political theory, the gist of enlighten perception was that the philosophies must be built on the basis of human reason in the place of superstitious assumption and blind faith or spiritual knowledge. They argued that if man is able to develop all these with the help of his rationality then only he would be able to find out true knowledge. The whole of the Enlightenment era was influenced by these thoughts. Voltaire, Rousseau, Montesquieu in France; Locke, Hume and Adam Smith in Britain; Gate, Kant and others in Germany; and Jefferson, Franklin and Thomas Pain in

America developed the same ideology of rationalism and all of them came to the conclusion that modern society is represented by human mind and his reason.

To build the political institutions based on human reason may also be found in the writings of C.L. Montesquieu (1689–1755). In the preface of his greatest and most lasting work, *The Spirit of the Laws* (1899), Montesquieu says:

> I have not drawn my principles from my prejudices, but form the nature of things .... Every nation will find here the reasons on which its maxims are based.[41]

As a liberal, Montesquieu's first concern was with individual freedom and he endeavoured to discover the checks on political authority by means of which it might be secured. To this end, he developed a theory of the separation of powers, which has had far-reaching effect.

Montesquieu begins his treaties on *The Spirit of the Laws* by declaring that the entire universe is regulated by laws: "all beings have their laws: the Deity His Laws, the material its laws, the intelligences superior to man their laws, the beasts their laws, man his laws." Laws, he says, in the broadest sense of the term, "are the necessary relations arising from the nature of things". There is nothing capricious or arbitrary about the universe, it is governed by invariable laws of cause and effect, for if it were not so "it would inevitably perish".

Montesquieu elaborates the laws of political realm in a different manner. He says before man lived in a society they lived in a state of nature. In this state man had no knowledge but only the potentiality for learning. Feeling weak and impotent, gripped by excessive fears man was like a savage "trembling at the motion of a leaf, and flying from every shadow". His first concern, as a consequence, would be security and "peace would be the first law of nature". The second concern of man in the pre-social state of existence would be the satisfaction of his wants. Hence, another law of nature would prompt him to seek for nourishment. And "the attraction driving from the difference of sexes" would lead him, also, to seek the association of others and this "natural inclination ... would form a third law". A fourth law of nature results from man's social predisposition, the desire fostered by reason in the light of these other laws, to live in society.[42]

But as soon as man enters society, "he loses the sense of his weakness, equality ceases, and then commences the state of war".

This war breaks out not only between individuals but also between different nations. As a consequence of this strife, three kinds of law arise: political law, governing the relations of the governors to the governed; civil law, governing the relations of one individual to another; and the laws of nations, governing the relations between nations. The desire for self-preservation interpreted in the light of reason is the foundation of all these laws. "Law in general is human reason" and "the political and civil laws of each nation ought to be only the particular cases in which human reason is applied". Such laws "should be adapted ... to the people for whom they are framed" since what is suitable for one people may not be suitable for another. Moreover, "they should be in relation to the climate of each country, to the quality of its soil, to its situation and extent, to the principal occupation of the natives ... they should have relation to the degree of liberty which the constitution will bear; to the religion of the inhabitants, to their inclinations, riches, numbers, commerce, manners and customs".[43] Thus, we see in the writings of Montesquieu that even he accepts human reason as the foundation of all relations.

Similarly, it was John Wise (1652–1725) who successfully attacked the New England theocracy. In 1710, Wise published his *Churches Quarrel Espoused* and a few years later his *Vindication of the Government of New England Churches* (1717) came where he argued that all men are free by natural right. Wise writes:

> Every man ought to be conceived to be perfectly in his own power and disposal, and not to be controlled by the authority of any other. And thus every man must be acknowledged equal to every man since all subjection and all command are equally banished on both sides; ... every man has a prerogative to judge for himself, namely what shall be most his behoof, happiness and well-being.[44]

It does not sound that men are free from all authority. All men are subjected to the authority of God and to those ordinances of reason, which are the embodiment of God's will. However, it does mean that men should be freed from all arbitrary and personal compulsion in order that they might be free to follow the dictates of reason. For by giving men the faculty of reason "God has provided a rule for men in all their actions, obliging each one to the performance of that which is right, not only as to justice, but likewise as to all other moral virtues, which is nothing but the dictates of right reason founded in the soul of man".

Further, Jean Jacques Rousseau (1712–1778) also worked on the project of rationalism. Rousseau, one of the propounder of the concept of social contract, believed that sovereignty lies in the General Will, which is absolutely free from any kind of divine obligations. General Will is the total of the ideal will of individual which emerged in the form of moral societal rule. It is that dictate of reason, which has its endeavour as welfare of society. According to Rousseau, "... the very essence of sovereignty is the creation, authorization and enactment of law according to the standards and requirements of the common good. And, the nature of the common good can only be known through public discourse and public agreement. Only citizens themselves can articulate, "the supreme direction of general will" which is the sum of their publicly generated judgments of common good".[45]

For Rousseau, sovereignty is identical with liberty. The sovereign, being formed wholly of the individuals who compose it, neither has nor can have any interest contrary to their's. The sovereign is absolute, indivisible, inalienable and infallible. Because, sovereignty is represented by general will, which is always right and tend to the public advantage. The people may be deceived but they are never corrupt, they may be misled but their will is always good because it is directed by the man's reason, not by any divinity.

Premised upon the presuppositions of the Age of Enlightenment, the Declaration of Independence declares:

> We hold these truths to be self-evident, that all men are created equal, that they are endowed by their Creator with certain unalienable Rights, that among these are Life, Liberty and the pursuit of Happiness. That to secure these rights, Governments are instituted among Men, deriving their just powers from the consent of the governed. That whenever any Form of Government becomes destructive of these ends, it is the Right of the People to alter or to abolish it, and to institute new Government, laying its foundation on such principles and organizing its powers in such form, as to them shall seem most likely to effect their Safety and Happiness.[46]

The above quotation connotes it very well that the Enlightenment has created such an atmosphere where man gets importance due to his rational capacity. At the same time, it was also realized that nature has created individuals equal and all of them are blessed to have rational mind. Therefore, human society must be built upon the edifice of rational rules. In the period followed the Enlightenment movement, it was insisted by the political thinkers that there was a fundamental law, binding upon individual will. On the one hand, it insisted that there is a fundamental law, binding upon individual will, which is eternal, universal and rational. On the other hand it also insisted upon the absolute value of human personality, the autonomy of human reason and of the individual will. All these developments sought to effect a compromise between these contradictory principles by an appeal to the Christian conscience. However, the Christian conscience, freed from the authority of the Church and progressively divorced from revelation, soon degenerated into a mere cult of the sentiment, without weight or sanction, and the will of the individual was left without any substantial limitation. As the tenets of the orthodox Christian faith were gradually abandoned, one by one, the "religion of justification by faith" was soon converted into a "religion of justification by self-esteem". And, at last, in the eighteenth century, self-love achieves its broadest, most satisfying rationalization, the conception of a universal harmony in which God, man and nature are pantheistically interfused. In this 'closed system of benevolence', man shares immanent divinity with nature. Self-love, social love and divine love are indistinguishable. Nature's God has confirmed man's longing to find goodness, wisdom and creative power in the depths of his heart. In this way, it may be concluded that rationalism was the first and foremost tenet of modernism.

Individualism

Individualism may be regarded as the second important feature of modernism. The conceptualization that individual is the starting point for all the knowledge and action, and that individual reason cannot be subjected to a higher authority, is the basic concern for modernity. Society is thus sum or the product of the thought and action of a large number of individuals.[47]

Now, it is clear that modern thoughts were the outcome of the Renaissance and Reformation. Up to the medieval era, the importance of an individual being was regarded only within the context of society. How an individual should lead his life, what should be the aim of an individual's life – answer of all these questions were sought out not by the individual himself, but by the political, social, religious and other related institutions. However, it was the renaissance through which, an individual's life got importance and those conceptions were accepted which were aimed at fulfilling individual's present life. It is said that if a man was not going to start as member of a system, accepting that system and his own place in it, then he must start with his own isolated self. Of course, he would submit to the authority of conscience, but it would be his conscience. He would submit to the voice of God, but it would be as he heard it. Therefore, the modern movement was bound to be a movement of individualism.[48]

Like in other fields individual-centric studies were also started in the field of political theory. Various political thinkers presented their own perspectives about individual's nature in political philosophies. Niccolo Machiavelli (1469–1527) may be regarded as a first modern thinker in this regard. He explained at length about the human nature and accordingly he presented the nature of politics, administration, religion and ethics. He was the first thinker who shifted his focus of attention from God to man and greater emphasis was laid down upon temporal security than upon eternal salvation.

Concerned with the politics as it is rather than politics as it ought to be, Machiavelli laid the foundations for modern political science and anticipated the attempts of the nineteenth century's positivists to find a natural science of politics. It is in this sense that *The Prince* is to be understood, i.e., as technical treatise on the means of gaining and keeping power. Machiavelli is less concerned with the uses to which power is to be put, with the ends in terms of which power is to be sought, and with the technical means of acquiring and keeping it. He says:

> A Prince then should know how to employ the nature of man and that of the beasts as well ... it being necessary then for a prince to know well how to employ the nature of the beasts, he should be able to assume both that of fox and that of the lion; for whilst the latter cannot escape traps laid for him, the former cannot defend himself against the Wolves. A Prince should be a fox, to know the traps and snares; and a lion, to be able to frighten the Wolves; for those who simply hold to the nature of the lion do not understand their business.[49]

Machiavelli goes on to say that the prince should learn how to be a 'hypocrite'; he should know, for example, how to "seem to be merciful, faithful, humane, religious and upright, and should even be so in reality; but he should have his mind so trained that, when occasion requires it, he may know how to change the opposite". The prince must be able to change "as the winds and changes of fortune bid him" for he will often be obliged "for the sake of maintaining his state, to act contrary to humanity, charity, and religion". Machiavelli clearly holds human nature in low esteem and if a prince would be successful in the maintenance of his state, it is better to appear to have good qualities than it is to observe them in every situation. The maintenance of the state appears in Machiavelli's thought to override all other considerations. In an age of violence and political instability he would appear to value stability above justice, not understanding, apparently, that genuine order is a product of justice. "Putting all other considerations aside", he wrote, "the only question should be, what course will save the life and liberty of the country?"

Hence, in Machiavelli's opinion, the nature of state depends on the nature of man. Whatever Machiavelli produces the concept of the origin of state, its extension and preservation, morale and ethics of king, is totally influenced by the nature of men. Thus, he was the first thinker who made politics individualized.

The Protestant reformists Martin Luther (1483–1586) and John Calvin (1509–1564) have also raised the question upon the relevance of the existence of Church and Pope. They were of the opinion that the Church had been corrupted and was in need of reform. The spirituality of Church was almost lost in secular and temporal ambitions and the Church appeared to be much more concerned about the increase of its revenues than about the salvation of individual souls. They emphasized that man by his own efforts or works alone can get salvation. Justification is a personal experience requiring neither priesthood nor Church for meditation. Having derived both the authority of the Church and the authority of reason the reformers were forced into the position of claiming that the scriptures were 'self-authenticated'.

The famous English political philosopher Thomas Hobbes also developed his theory on the basis of individual nature. He starts his political thinking with the nature of man. According to Hobbes, men are naturally selfish because they are naturally attracted to that which they desire. When their desires conflict they are at war with one another, and it is the natural condition of man. He writes:

> Nature hath made men so equal, in the faculties of the body, and mind; as that though there be found one man sometimes manifestly stronger in the body, or quicker mind than another; yet when all is reckoned together, the difference between men, and man, is not so considerable as that one man can thereupon claim to himself any benefit, to which another may not pretend, as well as he.[50]

Hobbes further adds that from this equality of ability there arises equality in the hope of attaining our desires. Thus equality of hope makes enemies of men especially when they desire something which they cannot get, which they cannot enjoy. We find in the nature of man, Hobbes says, three principal causes of quarrel, viz., competition, difference and glory.

Hobbes says, "The first maketh men invade for gain; the second, for safety; and the third, for reputation. The first use violence, to make themselves masters of other men's persons, wives, children, and cattle: the second to defend them; the third, for trifles, as a word, a smile, a different opinion ..."

Hereby it is manifest that during the time men live without a common power to keep them all in awe, they are in that condition which is called war; and such a war, as is of every man, against every other man.[51]

Thus, in a condition of nature, prior to the establishment of civil society, man is at war with man seeking to gratify his own desires, to keep what he has or to preserve his reputation. In such a condition men live in "continual fear" and in "danger of violent death", the "life of man" in such a condition being "solidarity, poor, nasty, brutish and sort". In this war of every man against every man, there is nothing just or unjust, right or wrong, but force and fraud everywhere prevail. It is not until men enter society that such a thing as justice is possible for "where there is no common power, there is no law; where no law, no injustice".[52]

Confronted with such a condition man is impelled partly by his passion, partly by his reason to seek peace by entering society. "The passions that incline men to peace, are fear of death; desire of such things as are necessary to commodious living; and a hope by their industry to obtain them. In addition, reason suggesteth convenient articles of peace, upon which men may be drawn to agreement. These articles, are they, which otherwise are called the Laws of Nature."[53] For Hobbes, a law of nature is not a moral law but a counsel of prudence, for, he says, "a law of nature ... is a precept or general rule, found out by reason, by which a man is forbidden to do that, which is destructive of his life, or taketh away the means of preserving the same". It is not love or desire for justice that implies us to take these steps to develop law of nature but fear of death and a calculated prudence. Due to this fear of death, state or commonwealth comes into existence, which is result of a contract or agreement in which every man covenants with every other man to give up his natural right of governing himself to some designated sovereign person or assemblage of persons. It is an oath where each man said, "I authorize and give up my right of governing myself to this man, or to this assembly of men, on this condition that thou give up thy right to him and authorize all his actions in like manner ... . This is a generation of the great *Leviathan* to which we own under the immoral peace and defense".[54] The power of the sovereign is unlimited and absolute: "there can happen no breach of covenant on the part of the sovereign; and consequently none of his subjects, by any pretence of forfeiture, can be freed from his subjection". There is only one liberty which Hobbes believes to be consistent with the unlimited power of the sovereign and that is the liberty which individuals retain "to defend their own bodies, even against them that lawfully invade them". "If the sovereign command a man, though justly condemned, to kill, wound, or maim himself; or not to resist those that assault him; or to abstain from the use of food, air, medicine, or any other thing, without which he cannot live, yet hath that man the liberty to disobey."[55]

It sounds that in Hobbesian thoughts state is a means and man is an end. State is existed for the sake of man, not man for the state. It implies that Hobbes develops his concept of state by keeping individual in its centre.

John Locke also starts his studies by analysing human nature. Men are the focus of attention in the Lockien philosophy. Elaborating this, he writes:

> ... man is a rational being, capable of living in a society. He is not selfish, competitive or aggressive. He is also capable of noble feelings like sympathy, love tenderness and charity towards his fellow beings. The first instinct of man was to live in peace and harmony with others.[56]

In fact, Locke was of the opinion that man is a rational being. With his power of rationality man can develop ethical system within which he tries to obey all the commands. It is his duty to follow it. On the basis of these ethical qualities, Locke provides an individual the right to life, liberty and property.

> The end of the government is the good of mankind, and which is best for mankind, that, the people should be always exposed to the boundless will of tyranny or that the rulers should be sometimes liable to be opposed when they grow exorbitant in the use of their power and employ it for the destruction and not the preservation of the properties of their people.[57]

Locke's state can use only those powers that are provided to it by the people because state is an agent for people. For Locke, state comes into the existence for the welfare of society. State, like a trust, is a legal institution based on the consent of individual. Whensoever, therefore, the legislative shall transgress this fundamental rule of society, and either by ambition, fear, folly, or corruption, endeavour to grasp themselves or put into the hands of any other an absolute power over the lives, liberties and estates of the people, by this breach of trust they forfeit the power the people had put into their hands, for quite contrary ends, and it develops to the people, who have a right to resume their original liberty, and by the establishment of the new legislative (such as they shall think fit) provide for their own safety and security, which is the end for which they are in society. It means if state could not able to maintain welfare, security or safety of its people, it should be abolished. It reflects importance of individual in Locke's philosophy. He not only makes studies individual-centric, but also tries to individualize the whole socio-economic fabric of society.

After Locke, the Enlightenment thinkers carried on his individual-centric studies further. As the leaders of the movement, they regarded their intellectual labours as the emancipation of men from prejudice, superstition, convention and tradition. It was an age marked by a passionate avowal of the self-sufficiency of human reason and by a faith in the capacity of men to establish paradise on earth by their own powers and in their own image. Rejecting the orthodox Christian trinity, the Enlightened intellectuals of the eighteenth century proclaimed their faith in the new trinity of reason, nature and humanity. For the love of God, they substituted the love of humanity, for the vicarious atonement the perfectibility of man through his own efforts, and for the hope of immorality in another world they hope of living in the memory of future generation. The basic assumption of the Enlightenment movement was that to make the present life prosperous and healthy, not the life after death. It shows a revolutionary change in the whole scenario of the transitory period. Religion of Christianity had been replaced by the religion of Humanity to establish the importance of human beings.

C.L. Montesquieu also made a valuable contribution in developing the basic norms of individualism. He was the great advocate of individual freedom and that is why he endeavoured to discover the checks on political authority by means of which it might be secured. To this end, he developed a theory of 'separation of powers', which has had following essence:

> the political liberty of the subject is a tranquillity of mind arising from the opinion each person has of his safety. In order to have this liberty, it is requisite the government be so constituted as one man need not be afraid of another ... When the legislative and executive powers are united in the same person, or in the same body of magistrates, there can be no liberty, because apprehensions may arise, lest

> the same monarch or senate should enact tyrannical laws, to execute them in a tyrannical manner ...[58]

Being a liberal, Montesquieu's first concern was for individual freedom, and he endeavoured to discover the system through which it might be secured. To this end, he developed a theory of 'separation of powers'. He was of the opinion that there would be an end to everything, where the same man or the same body, whether of the nobles or of the people, to exercise those three powers, that of enacting laws, that of executing the public resolutions, and of trying the causes of individuals. That is why, he demanded that power should be a check to power. It is the only condition where an individual can exercise his power freely within the limitation of laws.

Although within the shadows of liberalism individual has became focal point of various discourses, yet with the destruction of the liberal conception, liberalism in the nineteenth century forced to seek a new foundation for freedom. To preserve individual's natural rights to life, liberty and property, which was the objective of any state, was challenged and there came a radical change in the nature of state. Now state is regarded as an institution, which not only preserves the natural rights of individuals but also aims at promoting the utilitarian philosophy of "the greatest happiness of the greatest number".

Utilitarianism was an attempt to establish ethical and political theory upon a thoroughgoing scientific empiricism. Hume, Holbash, Helevetius etc. were the noted utilitarian philosophers of the eighteenth century. All of them studied the individual with a new perspective and they concluded that an individual works within the two motivational factors – pain and pleasure.[59]

Jeremy Bentham (1748–1832), by rejecting all the previous theories like natural rights, law of nature and the theory of social contract says, that there are no eternal and immutable rule of right, no law of reason, no moral law of nature, no natural justice. Unnatural never means anything more than infrequent. According to him:

> Nature has placed mankind under governance of two sovereign masters, *pain* and *pleasure*. It is for them alone to point out what we ought to do, as well as to determine what we shall do. On the one hand, the standard of right and wrong, on the other the chain of causes and effects, are fastened to their throne. They govern us in all we do, in all we say, in all we think; every effort we can make to thrown off our subjection, will serve but to demonstrate and confirm it ... *The principle of utility* recognizes this subjection, and assumes it

> for the foundation of that system, the object of which is to rear the fabric or felicity by the hands of reason and of law.[60]

In fact, Bentham was of the opinion that men obey the laws of government not because they have consented to do so, not because the laws embody principles of justice to which their reason inclines them to render obedience, but because the probable mischiefs of obedience are less than the probable mischiefs of resistance. "When a number of persons are supposed to be in *habit* of paying obedience to a person, or an assemblage of persons, of a known and certain description, such persons altogether are said to be in a state of *political* society."[61]

To Bentham the state is primarily a law-making body. As already mentioned, the state is a group of persons organized for the promotion and maintenance of happiness. Law is a command and a restriction. It is opposed to liberty, more precisely, natural liberty (natural liberty is unlimited liberty or freedom to do whatever one wants to do). The great task of law is to reconcile the conflicting social and economic interests. It should regulate the selfish interest of man to promote the greatest happiness. This is possible only through a system of punishment. Punishments are described as artificial pains. Bentham added that law need not concern itself with all actions of individual but only with those actions which may affect the general happiness of the community. The aim of law is "to increase the net balance of pleasure and to decrease the net balance of pain".

Similarly, J.S. Mill (1806–1873), who is universally regarded as the foremost champion of liberty, believed that all changes of society are bought about by man's mind. He was convinced and rightly feared that the increasing legislative power of the state may bring about a cult of personality by casting citizens in a common mould. The individual needed protection from over-regulation by the state. Moreover, the individual is the only source of all that is wise and noble in human culture. Thus, the individual personality should be cherished and allowed to flourish in an atmosphere of maximum freedom. In other words, free men should be allowed to move with free minds. Mill argued that "liberty is also necessary for the happiness of society: it is clear that liberty is not to be expressed in terms of utility, but is yet more fundamental than it".[62]

In fact, Mill has two definitions of liberty. First, he defines liberty as the "sovereignty of the individual over himself and over his own body and mind". This implies "being left to oneself". Mill further says, that "all restraint qua restraint is an evil". The state should not interfere with the individual action unless it harms others. In this context, Mill divides all human actions into two categories: (a) self-regarding actions, and (b) other-regarding actions. Self-regarding actions are those actions, which are concerned with the individual himself. The state has no right to interfere in these actions, except through persuasion and advice. Mill thus provides immunity from state interference over a wide range of activities of the individual, which may be turned 'personal'.

Other-regarding actions are those actions, which have their influence or impact on the members of society. The moment an individual act invades or infringes upon others, the sanctity of that act is lost and it is open to state regulation or state interference. The state can so interfere, if the "other-regarding" actions produce "positive, demonstrable harm to other". Mill further added that the sole end for which mankind is warranted individually or collectively in interfering with the liberty of action of any of their number is self-protection. The only purpose for which power can be rightfully exercised over any member of a civilized community, against his will, is to prevent harm to others. His own good, either physical or moral, is not a sufficient warrant. The only part of the conduct of anyone, for which he is amenable to society, is that which concerns others. In the part which merely concerns himself his independence is, of right, absolute; over himself, over his own body or mind, the individual is sovereign.

A closer examination of Mill's views on liberty shows that according to his conception all restriction is evil. Mill gave lots of importance to liberty of thought and expression. Society must allow the individual freedom of thought and expression although the opinion expressed may be unpopular, heterodox or both. Debates and discussion lead to a clash of ideas and pave the way to truth. Mill firmly believes that truth alone will ultimately triumph and survive, although it may be temporarily suppressed or driven underground. Moreover, freedom of thought and expression also provides a congenial atmosphere for the development of individual personality, which is very essential in a participatory democracy.

Similar to Mill's concept of individual liberty, Herbert Spencer (1820–1903) put forth the biological argument in favour of individualism and said, Survival of the fittest is the law of nature and the progress of society depends upon the elimination of the unfit by the fit. The duty of the state is simply to allow the fullest scope in the struggle for existence. The state has no business to come forward to help the poor, the aged and the sick. Any attempt by the state to interfere in the struggle for existence is an attempt to modify nature. Thus, society gets the benefit of the best individuals.[63]

Thus, the thinkers of the nineteenth century have presented a norm that institutions are there for preservation and promotion of individual's rights. Accordingly, state is the best institution, which rules at minimum possible level of authority and tries to promote the maximum possible level of opportunity to individual's liberty. Hence, individualism, as a fundamental characteristic of modern philosophy, places the individual at the centre of all discourses. He and his temporal life on this earth have its importance than the eternal life. To improve individual's personality, it is needed to improve the physical society with the help of instruments, where he is living. State is the means and men are its end. Thus, in short, it may be stated that modernism is a rational ideology, where individual's personality gets dignity.

Universalism

Universalism may be regarded as the third important characteristic feature of modernism. In fact, universalism is an ideology, which believes that human nature would always and everywhere be the same. Thus, societal rules and regulations should also develop in such a way so that they can be applied anywhere without any boundation of time and limitation of space.[64]

Different fields of knowledge get influenced by the concept of universalism. Even in the political theory, universal values were accepted. Thinkers have expressed that all men are rational being and rationality is the basis of all political philosophy, thus universalism of thoughts and theories is very natural. In fact, it was the Stoic philosophy from where universal or essential conception of human being was emerged. Stoic philosophers were of the opinion that "the universe is governed by natural laws of reason, which are immanent in nature and the individual achieves happiness and sincerity by comprehending the inevitability of natural causation."[65]

To Stoic thinkers man's reason is the representative of natural laws. These natural laws, which are based on reason, are supreme and universal in nature. Human society must be governed by these natural laws only. The wise man lives according to nature, i.e., he allows his reason to guide his conduct and restrain his emotions and thus cooperates with natural necessity. It shows that Stoicism did exalt not only the life of reason but it also emphasized the essential equality of all men. Stoic philosophers assumed:

> Although individuals may differ in wealth, social position, reputation and in other respect, they are nevertheless, essentially equal since all are equally endowed with reason and equally able, if

they will, to comprehend the laws of natural necessity, which direct the destinies of each.[66]

For the ancient *polis,* which was being swallowed up in great empires, the Stoic substituted the concept of the *cosmopolis* and for the first time man could be conceived as a citizen not of a particular city-state but as a citizen of the world. There was then born a concept of the brotherhood of man. Man, was linked to man by a common necessity to obey the universal law of reason and in the life of reason each could find equal freedom. Man, simply as man, achieved a new significance and a new status. Thus, two concepts, the universal brotherhood of man and the universal law of reason were the principal contributions of Stoicism to the Western philosophy.

The Stoic philosophy of universalism may also be seen in the philosophy of Roman jurisprudence. It was in the writings of Cicero that Stoicism was best exemplified in the Roman world and through him passed into Roman jurisprudence. He taught:

> True law is right reason consonant with nature, diffused among all men, constant, eternal; which summons to duty by its command and hinders from fraud by its prohibition, which neither command nor forbids good men in vain nor moves bad ones by either. To make enactments infringing this law, religion forbids, neither may it be repealed even in part, nor have we power through senate or people to free ourselves from it. It needs no interpreter or expounder but itself, nor will there be one law in Rome and another in Athens, one in the present and another in the time to come, but one law and that eternal and immutable shall embrace all people and for all time, and there shall be as it were one common master and ruler, the good of all, the author and judge and proposes of this law. And he who obeys him not shall flee from himself, and in spinning the nature of human kind by that very act he shall suffer the greatest of torments, though he escapes others, which men consider pain.[67]

This concept of natural law dominated all streams of western political thought for at least eighteen hundred years. Not until the nineteenth and twentieth centuries have men seriously challenged the idea of the existence of a law of reason, which is eternal, absolute, universal and immutable. For centuries men have distinguished between this law and the laws which are enacted by men insisting that the later is only truly law when it conforms in principle and content to the dictates of right reason. Justice, hereafter, is conceived as the expression of this natural law of reason.

According to Cicero, and to Roman thought generally, this law, which is common both to God and to men, is also the foundation of the state since it existed "before any written laws or any state had been founded". The state is nothing, neither more nor less, than a "partnership in law" (*juris societas*); it is "an assemblage of men associated in consent to law".[68]

The idea of a universal law and the idea of the state being founded upon consent together laid the foundation for the conception of individual rights – a conception which was lacking in ancient Greek political thought. These ideas were passed on the Middle Ages through the medium of the writings of the great Roman jurists. And it was carried on further by the Christian philosophers and paved the way for the development of modern universalism.

Christian philosophers like St. Paul, St. Ambrose, St. Augustine, St. Gogori-I, Pope Glacious-I etc. have placed the concept of universalism and that of equality of human being at the centre of their studies. In Jesus, at first, only a few and later many, came to recognize the Christ, of whose coming the Jewish prophets had foretold any they called him the Son of God. They recognized one who was perfectly God and perfectly man who through his life, death and resurrections had reconciled man to God in love and suffering. They recognized one who was the perfect embodiment in human form of perfect love and perfect wisdom. His disciples, who were plunged into despair as He lay dying in agony upon the cross condemned by the world for his innocence hastened later when He appeared to them in life to bring this good news to all who would listen.

Christianity as a body of thought merged the teachings of Greek philosophy with those of the Jewish prophets and added the incarnation of the word. Prepared by the Greeks to conceive of God as the embodiment of cosmic reason and by the Jews to conceive of God as the embodiment of perfect righteousness, the western man was prepared to recognize in Jesus the incarnation of perfect wisdom and perfect justice.

Christianity taught that man is the creature of God, that essentially he is a spiritual being with a nature and destiny that transcends time and space. Beyond the Kingdom of man there is the Kingdom of God and if an individual would enter that Kingdom he must surrender his will to God and put an end to his rebellion. Thus, there is introduced into life a duality unknown in the Greek world, that man is not only a citizen of the world (the Kingdom of man) but is also, potentially at least, a member of the Kingdom of God. Man is confronted for the first time with a dual loyalty – a loyalty to Caesar and a loyalty to God. He is admonished to render into Caesar that which is rightfully his but into God that which belongs to Him and if there is a conflict of loyalties he must choose, if he would be saved, that which is God's. The Repentance for one's sins, a change of heart, the reorientation of one's will and thoughts from self to God, is the only requirement for entrance into the Kingdom of God which, unlike the Kingdom of man, endures forever.[69]

Throughout the Middle Ages all the branches of knowledge, viz., metaphysics, logic, ethics, politics and economics, were held together in one coherent whole through the mediation of the "queen of the sciences" – Theology. In the thirteenth century, in the realm of nature and the realm of grace, the knowledge yielded by natural reason and the knowledge yielded by revelation were conceived as complementary. But, in the fifteenth and sixteenth centuries, the authority of the Church, as the guardian of theology, was challenged by nationalistic and intellectual forces with which it was unable to cope successfully. The Church itself lacked the moral authority necessary to harmonize the new intellectual forces with the old. With the repudiation of the authority of the Church and the disintegration of scholasticism the medieval edifice of thought collapsed – the key of its arch, theology, discredited. The concept of natural law developed by the Stoics and perpetuated by the Roman jurists is retained by Christianity and identified as a species of divine law. The law as conceived both by the Greeks and as conceived by the Jewish prophets is not abrogated but transcended by the principle of love – justice is recognized as an imperfect manifestation of God's love for men and henceforth men are enjoined to temper justice with mercy, to administer justice with the compassionate knowledge that the sins of others are our own sins and that in their sinning we sin as well.

The Stoic conception of the universal community in which all men are brothers was given spiritual content by the Christian conception of the Kingdom of God. All men are brothers because all men have common father and the Kingdom of God knows neither male nor female, freeman or slave, Gentile or Jew, Greek or barbarian. This Kingdom is not a partnership of law but a partnership of love. It is through love of God that men learn to love one another. This tendency of brotherhood, which characterized the period of the Renaissance, necessitated the search for some substituted method of admiring at knowledge and the intellectual activity of the fifteenth, sixteenth and seventieth centuries was directed towards the search for that new method through which it may be universally applied. Within the intellectual climate of the period of Enlightenment movement there emerged a new scientific society. Copernicus (1473–1543), Galileo (1564–1641), Newton (1493–1543), Kapler (1642–1727) and Francis Bacon (1561–1626) were some of the famous scientists of this age. They were of the view that the method of discovery and proof, according to which the most general principles are first established, and then intermediate axioms are tried and proved by them, is the parent of error and the curse of all science. For the demonstration of truth, these scientists would substitute a method of discovering truth.[70]

For until the fifteenth and sixteenth centuries it was nowhere seriously disputed that knowledge is a knowledge of real objects. It is the external world of real objects which is the starting point of modern philosophical speculation but rather the individual mind or experience. Following the scientific discoveries it was also founded in the philosophical streams that like the general scientific principles the societal norms should also be generalized. Political thinkers developed those theories and conceptions, which can be applied beyond the limitation of time and space. That is why, the modern political theory represents not any particular caste (Greek or Romans), not or particular state (Athens or Sparta), particular religion or community (Christianity or any other), but the whole of world community.

The first modern political philosopher Niccolo Machiavelli, through his studies, presented the similar conception. Machiavelli started his studies of politics by analysing human nature. He takes a pessimistic view of human nature. Accordingly, men by nature are purely selfish and they, in their lives, are always motivated by selfish desires. Machiavelli points out that men are ungrateful, fickle, deceitful, cowardly and avaricious. Thus, a prince must be able to change "as the winds and changes of fortune bid him" for he will often be obliged "for the sake of maintaining his state, to act contrary to humanity, charity and religion". Machiavelli clearly holds human nature in low esteem and if a prince would be successful in the maintenance of his state, it is better to appear to have good qualities that it is to observe them in every situation. The maintenance of the state appears in Machiavelli's thought to override all other considerations. In an age of violence and political instability he would appear to value stability above justice, not understanding, apparently, that genuine order is a product of justice. "Putting all considerations aside", he wrote, "the only questions should be what course will save the life and liberty of the country". In the *Discourses,* Machiavelli declares:

> … as regards prudence and stability, I say that people are more prudent and stable, and have better judgment than a prince; and it is not without reason that it is said. The voice of the people is the voice of God … if we compare the faults of a people with those of princes, as well as their respective good qualities, we shall find the people vastly superior in all that is good and glorious. And if princes show themselves superior in the making of laws, and in the forming of civil institutions and new statutes and ordinances, the people are superior in maintaining those institutions, laws and ordinances, which certainly places them on a par with those who established them.[71]

A reading of the *Discourses* reveals that Machiavelli was one of the first to recognize the nature of the new secular state which was emerging at the time of renaissance. The distinctively modern characteristic of his theory was his attempt to divorce the foundation of the state from all theological considerations and to develop a universal theory of state based on human-nature.

To Thomas Hobbes, universe is a machine made up of particles moving according to the mechanical law. This mechanical law is the theory of universe. Man is a microcosm, an epitome of the great universe. He is also a machine, more complicated then plants and beasts, but composed as they are, and as the universe is, of moving particles. In fact, Hobbes was influenced by the development of his time, especially in the field of science, and tried to develop some general or universal conceptions within the realm of political science. Actually, Hobbes' ultimate objective was to evolve a universal philosophy; and the philosophy, related with politics, was only a part of that universal philosophy. Hobbes' endeavour was to formulate a doctrine of man and a theory of state wholly based upon naturalistic or universalistic assumptions.[72]

It was on these naturalistic or materialistic grounds that Hobbes argued that whatever exists is matter and whatever changes is motion. Underlying anything is matter in motion. Our thoughts are but motions in our brains. It was upon this underlying assumption, derived, from natural science that he sought to erect a doctrine of man and a theory of the state.

As an empiricist, Hobbes argued that "there is no conception in a man's mind, which hath not a first, totally, or by parts, been begotten upon the organs of sense. The rest are derived from that original". Anticipating modern behaviouristic psychology, he argued that it is physical stimuli 'pressing' upon our sensory organs which gives rise to mental impressions in some automatic fashion. All the different phenomena of sensation can ultimately be explained in terms of the fundamental laws of motion, i.e., in terms of physics or of a kind of physiological psychology. Just as the cognitional attributes of man's nature can be explained in physical terms so also can his volitional activities. He equates good with pleasure and evil with its absence.

Further, Hobbes explains that good and evil are matters of individual taste, that which we happen to like or dislike. We are not attracted to something because it is good but 'good' is the name we call that to which men are attracted. Men are naturally selfish because they are attracted to that which they desire. When their desires conflict, they are at war with one another and being at war with one another is the natural condition of man,. From this equality of ability there arises equality in the hope of attaining our desires. This equality of hope makes enemies of men, especially when they desire something which they cannot, get enjoyable. We find in the nature of man, Hobbes says, three principal causes of quarrel, viz., competition, difference and glory. In this condition of nature, prior to the establishment of society, man is at war with man seeking to gratify his own desires, to keep what he has or to preserve his reputations. In such a condition, men live in "continual fear" and in "danger of violent death", "the life of man" in such a condition being "solitary, poor, nasty, brutish and short".

In this way, Hobbes through his philosophy of politics tried to evolve a general or universal theory of human being. Thus, by producing the systematic concept, Hobbes first of all presented the universal concept of human nature, then, the fundamental law of nature, concept of contract and at the last, the theory of state that can be applied anywhere beyond any restriction of times and spaces.

One can explore the universalistic feature even in the philosophy of John Locke. To Locke men have some natural rights by virtue of being human. These rights, Locke describes, are the natural right of "life, liberty and property". Like Hobbes, Locke also described the universal nature of men. To him, "Man is a rational being, capable of living in a society. He is not selfish, competitive or aggressive. He is also capable of noble feelings like sympathy, love, tenderness and charity towards his fellow human beings. The first instinct of man is to live in peace and harmony with others." Locke also believed that people in the state of nature did not live in a state of war or in constant fear. Men were equal and free, to act within the limitations of the law of nature. They enjoyed liberty. They enjoyed the natural rights to life, liberty and property. They were governed by the law of nature in the state of nature. The law of nature demands that no person should harm another person in his life, health, liberty or possessions. To avail these rights an individual must have the reason.

Thus, it is clear that the Lockian philosophy also starts with human nature. Locke put his best efforts to develop those universal laws which can be applied universally beyond any limitations of times and spaces and which can be proved on the criteria of reason.

The above mentioned Lockian philosophy developed in stream of liberalism within the philosophical scenario of politics. As a father of liberalism, Locke believed that being a rational human, an individual should have some natural rights, but these rights are bound by law of nature. Liberalism endeavours to find out those general principles which can be applied upon the entire individual community at the same time, irrespective of times and spaces. The concept of universal laws and universal theories were contributed by the liberalists. It is the liberal principle, which sees the whole world with equal eyes. The central problem with which liberalism is concerned is the relation between the individual and authority. But if the individual, because of the absolute value of human personality, cannot submit to any personal authority capable of acting capriciously and arbitrarily, to what authority can be submit? And the liberal answered. He can submit only to the authority of law; it alone can command and restrain him. Accordingly, liberalism advocates freedom from every form of social control except law.[73]

Thus, the authority, which had necessarily to be impersonal, objective and independent of will, could be nothing else than the law. The law, moreover, had to be conceived as eternal, universal, immutable and rational. If the authority was not to be arbitrary, it could not emanate from any personal will that was capable of acting capriciously; it could not change from day to day or place to place; it must be predictable and rational or universal in nature. Hence, it is clear that politics was like science. Similar to that of natural sciences, the philosophy of government was studied by the thinkers as a science of government. Constitutional government, democratic government etc. were studied within the scenario of liberalist philosophy. It was the era when the wars were fought not simply to protect the rights of property in a narrow sense, but to establish those liberties which the liberalists believed essential to human dignity and moral worth. The 'rights of man' established by the Revolution of 1688 and enumerated in the Bill of Rights of 1689 gradually were proclaimed beyond the confines of England, notably in the American Declaration of Independence of 1776 and in the French Declaration of the Rights of Man of 1789.

When the political doctrine, that the government rests upon the consent of the governed, found effective expression in the practice of representative government, modern constitutionalism was born. It was through the "power of the purse" that modern constitutional government came into being.

> The principle that supply and redress of grievances go hand-in-hand is the key to modern constitutional development, and when it was accompanied by the decline of the kings' feudal revenues, the growth of representative institutions, and a feeling of national solidarity, it tended to make real and effective the limited, as well as the national, character of kingship.[74]

It was the Enlightenment movement through which the universal nature of political philosophy was extended. The sixteenth century has long been characterized as the Age of Enlightenment. Enlightenment has it great impact on human thinking. According to the thinkers of Enlightenment:

> ... man in general is natively good, easily enlightened, disposed to follow reason and common sense, generous and humane and tolerant, more easily led by persuasion than compelled by force; above all a good citizen and a man of virtue, being well aware that since the rights are claimed by himself are only the natural and imprescriptibly rights of all men, it is necessary for him voluntarily to assume the obligations and to submit to the restraints imposed by a just government for the commonweal.[75]

Thoughts, which were related with the equality of human nature throughout the universe and that of scientific advancement, have paved the way for modern political thought. In such a situation, thinkers tried to develop such a system which can be generalized throughout the world. In this enlightened surroundings, Montesquieu presented focused and effective thoughts in the fields of politics and law. He established the universality of law by replacing the universality of Church and that of state. To Montesquieu man by nature is lover of liberty and liberty consists in the free exercise of the will in a political sense, it consists of the power of doing what we ought not to will. "Political liberty does not consist in an unlimited freedom but is a right of doing whatever the laws permit. Although, all governments have the same general end. Or nation there is ... in the world that has for the direct end of its constitutional political liberty."[76] In this way,

Montesquieu established the notion of universality of law and evolved that an individual's liberty and all the opportunity to flourish his personality depends only by following the universal laws.

Renowned American philosophers like Thomas Hooker (1586–1649), Roger Williams (1603–1684), John Wise (1652–1725) etc. also propounded the similar concept of universalism on the basis of human reason, instead of Church, religion or God. Human rationality may be represented by the universal laws. Wise argued, "Every man ought to be conceived to be perfectly in his own power and disposal, and not to be controlled by the authority of any other. And thus every man must be acknowledged equal to every man, since all subjection and all command are equally barristred on both sides; ... every man has a prerogative to judge for himself, namely what shall be most his behoof, happiness and well-being."[77]

We can find the universal political philosophy even in the works of utilitarian thinker, Jeremy Bentham. While presenting the universal conception of human nature, he said, "Nature has placed mankind under the governance of two sovereign masters, *pain* and *pleasure*. It is for them alone to point out what we ought to do, as well as to determine what we shall do. On the one hand, the standard of right and wrong, on the other, the chain of causes and effects, are fastened to their throne. They govern us in all we do, in all we say, in all we think; every effort we can make to throw off our subjection, will serve but to demonstrate and confirm it ... The principle of utility recognizes this subjection, and assumes it for the foundation of that system, the object of which is to rear the fabric of felicity by the hands of reason and of law."[78] In this manner, Bentham made the utility as universal law and came to the conclusion that it was the duty of the state to develop such a kind of law which can provide maximum pleasure to maximum number of individuals. Similarly, John Stuart Mill also described the importance of the theory of liberty within the political sphere.[79]

Hence, all the above discussion substantiates it very well that there are some universal laws. By following these universal laws an individual can develop his best self. It reflects that the pre-modern notion of the eternal law of spirituality got replaced by modern universal law of rationality.

Critical Evaluation

Modernism, characterized by rationalism, universalism, and individualism had to face a vehement criticism from the thinkers belonging to different disciplines like philosophy, sociology, psychology as well as politics. Critics argued that modernism presented only one aspect of human society. It is a partial and ill-conceived theory. They were intended to criticize the modernist perspective and to explore new dimensions.

By criticizing rationalism, which is the foremost feature of the modern philosophy, the critics argued that man is not only a rational being, he is also a creature of irrational forces. They were of the opinion that the attempt to reduce human life to a mathematical equation, a purely biological fact, or a physical apparatus, could only end in the repudiation of human personality and dignity.[80]

These conclusions have been fostered in part by a new 'science' of human nature – psychology – which emerged during the second half of the nineteenth century. First conceived as a science of mind or consciousness, it later developed as a science of behaviour. A broadly defined functional psychology starts with the question "what man *does*" and proceeds to the question, how and why man does? These questions demands introspective methods along with the experimental and scientific methods.[81]

One of the first scholars to define psychology as a science of human behaviour was William McDougall (1871–1938). He was also one of the founders of social psychology. His general assumption was that there must be a number of fundamental motives, which are natural and hereditary and that all other motives, must be derived from these primary motives in the course of the individual experience. In 1908, McDougall published a list of these primary motives, which he first called *instincts* and later *propensities*. His list of propensities included:

1. To desire food periodically (hunger),
2. To reject certain substances (disgust),
3. To explore new places and things (curiosity),
4. To try to escape from danger (fear),
5. To fight when frustrated (anger),
6. To have sex desire (mating propensity),
7. To care tenderly for the young (mothering propensity),
8. To seek company (gregarious propensity),
9. To seek to dominate (self-assertive propensity),
10. To accept obvious inferiority (submissive propensity),
11. To make things (constructive propensity), and
12. To collect things (acquisitive tendency).[82]

These propensities tells us that man is not motivated by any logical or rational principles or by any rationally calculated desire for a preponderance of pleasure over pain. He is primarily a creature of instinct or impulse, which is motivated by these propensities. In fact, McDougall added that the individual is motivated, however, not only by these primary instincts or propensities, but also by the influence exerted by the social environment. He said:

> Each man is an individual only in an incomplete sense, he is but a unit in a vast system of vital and spiritual forces which are expressing themselves in the form of human societies and working towards ends which no man can foresee.[83]

It is the group to which an individual belongs that largely conditions how he shall think and how he shall act. As a product of long evolution, "society has ideals and aims and traditions loftier than any principles of conduct the individual can form for himself unaided, and only by the further evolution of organized society can man be raised to higher levels".[84] The individual apart from society yields to "non-moral and purely egoistic tendencies" but under the restraint imposed by social living "man's conduct" is raised "above the plane of pure egotism" and he led "to think and care and work for others as well as himself".[85] McDougall writes:

> The collective actions of the well organized group become truly volitional actions expressive of a degree of intelligence and morality much higher than that of the average member of the group, and even, by reason of exultation of emotion and organized cooperation in deliberation, above that of its highest members.[86]

Society has not only a mind, but a life and destiny, apart from that of the individuals which happen to compose it at any given time.

Similarly, Sigmund Freud (1856–1939) had proved it very well that unconscious mind also has its great impact along with conscious mind. He gave much more importance to the unconscious mind in his psychological studies:

> Every human action, thought and emotion is motivated and when there is no conscious motive there is always an unconscious motive that can be unearthed by psychoanalytic methods of analysis.[87]

To Freud every human behaviour is motivated not only by conscious motive but also by unconscious motives. Psychoanalytic method of analysis shows that human behaviour is the result of social, natural and individual stimuli.[88] Reason, in the form of conscious motive, has an instrumental function only. It can tell us how to do what we want to do but not why or whether. It can supply us with good reason for bad motives or to prefer one to another. Cut loose from its moorings in faith, reason drifts with the currents of fashion unable to distinguish the real from the unreal, the true from the false, and the good from the bad. Thus, the psychological perspective took modernist conception of rationality as a partial or one-sided theory.

Further, socialist thinkers have also presented their vehement criticism against the rationalist concept of modern philosophy. They argued that sociology cannot be studied only through the rational action of human being. They assumed that in his social behaviour man usually follows the unconscious motives, rather than conscious motives. Eminent Sociologist Max Weber (1864–1920) categorized the man's social actions into following four categories:

1. *Rational action in relation to goal:* Those actions, where an individual uses his rational capacities to achieve goal with the help of available facilities.
2. *Rational action in relation to value:* Those actions, where an individual achieves his goal with the help of traditional and social values. The goal would be decided by the subject with the help of reason but its aim would be depended on social values.
3. *Emotional action:* Those actions, which are totally related with an individual's emotions. While implementing these actions, he becomes emotional.
4. *Traditional actions:* Those actions, which are backed by traditional, conventional customs. These actions are neither goal-oriented, nor rational or value-based. Rather, as groups are accustomed to follow these pre-decided actions, an individual follows it automatically. Otherwise, these actions are emotionless.[89]

Thus, it reflects that an individual's actions are resulted not only due to his rational capabilities, but also, directly or indirectly, they are influenced by social values, traditional norms and practices.

In this context, famous sociologist Talcott Parsons (1902–1979) mentioned it succinctly that all the social actions can be categorized within the circumference of meaningful category. These actions always endeavour to achieve particular ends. To achieve these aims, men are not always directed or guided by reason, but sometimes also inspired by certain motivations. According to Parsons, these motivations can be listed into three categories as follows:

1. *Cognitive motivations:* Those motivations through which an individual receives informations which are related to him.

2. *Cathetic motivations:* Those motivations, with which an individual can develop his emotional and empirical attachments.
3. *Evaluative motivations:* Those motivations, which are related with individual's reasons. While implementing these an individual develops a relational perspective, means how much he is going to gain or lose.

In addition to these motivations, Parsons has also presented the classification of values:

1. *Cognitive values:* Those values, which are factual in nature and an individual evaluates them at the level of objectivity.
2. *Appreciative values:* Those values, which are appreciated by an individual, groups and societies.
3. *Ethical values:* Those values, which are related with the ethics of the society.

In this way, Parsons says that when a person does a particular action, his action contains both motivations and orientations. Due to these two factors only, an individual is motivated to achieve certain goals. Thus, reason is not the only factor having its impact on individuals' behaviour, but there are also many other factors which have also their direct or indirect impact on individuals' action.

Further, critics have also raised question on scientific knowledge, which is rational and follows the principle of experimental uniformity. Vilfredo Pareto (1848–1923) rejected this notion of science. To him, in the societal context, science usually follows the principles of logico-experimental, but at the same time it can never follow the principles of experimental uniformity. According to Pareto, all the streams of social sciences can be categorized within two necessarily contexts. First is logico-action and the other is non-logico action. Those actions, which are both objective as well as subjective, are called logico-actions.

For Pareto, social actions cannot be categorized only upto to the logical or rational actions. Instead, he classified the social actions within the class of non-logico-actions. He proved his words by giving the nature of rational actions. He said that all the actions which are directed by mind, depended on three stages: stage of mind, fact and expression. To Pareto ali those actions of an individual, which are represented by heart, are in fact state of mind. Although they can not be studied directly, yet can be realised through expressions. Thus, besides the logico actions, non-logico experiments are also responsible for individual's behaviour.[90]

Further, Pareto discarded the categories of 'cause' and 'effect' which he thought gave a one-sided and hence oversimplified and superficial view of social change, in favour of the terms 'variable' and 'function'. Society is composed of many variable elements, which react upon one another and it is impossible to select one and call it the 'cause' and another call it the 'effect'. The relationship between politics, economics, religion, ethics, learning, etc. is a functional, and not a casual relationship. In addition, he suggested that sociologists should confine their attention to those constant and uniform elements of a social system that could be measured quantitatively. For him, society is neither an organism nor a mechanism but simply a 'social system' in which the disruptive forces are held in check by integrating forces. Social system may take various forms. The form of a society is determined by all the elements which influence it. And, this influence cannot be examined only by reason. Reason has technical efficacy only. It can tell us how to do, what to do, what we want to do but it cannot tell us anything about the desirability or intrinsic goodness of our wants. As a consequence, most human conduct is motivated by non-logical factors. In science, reason reigns supreme, but in yielding knowledge it is of little or no use a guide to action.

In this context, William James (1842–1910) said that we cannot define truth as a universal rational conception acceptable to every one. To him, "We have to live today by what truth we can get today, and be ready tomorrow to call it falsehood."[91]

Our obligation to seek truth is part of our general obligation to do what pays. The payment true ideas bring are the sole why of our duty to follow them. Identical whys exist in the case of wealth and health.[92]

The truth of an idea is not a stagnant properly inherent in it. Truth happens to an idea. It becomes true, is made true by events. Its varity is in fact an event, a process: the process namely of its verifying itself, its verification. Its validity is the process of its valid action.[93]

To James, truth is not something to be discovered but something to be made. Truth is not something absolute and constant, but something relative and ever-changing. Truth is whatever 'works' here and now. But, who is to decide what 'works' mean?

According to James, the conception of truth is the idea of the "will to believe". He argued that all the moral and religious questions are of such a vital nature that their "solutions cannot wait for sensible proof" and on such questions we must consult our 'hearts', rather than our 'heads'.

In a similar way, Friedrich Wilhelm Nietzsche (1844–1900) said that truth is nothing but the will to power. "Truth is not something there, that might be found or discovered, but something that must be created."[94] And, the groups of the people who are creating this truth are those people who are sitting at the powerful position.

By declaring himself as anti-Christ, Nietzsche said that either it was Caesar, Napoleon or Cesare Borgia, they all used the Christianity to extend their power. Otherwise, Christian morality is fit only for slaves; it exalts weakness, engenders comparison, encourages submission, and condemns pride. It is a morality for the masses. The new morality is for the few, those supermen of the future who must learn to be self-reliant, hard and cruel if they are not to perish with the masses and to be engulfed by mediocrity. Life is tragic, hard and cruel but it is its own reward for those with strength and courage enough to do battle with it. Only the few can hope to win, to become 'new creatures', to be the supermen, but in their 'creation' lies the meaning of life itself. In Nietzsche's words:

> *I teach you the Superman.* Man is something that is to be surpassed. What have you done to surpass man? All beings hitherto have created something beyond themselves: and ye want to be the ebb of that great tide, and would rather go back the beast than surpass man?
>
> What is the ape to man? A laughing stock, a thing of shame. And just the same shall man be to the Superman: a laughing-stock, a thing of shame ..., I teach you the Superman! The Superman is the meaning of the earth. Let your will say: The Superman shall be the meaning of the earth![95]

To Nietzsche, if God is dead, there is no alternative but for men "to become Gods". Therefore, not matter, not ideas, but the will to power is an essential reality, which includes both spirit and matter. The world is neither an organism nor a machine but a chaos, without beginning or end, meaning or purpose. It is a process of Eternal Recurrence. Only one thing can redeem life in this world from futility and that is *courage*. If life is to be something more than "a tale told by an idiot, full of sound and furry, signifying nothing", it must be embraced in all its misery and tragedy with a passionate defiance or courage that "strikes even death dead". Of all the traditional virtues, only one – courage – survives in Nietzsche's philosophy and upon that one virtue he seeks to erect an entire philosophy of life.

Nietzsche agrees with Christianity in saying that man can be saved only by becoming a 'new creature' but the new creature envisaged by Nietzsche is the exact opposite of Christ. It is a man motivated by "voluptuousness, passion for power, and selfishness", he is devoid of all sympathy for his fellow men, cunning, treacherous, cruel.

Further, Nietzsche was very much clear in the sphere of science also. He said:

> No don't come to me with science when I ask for the natural antagonist of the aesthetic ideas. Science cannot escape an ideological character similar to that of religion. Since 'it too rests upon faith' ... this is the great error that has every committed; one believed one possessed a criterions of reality in the form of reason while in fact one possessed them in order to misunderstand reality in the shrewd manner.[96]

In fact Nietzsche was under no illusion that science could do what religion had failed to do and, more consistently than most of those who rejected reason, he refused to worship at the alter of science when he could no longer worship at the alter of God. In Nietzsche the tortured soul of modern man is laid bare for all to see, in him all the conflicts of modern thought find a local point, in him are embodied all the anxieties that the separation of reason from faith has engendered. Actually, Nietzsche's gentle and delicate nature is often pleaded in extenuation. The truth remains that his doctrine is, what it professes to be, a philosophy of force and nothing but force, that it is certain to stimulate that pride from which tyranny comes in its disciples, and that it ministers to the worst prejudices of cultivated men that other people are of no account.

This is the reason why Nietzsche predicated and welcomed the coming of the "new barbarians" – the cynics, experimentalists and conquerors – who would unite in their person intellectual superiority and physical prowess. He said:

> ... the illogical is a necessity for mankind and much good proceeds from the illogical. Once one found truth, is supposed to eliminate ignorance and error, but as a result, the will to examination, investigation.[97]

Thus, it is clear from Nietzsche's philosophy that truth is neither rational nor religious in nature; it is something contemporary, which can contribute in the development of the society. To Nietzsche, the idea of a pure knowledge is impermissible because reason and truth are ""nothing more than the expediency of a certain race and species – their utility alone is their truth". Nietzsche characterizes truth as a "mobile army of metaphors and metonyms", that is, sentences are the only things that can be true or false. Knowledge is the question not of true discovery but of the construction of interpretations about the world that are taken to be true. For Nietzsche, truth is not a collection of facts, for there can be only interpretations and there is no limit to the ways in which the world can be interpreted. In so far as the idea of truth has a historical purchase, it is the consequence of power, that is, of whose interpretations counts as truth. Consequently, Nietzsche rejects the Enlightenment philosophy of universal reason and progress.

The proponents of Frankfurt School (Germany, 1932), like Max Horkheimer and T.W. Adorno, also criticize the Enlightenment philosophy of reason. In their book *Dialectic of Enlightenment,* Horkheimer and Adorno argue that the Enlightenment rationality is logic of domination and oppression. The very impulse to control nature through science and rationality is, they argue, an impulse to control and dominate human beings. In this view the Enlightenment thinking is inherently an instrumental rationality whose logic leads only to industrializations. Epistemologically speaking, Horkheimer and Adorno characterize the Enlightenment thinking as positing an 'identity' between thought and its objects, which seeks to capture and subsume all that is different from itself. They regard the Enlightenment reason as turning rationality into irrationality and deception as it eliminates competing ways of thinking and claims itself as the sole basis for truth. As Best and Kellner put it:

> In their [Horkheimer and Adorno's] interpretation, a synthesis of instrumental rationality and capitalism employed sophisticated modes of mass communication and culture, a bureaucratized and rationalized state apparatus and science and technology to administer consciousness and needs to ensure social integration so that individual would act in conformity with the system's dictates.[98]

For Horkheimer and Adorno the Enlightenment movement presents that kind of rationality through which an individual again comes into a strong grip of a new kind of intellectual shackles, instead of breaking and throwing it away.

Jurgen Habermas, another propounder thinker of the Frankfurt School, though accepted the Enlightenment movement as a positive development, yet he was of the view that the project of modernity has not been completed and can be completed only with the help of 'communicative rationality'.[99] Elaborating the meaning of the Communicative Rational Theory, Habermas said that science is the one aspect of knowledge, which is intended to fulfil man's particular interest. From this perspective Habermas has divided the concept of knowledge into following three categories:

1. *Applied knowledge,* which is intended to discover the various objectives of the physical/material world order.
2. *Historical knowledge,* which is intended to understand the essence of society with the help of historical text, scriptures and manuscripts.
3. *Analytical knowledge,* which is intended to bring out about those notices which are responsible for exploitation of a man by man.

In this very context, Habermas also talked about three kinds of interests of man in following manner:

1. *Technical or instrumental interests,* which correspond to empirical science.
2. *Practical or commutative interests* by which an individual tries to learn his present surroundings with the help of past.
3. *Emancipatory interests,* which govern historical sciences.[100]

On the basis of the above-mentioned three types of knowledge and interests, it can be said that if an individual wants to lead a secured and satisfied life he has to have proper control on environment with the help of advanced means of technologies so that he can liberate him from every kind of exploitation – natural as well as social.

Further, an individual may require various kinds of instruments to emancipate him from every kind of exploitation. Habermas discussed about these emancipatory instruments while discussing critical theory.

In fact, Habermas' critical theory rests upon a combination of casual explanations and is ultimately aimed at self-emancipation. Self-emancipation takes place whenever people are able to challenge past restrictions, which are a result of distorted communication.[101] Habermas divides those instruments in following manner:

1. *Interaction:* The aim of the interaction is to reveal to the patient the previously hidden causal mechanisms, which have hitherto influence on behavioural patterns.
2. *Language:* It is an empirical-analytical dimension of interests. It is the instrument with which an individual develops behavioural understanding.
3. *Hegemony:* The ultimate goal of the psychoanalytic encounter is the removal of these restrictions of the past.[102]

It is obvious that up to the question of technological development, the science is useful, but at the same time it is also true that it is not the concern of science at all that by whom the science and technology would be controlled. Accordingly, we should find out the reasons of interaction among the members of society, because these interactions are responsible for the theory construction and its psychoanalytical explanations. Thus, for a clear concept of society, a clear-cut knowledge of interaction is always required.

For Habermas, an action or a statement is rational if it can, in principle, be justified on the basis of an open debate with equal participation for each individual. This working definition can be used to address three aspects of the concept of rationality. One component is epistemological. Its leading question is, whether or not each culture incorporates its own rationality. Habermas' conceptualization of rationality as procedural leads him to reject relativist notion such as those of which, who relies upon Wittgenstein's philosophical investigations. A second concept of rationality operates at the level of social theory. It deals with the rational claims which are made in one's explanations of social conduct. The third component, to which Habermas pays most attention, refers to the sociology of culture and particularly the cultural process of transition, which the West has undergone since roughly the sixteenth century.

By focusing on the third component, Habermas reacts partly against Weber's notion of disenchantment and Adorno and Horkheimer's concept of instrumental reason. According to these authors, modern civilization is characterized by an increase in the logic of means-end rationality. As such, they are highly critical of the project of modernity. For Habermas, however, rationalization is not a single, but a two-fold, process. On the one hand, it indeed involves instrumental rationality, as it has been conceptualized by Weber and the Frankfurt School. Similarly, Habermas has also criticized excess focus on rationality. On the other hand, there is undoubtedly a more positive component to the rationalization process in the West. Habermas decides to call this positive aspect of the Enlightenment 'communicative rationality'. Communicative rationality refers to the institutionalization of mechanisms of open criticism. Whereas the instrumental rationality links it with the imperative of social system, the communicative rationality refers to the level of the life world. Communicative rationality becomes the cornerstone of Habermas' contribution to critical theory.[103]

Habermas argues that people possess specific practical skills, which allow them to draw particular distinctions. One of these distinctions is between three types of actions: 'instrumental', 'strategic' and 'communicative'. Instrumental and strategic actions are oriented towards success, but while the former refers to a relationship with external nature, the latter deals with strategic situations between people. Strategic and communicative actions are both social, but the latter is a social action oriented towards reaching 'understanding' with respect to all 'validity claims'. Obviously influenced by Karl Popper, Habermas argues that people are, in principle, to make an additional distinction between three different worlds: external nature, society and internal nature. Whereas the world of external nature refers to issues of a correct representation of facts, society refers to issues of moral rightness of social rules, and internal nature deals with issues of sincerity.[104]

One of Habermas' central claims is that the notion of rationality presupposes communications. To elaborate this argument, Habermas relies on the speech act theory. Habermas claims that every speech act can be divided into a propositional level and an illusionary level. Habermas combines this with his tripartite frame of words according to which there are three uses of language: cognitive, interactive and expressive. The cognitive use of language points to something in the objective world and draws upon construction as a type of speech action. The interactive use refers to the social world, and aims at establishing legitimate interpersonal relations and draws upon regulatives (like commands or promises). Finally, the expressive use refers to the subjective world, the intention or self-representation of the speaker, whilst drawing upon avowals. As will become clear in the following, these three uses of language tie in with three 'validity claims'.[105]

The core of Habermas' theory of communication is that whenever people are involved in a conversation with one another, four culturally invariant 'validity claims' are implicitly presupposed: 'intelligibility', 'truth', 'moral rightness' and 'sincerity'. Intelligibility refers to the presupposition that whenever one speaks, what one says has meaning and is not gibberish. Intelligibility is fulfilled within language use itself; it is not part of the subject matter covered within Habermas' universal pragmatics. Truth, the second validity claim, refers to the fact that by saying something, there is the implicit idea that the 'factual content' of what is said, is true. Moral rightness refers to the implicit claim that, by saying something, one has the right to say it at a given moment within a given context. Finally, sincerity is the implicit claim that, by saying what one says, he is not intending to deceive the other participants in the interaction.

The ability of people to differentiate between the three words ties in with the latter three validity claims. Truth belongs to the world of external nature; Habermas calls it the 'cognitive-instrumental sphere'. Moral rightness links in with the world of society; in Habermasian parlance, this is the 'moral-practical sphere'. Sincerity concerns the world of internal nature; Habermas calls it the 'evaluative or expressive sphere'. Although the validity claims are implicitly presupposed in communication, all are also potentially open to argumentation. Each validity claim is associated with a different form of argumentation. Theoretical discourse refers to the truth validity of propositions or efficiency of actions; Habermas calls this form of discourse the 'cognitive use of language'. Practical discourse refers to the rightness of norms; Habermas coins it 'interactive use of language'. Aesthetic criticism and therapeutic critique refer to adequacy of value standards and truthfulness and sincerity of expressions; this is the 'expressive use of language'.[106]

'Undistorted communication' differs from 'distorted communications' in that the people involved can openly defend and criticize validity claims. This is especially the case in an 'ideal speech situation', which is an unforced debate between free and equal individuals, and as such it is entirely dominated by one principle: the 'force of the better argument'. Furthermore, all individuals involved have equal right to enter the discussion, and there is no repressed motive or self-deceit which might affect the outcome.

About the societal development, Habermas argues that societal development goes through analogous stages to personal development. As opposed to modern world views mythical world views do not allow people to distinguish between the external world, the social world and internal nature – they tend to conflate nature and culture, or language and the world. Analogous to individual development, there is a trend towards increasingly discursive rationality in the transition from mythopoietic, cosmological and religious cultures, to metaphysical and modern societies. Habermas adheres to a unilinear evolutionism in that he sees this trend towards increasing rationality as the inevitable and irreversible outcome of a collective learning process. Rationality becomes a possibility once a differentiation of the system and life world takes place, plus a differentiation of the cognitive-instrumental sphere, the moral practical sphere, the evaluative and expressive sphere.

However, with the differentiation of the system and life world, two problems occurs. First, the maintenance of the economic and political dimensions of the social system might become eroded. This ties in with a 'motivation crisis' in the work sphere and a 'legitimation crisis' at the political sphere. Frankly speaking, Habermas' argument is that in advanced capitalism, politics is reduced to its pragmatic dimension; it is mainly in charge of macro-economic issues. However, if it fails to pursue its economic functions, it cannot rely upon legitimate authority, loyalty or commitment on the part of the citizens. Once politics is reduced to the solving of economic problems, recurrent economic crises are sufficient to erode its legitimacy.[107]

Further, the system imperatives tend to instrumentalize the life world, and this colonization of the life world leads to anomie or general loss of meaning. The subordination of the life world to systems imperatives is exemplified in the Marxist theory of labour where the commodification of labour leads to the erosion of its life world dimension. It is worth mentioning, however, that the Habermas' theory of colonization differs significantly from the view of classical social theorists and their followers. He differs from Weber in that he does not conceive of the colonization of the life world as part of an internal logic of modernization. In Habermas' view, the colonization of the life-world is not inevitable. This differs from a Marxist view in that Habermas' hope rests with the new social movements, and the latter do not operate within a tradition of Marxist agenda. These new social movements are concerned with issues relating to quality of life and self-realizations. Although these values are not incompatible with Marx's earlier writings, contemporary Marxists are reluctant to attribute such priority in these goals.[108]

Eminent British sociologist Anthony Giddens says that modernists have displayed an optimistic faith in the power of science, rationality and industry to transform our world for the better. Not that modernism is a culture of certainty; on the contrary, the very dynamism of modernization is premised on the perpetual revision of knowledge. Modern institutions are based on the principle of doubt, so that all knowledge is formed as a hypothesis open to revision.[109] Indeed, Giddens sees modernism as a 'risk culture'.[110] This does not, he argues, mean that modern life is inherently more risky as such. Rather, it is a reference to the way in which risk calculations play a central part in the strategic thinking of both institutions and the lives of ordinary people.

According to Giddens, the ambiguity, doubt, risk and continual change, which are makers of modernism, are manifested in the constitution of the self. 'Tradition' values stability and the place of persons in a normatively ordered and immutable cosmos, a firmness of parameters in which things are as they are because that is how they should be. By contrast, modernism values changes, life planning and reflexivity. In such a pathetic circumstances person's 'ontological security' gets affected. In the context of tradition, self-identity is primarily a question of social position, while for the modern person it a 'reflexive project', that is, "the process whereby self-identity is constituted by the reflexive ordering of self-narratives."[111] By identity project is meant the idea that identity is not fixed but created and built on, always in process, a moving towards rather than an arrival. For modernism, the self is a question not of surface appearance but of the workings of deeper structures so that metaphors of *depth* predominate. This is manifested by the ideas and concepts of psychoanalysis.

Herbert Marcuse (1898–1979), who claimed to be a neo-Marxist thinker, brilliantly analysed the problem of freedom in contemporary modern society. In his *One-Dimensional Man: Studies in the Ideology of Advanced Industrial Society,* Marcuse offered a penetrating critique of capitalism as regards its impact on human freedom. He said that capitalism exercises monopolistic control not only on production and distribution, it also creates the desire and demand for commodities through a clever manipulation of the mass media. The result is widespread craze for consumer goods, which develops into a distorted second nature of man. Consumer capitalism renders the oppressed sections insensitive to their original discontent, by stimulating their trivial, material desires, which can be easily satisfied. Under the spell of gratification of these trivial desires, the genuine urge for freedom disappears. In this background, the alienated human beings become unaware of their alienation. Under the circumstances, they should first be awakened to realize their condition of alienation in order to arouse their urge for freedom.

In his another book, *Eros and Civilization,* Marcuse has presented a blueprint of society where alienation will be removed and freedom will be restored. It will be a democratic community where work will become play, and necessary labour will be organized in harmony with liberated, and authentic, individual needs. Discontinuance of repressive performance will eliminate surplus repression, thus freeing the person from alienated labour. Marcuse concludes with an optimistic note that the Western society has already evolved a technology which is geared to meet most of the human needs. It is sufficient to enable men to live in freedom and dignity. Once they understand the necessary condition of freedom, they can transcend the era of violence and anarchy and build a new society where freedom will reign supreme.

American psychologist and sociologist, Erich Fromm has depicted the plight of aloofness of modern rational man. Fromm demonstrated that the capitalist system deformed the productive activity of man and caused his alienation in several ways. Accordingly, the alienation of man in contemporary society was an outcome of the system of commodity production, division of labour, private ownership, market economy, and monetarization of exchange and similar features of the capitalist system. Fromm identified that physical aloofness is unbearable in itself but here in contemporary world men are facing another kind of aloofness, which is called moral aloofness. Accordingly, when this moral aloofness is increasing with all its speed, then men have to face the problem of 'schizophrenia' – a mental syndrome. Spontaneous love and creative work are the only cure of this problem through which men can be reattached with the societal scenario.[112]

Karl Popper also criticizes the Enlightenment-scientific model by saying it as *pseudo-science*. According to Popper, we have to assume the fact that human knowledge can never be perfect. Any acceptance of the Enlightenment philosophers that they know the truth in absolute term cannot be accepted at all. Nature of truth is relative. Popper suggests that we should accept the concept of methodological individualism in the place of methodological wholism.[113]

Popper assumed that science and ideologies can only be developed in their fullest manner where society is open and free. It means society must always be ready for accepting new changes.[114] But the rationalist scientific society demands for following certain fixed rules and universal laws, which limit any initiatives.

Even communitarians, like Alsdair MacIntyre, criticize the scientific rationality for its craziness. He says that every individual is having a common identity and this identity is the result of the belief, and values, which are creating our system of faith. That is why, MacIntyre said, "What is good for me has to be good for one who inhabits these roles."[115]

By following the communication principle, MacIntyre says that an individual's pleasure is complementary to the co-members of the community where they are living. Hence, we cannot make difference between individualist pleasure and that of societal pleasure. If an individual is depended upon society or community for his development, then the society is also depended upon their inhabitants for its development. According to MacIntyre, man is not only a rational being as assumed by individualist modern philosophers, but he is also an emotional being. By certifying his argument, MacIntyre says that all our social interactions are the result of our emotional nature or intuitive nature. Even society or communities are the result of those laws or rules, which are oriented towards faith and belief system. According to MacIntyre:

> ... the eighteenth century moral philosophers engaged in what was an inevitably unsuccessful project; for they did indeed attempt to find a rational basis for their moral beliefs in a particular understanding of human nature, while inheriting a set of moral injunction on the one hand and a conception of human nature on the other which had been expressly designed to be discrepant with each other ...[116]

The above extract demonstrates that the Enlightenment philosophers have tried their best to define morality on the basis of rationality. Modernity had diluted all those moral standards of life upon which an edifice of societal life is created.

Communitarian thinker Charles Taylor has also criticized the modern individualistic trend in philosophy. According to Taylor, individual 'self' can never be different from that of societal 'self', which is the web of relations. All the shades of emotions like hunger, love, anger, thrust, competition, institutions are developed in between the societal circumference. Taylor says:

> ... One cannot be a self on one's own. I am a self only in relation to certain interlocutors: in one way in relation to those conversations partners who were identical to my achieving self-definition; in another in relation to those who are now crucial to my continuing grasp of language of self-understanding – and, of course, these classes may overlap. A self exists only within what I call 'web of interlocutors'.[117]

Accordingly, instead of being one-dimensional an individual's identity or his own 'self' is multi-dimensional in nature. He is not limited only up to his own self but his self is the part of the universal (societal) self. That is why, Taylor argued not for *located-self* but for *situated-self.*

Another communitarian philosopher, Michael Walzer, while criticizing the universal notion of modernity, said that we can never adopt any universal principle of justice in the real sense of the term. As, while conceptualizing the theory of justice, we have to see the context, where the theory would be implemented. A comprehensive study of the traditional values, assumptions and societal relationship is always required. According to Walzer:

> ... different social groups ought to be distributed for different reasons in accordance with different procedures, by different agents; and all these differences derive from different understandings of the social goods themselves – the inevitable product of historical and cultural particular.[118]

If the problem of justice is mainly concerned with the just distribution of social goods and benefits, then, we have to find out the rational basis of distribution. In this context, Walzer developed the theory of 'simple equality' and 'complex equality'. He was of the opinion that in this contemporary world scenario, which is so critical in nature, we are compelled to adopt the concept of 'complex equality' Thus, Walzer develops the concept of decentralized democratization of socialism where he demands for a strong welfare state.[119]

Hence, these comprehensive critical discussions have proved it very well that modernity and its various facets like rationality, universality and individuality are half-hearted concepts. Rational discussions have their importance, but irrational, emotional or sensitive and intuitive aspects of human personality have their own place in understanding human behaviour. Actually, irrational and intuitive behaviour are the intrinsic and inherent nature of any society.

Similarly, universalism gets its importance in modern philosophy but there is not any place for localism, which is responsible for individual identity in real sense of the term. These loopholes are showing that Enlightenment philosophy is not comprehensive and perfect at all. This incomplete project of modernism was completed by its following philosophy which was emerged in the late twentieth century, and called as postmodernism. The next part of the chapter deals with the same at length.

II
Postmodernism

Postmodernism has emerged as an important political current in the contemporary philosophical scenario and offered a deep and far-reaching criticism of modernism. It has challenged all the traditional as well as modern categories of thoughts within which social theories have been discussed and evaluated. Postmodernism offers sophisticated criticism of rationalism, essentialism and universalism. In fact, postmodernism is a perspective through which a new trend or a new aspect of society is emerged within the terrain of philosophy. Postmodernism, as the 'post' preface implies, is something that follows modernism. However, people who think about such things as postmodernism do not agree whether postmodernism is a break from modernism or a continuation of modernism or both. Before discussing about the conceptual analysis, it is essential to throw some lights on the sources of the origin of the philosophy.

Origin

The term 'postmodern', understood as distinguishing from the modern, seems to have been used first in 1917 by the German philosopher Rudolf Pannwitz, to describe the 'nihilism' of twentieth century's Western culture – a theme he took from Friedrich Nietzsche.[120] It resurfaced in the work of the Spanish literary critic Federico de Onis in 1934 to refer to the backlash against literary modernism.[121] It first appeared in English in 1939, used in two very different ways, by the theologian Bernard Iddings Bell, signifying the recognition of the failure of secular modernism and a return to religion,[122] and by the historian Arnold Toynbee to refer to the post-World War I rise of mass society, in which the working class surpasses the capitalist class in importance.[123]

It was then employed in the literary criticism in the 1950s and 1960s referring to the reaction against literary modernism. In fact, it is in the field of literary studies that the term 'postmodernism' has received widest usage and most verged debate. There have been many attempts to theorize the consequences and manifestations of postmodernism for literature, all usually running into problems of historical or formal definition.[124] The dominant characteristic of postmodernist novels is the pretence that it is impossible to write an original work and their paradoxical theme is writing about 'end of writing ...' consequently art rather than nature became the object of imitation and a self-conscious reflexivity emerged.[125]

Moreover, in 1970s, it came in architecture. The very universal nature of international style's application led to designs which failed to recognize the different functions of various buildings. Housing, offices and cultural institutions all looked similar, and this stylistic uniformity was criticized for its inability to add anything to their environment. The evisceration of historical reference demanded by international style was recognized as stylistically restrictive, rootless and meaningless; and consequently, in the rejection of modernist architecture, along with an explicit adoption of 'pop' style, historical traditions have become the source of contemporary quotation and imitation.[126] Robert Venturi, Charles Jenks and David Harvey have contributed a lot in this area.

During 1970s the concept of postmodernism began to be connected with that of the post-industrial society, the increasingly service or knowledge dominated economies of the most advanced societies after World War II.[127] A post-industrial society, characterized by the shift from industrial manufacturing to the service industries, now centred on information technology. This gives a key role to knowledge production and planning. In this view, technological change is the driving force of social change as information exchange and cultural production displace heavy industry at the heart of economy. New production processes, and a general shift of emphasis from production to consumption, make information technology and communications the industries of the future, and central to these processes are the role and capabilities of computers in managing the increase in volume, speed and distance with which increasingly complex information is generated and transformed.[128]

Pivotal to the conception of the post-industrial society is the place of knowledge, the shift taking place in the kinds of work people do and the related changes in the occupational structure as manual jobs give way to white-collar, professional and service work.[129] There has been both the sectoral redistribution of labour from the primary and secondary sectors to the service sector and a shift in the style or organization of labourer towards white-collar work increasingly organized on craft, rather than industrial, lines. The new class structure is centrally connected to the growing importance of knowledge and technical skills in post-industrial society. That is, the major class of the emerging new society is primarily a professional class, based on knowledge, rather than property. This service class are not primarily involved in the direct production of commodities. Rather, they sell their skill and depend on their market power. They usually have a high degree of autonomy, working either as professional experts or in directing the labour of others. Though they do not own the means of production, they may be shareholders and/or possess the ability, at least at the top of the spectrum, to manage the strategic direction of powerful companies.

Thus, the class structure of this post-industrial society would be constituted by a professional class, a technical and semi-professional class, a clerical and sales class, and a class of semi-skilled and craft workers. Noticeably absent is the manual working class to whom critics have said 'farewell'.[130] Their central argument is that, in the context of automation and post-industrial economies, new technologies have changed the employment patterns of societies removing the tendencies of the population from working class manual jobs and its associated class identity. Instead of a working class, we have a new cash-oriented post-industrial 'working' class, a secured and privileged labour 'aristocracy' and an unemployed underclass. In this post-industrial society the control of the information and knowledge would create new conflicts. Consequently, the dominant class in that group will be able to access and control information. Technocrats and bureaucrats are counterpoised to workers, students and consumers.[131]

In philosophy, it came in the 1980s to refer primarily to French post-structuralist philosophy, and secondarily to a general reaction against modern rationalism, utopianism and what came to be called 'foundationalism' – the traditional philosophical attempt to justify knowledge by rooting it in uncriticizable first principles or sense-data or both. Eventually, 'postmodern' burst into popular usage as a term for everything from rock videos to the demographics of Los Angles to the whole cultural style and mood of recent decades.

Despite the divergence among these usages of 'postmodern', one could find some commonality centring on: a recognition of pluralism and indeterminacy in the world that modern or modernist thought had evidently sought to disavow, hence, a renunciation of intellectual hopes for simplicity, completeness and certainty; a new focus on representation or images or information or cultural signs as occupying a dominant position in social life; and an acceptance of play and fictionalization in cultural fields that had earlier sought a serious, realist truth. This is a vague commonality, to be sure.[132] As the trust area of the present work is political theory, postmodernist philosophy would be studied here mainly in the context of political theory.

Development: A Philosophical Perspective

In the 1960s philosophy in France underwent a major change. A new group of the young intellectual people emerged there, who were not only deeply critical of the French academic and political society, but also of the very form of the radical philosophy that had given the establishment 'headaches' in the past, primarily, Marxism and existentialism, and to some extent, phenomenology and psycho-analysis as well.[133]

Accordingly, Marxism, existentialism and phenomenology had been, perhaps awkwardly, combined by the great French philosophers of the middle of the century, especially Jean-Paul Sartre and Maurice Merleau-Ponty, along with a dash of Freudian psychoanalysis. These intellectual movements had projected the individual human subject or consciousness as alienated in contemporary society, estranged from his or her authentic mode of experience and being – whether the source of that estrangement was capitalism (for Marxism), the scientific naturalism pervading modern western cultural (for phenomenology), excessively repressive social modes (for Freud), or bureaucratically organized social life and mass culture (for all of them). Methodologically, they rejected the belief that the study of the humanity could be moulded on or reduced to the physical sciences, hence they avoid behaviouralism and naturalism. Unlike physics, chemistry or biology, the human sciences must understood the experience – the first person point of view of their objects of study: they are concerned not merely with the fact but also with the meaning of the fact for human subjects. To diagnose contemporary alienation, they produced a historical analysis of how human society and the human self develop over time, in order to see how and why modern civilization had gone wrong. What was needed, it seemed, was a return to the true, or authentic, or free, or integrated human self as the centre of lived experience. This meant not an abandonment of modern industry, technology and secularism, but to some extent the whole reconstruction of the society (for Marx), or of moral culture (for Freud), or of our openness to the vices – studies of our own authentic experience (for phenomenology and existentialism).

Now, Marxism, existentialism, phenomenology and psychoanalysis never ruled the academic roots in France for anywhere else (exempting of course the case of Marxism in communist societies, where it had official status). They represented the major theoretical opposition to the status quo in the first half of the century. Young intellectuals dissatisfied with the neo-scholaristic, rationalistic, neo-Kantian, theologically- or scientifically-oriented forms of thought dominated in the academy – all of which seemed well suited to endorsing institutional and political authorities – tend to see these movements as the main alternatives. In the post-World War II period they constituted a major intellectual sub-culture in Europe, gradually influencing American thought as well. The new French philosophers of the 1960s – including Gilles Deleuze, Luce Irigary, Jean Francois Lyotard, and above all, Jacques Derrida and Michel Foucault – also wanted to fight the political and academic establishment. They had been schooled by another theoretical movement – structuralism developed by linguists Ferdinand de Saussure and Roman Jakobson, and championed in mid-century by the French anthropologist Claude

Levi-Strauss. Structuralism rejected the centrality of self and its historical development, characterized by Marxism, existentialism, phenomenology and psychoanalysis. The social or human sciences, like anthropology, linguistics and philosophy, needed to focus instead on the supra-individual structures of language, ritual and kinship, which make the individual what he or she is. Simply put, it is not the self that creates culture; it is culture that creates the self. The study of abstract relation within system or 'codes' of cultural signs (words, family, relations etc.) is key to understanding human existence. Structuralism seemed to offer the student of humanity a way of avoiding reduction to the natural sciences, while yet retaining objective, scientific methods, unlike the apparently subjective orientation of psychoanalysis. At the same time, it also implied that nothing is 'authentic', that there is no fundamental, original nature of the human self against which we could judge a culture.

The new philosophers of the 1960s accepted structuralism's residual to worship at the alter of the self. But they rejected its scientific pretensions. They saw deep self-reflexive philosophical problem in the attempt by human beings to be 'objective' about themselves. They applied the structural-cultural analysis of human phenomena to the human sciences themselves, which are, after all, human cultural constructions. Hence, they are commonly named "post-structuralist", meaning not that they rejected, but radicalized, structuralism. The importance of their work appeared radical in nature. They seemed to announce the end of rational inquiry into truth, the illusory nature of any unified self, the impossibility of clear and unequivocal meaning, and the oppressive nature of all modern western institutions. They appeared critically to undermine any and all positive philosophical and political position(s), to exhibit hidden paradoxes and modes of social domination operating within all products of reason.[134]

One another factor in the development of postmodernism since the early 1970s deserves special mention: the decline of Marxism. The New Left of the 1960s, and some of the new French philosophers, reinterpreted their Marxism through Freud and Ferdinand de Saussure, and so had already begun to shake off Marxist-Leninst orthodoxy. But a deeper disenchantment can be traced to the 1973 publication, in Paris, of the first volume of Alexander Solzhenitsyn's *The Gulag Archipelogy* – a monumental recounting of Stalinist atrocities in the Soviet Union. After this, it was no longer possible for people of the Left to look to the Soviet Union as a free society in any sense. The western European and North American academy became increasingly unsympathetic with Marxism and to some extent with socialism over next decade. This coincided with the popular turn to the Right in many western societies in 1998. In the last decade of the twentieth century the modern competitor to liberal capitalism – the qualifier 'modern' functioning here to exempt rejuvenated premodern competitors, like Islamic fundamentalism/utterly collapsed. The result of this change was profound, and not limited to yet another swing in the pendulum of popular opinion between the demands for greater governmental control over capitalism, a pendulum that will no doubt continue to swing. Marxism had provided a philosophy of history that served for a sizable segment of the secularized western intelligentsia as promise of worldly salvation, a fulfilment of the great modernist hope in progress, what Christopher Lasch called the "True and Only Heaven".[135]

For many irreligious intellectuals, the hope for a utopian socialist future gave badly needed significance to a life lived after the "Death of God". The loss of hope stuck a sizeable portion of this group much as the loss of the religion had already struck traditional society: absent a historical *telos* or goal, it seemed that the world had become centreless and pointless once again. Hence, Ernest Gellener dubbed it the 'second secularization'. Postmodernism in its French origins is a wayward stepchild of Marxism, and in this sense a generation's realization that it is orphaned. Logical empiricism, also called positivism, which had by the mid-century swept aside the indigenous American pragmatist philosophical tradition as well as English idealism and empiricism pursued a systematization of human-knowledge based in the certainties of a recently revolutionized logic combined with a scientific explanation of 'sense data'. Positivism was only one of a wide verity of philosophical movements of the first half of the twentieth century that attacked the very possibility of philosophical inquiry into the ultimate nature of reality, the existence of God, or a universally valid ethics.[136]

But, the subsequent philosophers of language, logic and science began to cast doubts on the adequacy of the positivist picture. A complete and consistent logic complex enough to include arithmetic was shown to be impossible, rendering unrealizable not only the complete axiomatization of mathematics, but the greatest hopes of an ideal language philosophy as well. The distinction between analytic or logical statements and synthetic or empirical statements, and the distinction between statements of observed sense data and theoretical explanations of those data, appeared more and more to be porous: there seemed no way to say what we sense without already using some unverified theoretical language in order to say it. But that implied that verification in a strict sense is impossible, since any statement of 'fact' (sense experience) must presuppose the theoretical perspective it might be offered to verify.[137] In the later philosophy, even Wittgenstein suggested that the attempt to discover the foundation of knowledge was senseless as that of speculative metaphysics.

Even in science, the model of knowledge for so many philosophers came to be seen as non-systematic, hence perhaps non-rational, in its development.[138] And throughout the twentieth century certain scientific discoveries generated new kind of theories that eventually, since 1970s, have contributed to the development of what may be called a 'scientific postmodernism'. This arguably began with quantum theory in the 1920s, which was forced by the nature of its objects to abandon determinism as an ideal of explanation and to accept the inescapable effect of observation on the phenomena observed. In the last decades of the century developments in the theory of self-regulating system in biology and cybernetics, chaos and catastrophe theory have been exploited as part of 'new science' with postmodern implications.

Returning to the early post-World War II period, outside philosophical and scientific inquiry, new tendencies in art, literature, music, and especially architecture, were critically superseding movements that had earlier been considered radical. Through the first half of the twentieth century modernist art and literature had seemed to critique the bourgeois, capitalist social order that carried the economic load of modernity.

By the time of the 1960s, a new generation of writers, painters and architectures began to react against aesthetic modernism. The 'end' of modernism in literature was recognized as early as in the 1950s by Irving Howe and in the 1960s by Leslic Fiedler.[139] Literary irony and camp seemed to capture the sensibility of the time more than the seriousness of the modernist search for the alienated soul and the essence of reality. This period saw the development of art that seemingly renounced unity of style for *pastiche* and threatened to break down the very notion of the 'aesthetic', hence the distinctiveness of the art object.

It was in the most socially consequential of arts, architecture, that postmodernism had its most widespread influence in the 1960s and 1970s.[140] The groundwork had been laid in 1961 by Jane Jacobs' devastating book, *The Death and Life of Great American Cities*.[141] Jacobs lashed out at the orthodox urban reform movement of the day, in which modernism had been joined with welfare state policy to create vast "single use" housing complexes for the poor. She exposed the virtually anti-urban, anti-human impulses of this alleged humanitarian policy, whose abstract grids undercut the social mechanisms by which urban neighbourhoods had traditionally maintained themselves as viable communities. Then, in 1966, in his *Complexity and Contradiction in Architecture,* Robert Venturi insisted that architectural communication requires not simplicity but complexity and even contradiction. Modernism's search for a signified universal style had been summarized by Mies Van Der Rohe's slogan "less is more", to which Venturi replied, "less is bore".

In the late 1970s, three books viz., Charles Jenck's *The Language of Post-Modernism Architecture* (1977); Jean Francois Lyotard's *The Postmodern Condition : A Report on Knowledge* (1984); and Richard Rorty's *Philosophy and the Mirror of Nature* (1979) galvanized postmodernism as a movement. The last, while not employing the term 'postmodern', argued that the developments of post-Heideğgerian continental philosophy and post-Wittgenstenian analytic philosophy were converging on a kind of pragmatic anti-foundationalism. Rorty thereby became an American representative of postmodernism, albeit in pragmatic garb, giving 'postmodern' a meaning for philosophers outside the European tradition.

Thus, postmodernism is not a philosophical*ism* develop recently to rebel against what might be considered the dominant strains of modern thought. As postmodernism developed, others responded to the problems of late twentieth century society and culture with a call for a return to traditional cultural form.

In political theory, the 'premodernist' elements of conservatism and communitarianism echoed, in far milder tones, the global resurgence of nativism, nationalism and militant fundamentalism that began with Iranian revolution of 1980 and was accelerated in the Balkans and Central Asia after the fall of the Soviet empire. MacIntyre's philosophical choice "Nietzsche or Aristotle" is thus matched by political theorist Benjamin Barber's geo-political opposition, "Jihad versus McWorld", the postmodern global service economy and mass culture versus an anti-modern traditionalism, fundamentalism, and/or nationalism. At the same time, of course, other intellectuals, like Jurgen Habermas, continue to defend the modern legacy of rationalism and liberal individualism by developing a non-foundational version of the Enlightenment thought. Their reformed 'postmodernism' seeks to obviate either a fearful return to postmodern past or an impulsive leap into the postmodern future.

Definition and Meaning

The diverse factors behind the origin of postmodernism show that it could not be developed on a particular basis. Philosophers have tried their best to define the meaning of the term 'postmodernism' from different perspectives but it is difficult to summarize what postmodernism actually means. Even then, by analysing the different perspectives given by various philosophers, we can find out its basic features and fundamental characteristics more clearly.

French philosopher Jean-Francois Lyotard (1926–98) is regarded as one of the propounder of the philosophy of postmodernism. He says, "Simplifying to the extreme, I define *postmodern* as incredulity towards meta narratives. This incredulity is undoubtedly a product of progress in sciences: but that progress in turn presupposes it."[142]

Lyotard defines postmodernism in the absence of any concept of totality. Accordingly, society is full of diversity: various kinds of culture and traditions are there, including varieties of language, music, dance and economic systems. Thus, it is impossible to some extent to develop a unique universal model by ignoring these different shades of the society, which is multicultural and multidimensional in nature. Lyotard said, to the obsolescence of the meta-narrative apparatus of legitimization corresponds, most notably, the crisis of metaphysical philosophy and of the university institution, which in the past relied on it. Accordingly, the narrative functions in loosing its functions, its great heroes, its great damages, its great wages, its great goal. It is being dispersed in clouds of narrative language elements – narrative, but also denotative, prescriptive, descriptive and so on. Conveyed within each cloud are pragmatic valences specific to its kind. Each of us lives at the intersection of many of these. However, we do not necessarily establish stable language combinations, and the properties of the ones we do establish are not necessarily communicable. Hence, according to Lyotard, postmodern may mean faith in diversity or fragmentation.

Marxist French philosopher Jean Baudrillard is one of the foremost critics of contemporary society and culture, and is often seen as a proponent of the principle of postmodernism. He tried to depict the consumerist nature of postmodernist society with the help of the means of communications. In fact, Baudrillard took the postmodern turn in the mid-1970s, developing a new kind of social analysis that went beyond the confines of modern social theory. While offering a critique of modern society and theory, Baudrillard claims that the era of modernity and the tradition of classical social theory has become obsolete and that we need a novel mode of social analysis adequate to the era of postmodernity. A prolific author, who has written over twenty books, Baudrillard has commented on the most salient cultural and social phenomena of the contemporary era and developed one of the most influential modes of postmodern theory.

In his early writings, by criticizing the Marxist philosophy, Baudrillard argues that Marxism, first, does not adequately illuminate premodern societies, which were organized around symbolic exchange and not production. He also argues that Marxism does not criticize capitalist societies radically enough and calls for a more extreme break. At this stage, Baudrillard turns to anthropological perspectives. Yet, it is important to note that this critique of Marxism was taken from the Left, arguing that Marxism did not provide a radical enough critique of, or alternative to, contemporary productive societies – capitalist and communist. Baudrillard distinguishes between the logic of production and utility that organized modern societies and the logic of simulation that he believes in the organizing principle of postmodern societies. He postulates a rupture between modern and postmodern societies as great as the division between modern and premodern ones that are foundation of classical social theory. In theorizing the epochal postmodern repute with modernity, Baudrillard declares the "end of political economy" and of an era in which production was the organizing principle of society. He defines the postmodern society in following manner:

> The end of labour. The end of production. The end of political economy. The end of signifier/signified dialectic, which facilitates the accumulation of knowledge and of meaning, the linear syntagma of cumulative discourse. And at the same time, the end simultaneously of the exchange value/use value/dialectic, which is the only thing that makes accumulation and social production possible. The end of linear dimension of discourse. The end of linear dimension of the commodity. The end of the classical era of the sign. The end of the era of production.[143]

Baudrillard argues that the modern epoch was the era of capitalism and the bourgeoisie, in which workers were exploited by capital and provided revolutionary force of upheaval. Baudrillard, however, declared that in postmodern society the political economy of the modern era would be ended and thus the end of the Marxist problematic and of the modernity itself. The discourse of "the end" signifies his announcing a postmodern break or rupture in history. We are now, Baudrillard claims, in a new era of simulation in which social reproduction (information processing, communication, knowledge industries and so on) replaces production as the organizing principle of society. In this era, labour is no longer a force of production but is itself "one *sign* amongst many".[144] Labour is not primarily productive in this situation, but is a sign of one's social position, way of life, and mode of servitude. Wages too bear no rational relation to one's work and what one produces, but to one's place within the system.[145] But, crucially, political economy is no longer the foundation, the social determinant, or even a structural 'reality' in which other phenomena can be interpreted and explained.[146] Instead, we live in the 'hyper-reality' of simulations in which images, spectacles, and the play of signs replace the logic of production and class conflict as key constituents of contemporary societies.[147] Baudrillard further says:

> ... modern societies are organized around the production and consumption of commodities, while postmodern societies are organized around simulation and the play of images and signs, denoting a situation in which codes, modes, and signs are the organizing principles of a new social order where simulation rules. In the society of simulation, identities are constructed by the appropriation of images, and codes and models determine how individuals perceive themselves and relate to other people. Economics, politics, social life, and culture are all governed by the logic of simulations, whereby codes and models determine how goods are consumed and used, politics, uphold, culture is produced and consumed, and everyday life is lived.[148]

Baudrillard's postmodern world is also one of radical *implosion,* in which social classes, genders, political differences, and one-autonomous realm of society and culture collapse into each other, erasing previously defined boundaries and differences. If modern societies, for classical social theory, were characterized by differentiation, for Baudrillard postmodern societies are characterized by de-differentiation, or *implosion*. For Baudrillard, in the society of simulation, economies, politics, culture, sexuality and the social values all implode into each other, such that economics is fundamentally shaped by culture, politics, and other spheres, while art, once a sphere of potential difference and opposition, is absorbed into the economic and political while sexuality is everywhere. In this situation, differences between individuals and groups implode in a rapidly melting dissolution of the social and the previous boundaries and structures upon which social theory had once focused.

In addition, Baudrillaid's postmodern universe is one of *hyper-reality* in which entertainment, information and communication technologies provide experiences more intense and involving than the scenes of banal everyday life, as well as the codes and models that structure everyday life. The realm of the hyper-real (i.e., media simulations of reality, Disneyland and amusement parks, malls and consumer fantasylands, TV sports, and the other excursions into ideals worlds) is more real than real, whereby the models, images and codes of the hyper-real come to control thought and behaviour. Yet, determination itself is aleatory in a non-linear world where it is impossible to chart causal mechanisms and logic in a situation in which individuals are confronted with an overwhelming flux of images, codes, and models any of which may shape an individual's thought or behaviour.[149]

Postmodern theory has consistently been seen to challenge and undermine the central tenets of Marxist thought, especially the centrality it accords to class struggle as the driving force of history, the need for an analysis of the social as a 'totality', and the primacy of the economic over political and cultural concerns. According to Lyotard's influential formulation, postmodernity is characterized by incredulity to all grand universal or master narratives: the Enlightenment narrative of progressive instrumental reason, the psychoanalytic narrative of desire, and above all the Marxism narrative of human emancipation. In its stridently nominalist and anti-foudationalist rhetoric postmodernism rejects all universal explanatory systems, and the privileging of homogenized groups, such as the working class, in favour of an analysis of discrete micro-narratives and particular identities. Postmodernism, in short, represents, a fundamental epochal shift in which the older forms of explanation are no longer adequate or credible. Baudrillard has pursued this argument further through his claim that a radical break has taken place within capitalism itself whereby we now exist in a hyper-real world of cyberspace, free-floating images, and mediatized events. Therefore, key Marxian categories, such as the distinction between use value and exchange value, are now obsolete as they depend upon an essentially anthropological conception of human, which has been eclipsed by a new economy of signs and simulacra. Marxism, with its nostalgia for the historical referent and latent essentialism, is quite simply redundant in this 'unreal' reality of the postmodern world.

To many Marxists thinkers, the concept of postmodernism has been hostile among themselves. For example, the value of postmodernism in placing on the political agenda issues of gender, race, ethnicity and identity, but at the same time it seems as a radically imported resource. Postmodernism, they argue, tends to undermine its own radicalism by promoting a series of caricatures or 'straw-figures' – the Enlightenment, Marxism, totality, History (with a capital H), the subject, essentialism, hierarchy, and identity – which it can then extravagantly and ostentatiously knock down. Postmodernism thus undercuts the very foundations of political solidarity and agency ultimately denying the possibility for any real or meaningful social change.

The North American Marxist theorist, Fredric Jameson, in 1984, published his monumental work, *Postmodernism Or The Cultural Logic of Late Capitalism*[150] which served to redraw the whole map of the postmodern world at one stroke.

Postmodernism and consumer society first attempt to dilute the key features of this culture, albeit with a rather heterogeneous list of names, styles, and forms, ranging from the poetry of John Ashbeny to the films of God and, from the architecture of Robert Venturi to punk rock of the clash, from the music of Phillip Glass to the French new novel. The importance of this essay, however, lies not with who is included or excluded from this taxonomy but in its development of two essential characteristics of Jameson's theorization of postmodernism, that is, his contention that postmodernism ushers in a radically new experience of space and time. There has been a significant decline, according to Jameson, in our sense of history, narrative and memory, and simultaneously an erosion of aesthetic depth and critical distance. This experience finds aesthetic representation through the related concepts of particle and schizophrenic temporality. For Jameson:

> Postmodernism is implicated in a depthless sense of the present and a loss of historical understanding. We live in a postmodern hyper space in which we are unable to place ourselves, the specific manifestations of which includes the cannibalization of styles from past and present; the loss of authentic artistic style in favour of pastiche; the transformation of representations of the world into images and spectacles; the breakdown of a firm distinction between

> high and low culture; the culture of the simulacrum or copy (for which no original existed); the fashion for nostalgia in which history is the object not of representation but of stylistics connotation.[151]

Jameson's description of the postmodern world as one marked by fragmentation, instability and disorientation is one that has much in common with Baudrillard. However, he parts company on the level of explanation. Jameson is at pains to point out that postmodernism has genuine historical reality. He argues that postmodern cultural practices are not superficial but expressive of developments and experiences in deep 'reality'. For Jameson, postmodernism is expressive of a world system of multinational or late capitalism and represents the cultural style of late capitalism operating in a new global space. It is late capitalism which, by extending commodification to all realms of personal and social life, transforms the real into the image and simulacrum.

Michel Foucault (1926–94) defines the concept of postmodernism in the context of power/knowledge and in his unique way of thinking Foucault breaks the premises of 'classical' Enlightenment thought. He said that knowledge is not metaphysical, transcendental or universal. Rather, it is specific to particular times and spaces.[152] Foucault talks not of truth *per se,* but of 'regimes of truth', that is, the configurations of knowledge that 'counts as truths', under determinate historical conditions. He says, knowledge is perspectival in character. There can be no one totalizing knowledge, which is able to grasp the 'objective' character of the world. Rather, we both have and require multiple viewpoints or truth by which to interpret a complex heterogeneous human existence. Knowledge is not regarded as a pure or natural way of understanding. It is implicated in regimes of power.

Foucault breaks with the central Enlightenment metaphor of 'depth'. He argues against interpretative or hermeneutic methods which seek to disclose the hidden meanings of language. In fact, the idea that there is a clear, distinctive and final break between the Enlightenment and post-Enlightenment thought, or between the modern and postmodern, is challenged by Foucault when he suggests that we do not have to be 'for' or 'against' the Enlightenment. It is a question not of accepting or rejecting the Enlightenment rationality but of asking:

> What is this reason that we use? What are its historical effects? What are its limits, and what are its dangers? [If] philosophy has a

> function within critical thought, it is precisely to accept this sort of spiral, this sort of revolving door of rationality that refers us to its necessity, to its indispensability, and at the same time to its intrinsic dangers.[153]

Foucault is concerned with the description and analysis of the surfaces of discourse and their effects under determinate material and historical conditions. Foucault casts doubt on the Enlightenment understanding of progress. Knowledge as discourse does not unfold as an even historical evolution but is discontinuous. That is, Foucault identifies significant epistemological breaks in knowledge across time and rejects any notion of *telos* or the inevitable direction of human history. Hence, he adopts new methodologies like fragmentation, archaeology and genealogy to have knowledge and to know the truth in real sense of the term.

Jacques Derrida (1930–2004), born in Algeria, is one of the two most famous instigators of what is called postmodernism in contemporary philosophy. More accurately labelled a post-structuralist, his reputation was established in the late 1960s with a series of books known for careful analysis of texts, novel critical perspective and difficult style. The term 'post-structuralism' implies "after structuralism", embodying notion of both critique and absorption. That is, post-structuralism absorbs aspects of structural linguistics while subjecting it to a critique which, it is claimed, surpasses structuralism. In short, post-structuralism rejects the idea of an underlying stable structure which finds meaning through fixed binary pairs (black-white; good-bad). Rather, meaning is unstable, being always deferred and in process. The meaning cannot be confined to single words, sentences or particular texts but is the outcome of relationships between texts, that is, intertextuality. Like its predecessor, post-structuralism is anti-humanist in the decanting of the unified, coherent human subject as the origin of stable meaning.

Derrida's focus is on language and the deconstruction of immediacy, identity between words and meanings. He accepts Saussure's argument that meaning is generated by relations of difference between signifiers rather than by reference to an independent object world. However, for Derrida, the consequence of this play of signifiers is that meaning can never be fixed. Words carry many meanings, including the echoes or traces of other meanings from other related words in other contexts. For example, if we look the meaning of a word in a dictionary, we are referred to other words in an infinite process of defferal. Meaning slides down a chain of signifiers abolishing of stable signified. Thus, Derrida introduces the notion of *difference*, 'difference and defferal', and says that the production of meaning on the process of signification is continually deferred and supplemented in the play of more than one.

Given this instability of meaning, Derrida proceeds to deconstruct the 'stable' binaries upon which structuralism, and indeed western philosophy in general relies. He argues for 'undesirability' of binary oppositions. In particular, deconstruction involves the dismantling of hierarchical binary oppositions such as speech/writing, reality/appearance, nature/culture, reason/madness etc., which exclude and devalue the 'inferior' part of the binary.[154]

Thus, for Derrida, in postmodern world we think only in signs. There is no original meaning circulating outside of 'representation' so that writing is crucial to the generation of meaning. Derrida's argument is that writing is always present in speech. There is no primary source of meaning and no self-present transport meaning, which can fix the relation between signifiers and signifies. It is in this sense that there is nothing outside of texts or nothing but texts (by which is *not* meant that there is no external material world), so that texts are constitutive of practices.[155]

Anthony Giddens examines the concept of postmodernism as a pluralistic philosophy. Decentralization is its basic feature. Accordingly, doubts and uncertainty are the fundamental features of contemporary knowledge. Postmodern epistemology is seen by Giddens as the condition not of postmodernity but of a 'radicalized modernity'. In his view, "relativity, uncertainty, doubt and risk are core characteristics of low or high modernity."[156]

Similarly, Terry Eagleton defines the philosophy of postmodernity in following manner:

> Postmodernity is a style of thought which is suspicious of classical notion of truth, reason, identity and objectivity, of the idea of universal progress or emancipation, of single frameworks, ground narratives or ultimate grounds of explanation. Against these Enlightenment norms, it sees the world as contingent, ungrounded, diverse, unstable, indeterminate, a set of discriminated cultures or interpretation which breed a degree of skepticism about the objectivity of truth, history and norms, the givenness of natures and the coherence of identities.[157]

It means postmodernism is a style of culture, which reflects something of this epochal change, in a depthless, decentred, ungrounded, self-reflective, playful, derivative, electric, pluralistic art, which blurs the boundaries between 'high' and 'popular' culture as well as between art and everyday experience. Thus, on the basis of the above discussions, we can define the postmodernism in the following manner:

- Postmodernism, as the term itself denotes, is off-suit of modernism. It rejects all the fundamental modern principles like universalism, rationalism and essentialism.
- It also rejects the concept of meta-narratives or grand-narratives.
- It also deny the modernist faith on truth, as the ultimate foundation.
- It believes in hyper-reality and simulacrum.
- It develops various new methodologies viz., localism, deconstruction, fragmentation, etc.
- It accepts the differences of truth, reality, rationality, culture and language so that each and every section of society can find their due representation.

Hence postmodernism is such a contemporary philosophy, which keeps its faith on deconstruction, fragmentation or diversity and has its impact on every branch of knowledge in a different and unique manner.

Characteristics of Postmodernism

On the basis of various definitions given above by various thinkers, the postmodernism may be characterized by localism, rejection of rationalism and anti-essentialism. In this part we would delve into these characteristics.

Localism

Postmodernist thinkers do not have faith in meta-narratives. They reject the idea that there are any essential, universal concepts such as class, history, mode of production etc. that refer to unchanging entities in the world. Instead, they argue that truth, knowledge and understanding are located within particular context.

> "Completeness and consistency of a representation are impossible. Analysis never ends. As a result postmodernists are critics of unity whatever it is claimed to appear, the unity of the world; of the knowledge; of the society; of the self; of the meaning of a world."[158]

Postmodernist thinkers have no tolerance for the Enlightenment values. Reason, universality, morality, progress all these Enlightenment pretences meant nothing to them. They see the world as the dance of the destructively creative and creatively destructive God. Any man who acted in such a way would be Superman. Accordingly, many twentieth century Supermen like Hitler, Mao, Stalin, etc. have proved that one has to destroy these meta-narratives in order to create this world more conducive to live. They proclaime not only the "Death of God" but also the "Death of Christian Morality" and metaphysical world, the central symbols, institutions and beliefs of western culture, which had already suffered a tremendous blow by the Age of Reason, disappeared.

For French philosopher Jean-François Lyotard, postmodern society is a society in which no one narrative – big or little – no one language game dominates. In postmodernist societies, many micro-narratives are jumped together. And this carnival of narratives replaces the monolithic presence of one meta-narrative.[159]

In his monumental work *The Postmodern Condition*, Lyotard says:

> I define postmodernism as incredulity towards meta-narratives. This incredulity is undoubtedly a product of progress in the sciences: but that progress in turn presupposes it. To the obsolescence of the meta-narrative apparatus of legitimation corresponds, most notable, the crisis of metaphysical philosophy and of the university institution, which in the past relied on it. The narrative function is loosing its factors, its great hero, its great danger, its great voyages, and its great goal. It is being dispersed in clouds of narrative language elements-narrative, but also denotative, prescriptive valencies specific to its kind. Each of us lives at the intersection of many of these. However, we do not necessarily establish stable language combinations, and the properties of the ones we do establish are not necessarily communicable.[160]

Here, Lyotard argues that for past few decades science has increasingly investigated language, linguistic theories, communications, cybernetics, informatics, computers and computer languages, information storage, data banks and problems of translation from one computer language to another. He proclaimed that these technological changes would have a major impact on knowledge discourse.

In 1974, he predicted that no knowledge will survive that cannot be translated into computer language – into quantities of information. Learning will no longer be associated with the training of minds – with teachers training students. For, the transmission and storage of information will no longer depend on individuals, but on computers. Information will be produced and sold. Nations will fight for information, the way they used to fight for territory. Information will zip around the globe at the speed of electricity, and people will try to steal it. The role of the state will grow weaker. Taking the place of state, huge multinational corporations will dominate.

But having said all this about the direction of scientific knowledge, Lyotard adds that scientific knowledge is not the only kind of knowledge. His interest, as it turned out, is not so much in scientific knowledge and the scientific method, *per se,* but in how scientific knowledge and method legitimize themselves – how they make themselves believable and trustworthy. And, at this point, Lyotard makes a distinction between scientific discourse and narrative discourse.

According to Lyotard, science has depended upon two other narratives. The first is political and the second is philosophical. The first narrative science relies upon, in order to legitimize itself, is associated with the eighteenth century, the Enlightenment and the French Revolution. The eighteenth century was also called as the Age of Reason because the great thinkers of the era, such as Voltaire, Rousseau, Buffon, Condillac and Diderot, applied reason to every area of life: religion, morality, politics, and social life.

The idea of a place in society for a kind of generalized critical intellect – in fact, the very idea of an intellectual – was a product of the Enlightenment intellectuals, were called philosophers, where they enjoyed great celebrity and prestige.

Joined to this French political narrative of freedom is a German narrative: Hegel's philosophy of the unity of all knowledge. For Hegel, knowledge played an essential part in the gradual evolution of the human mind from ignorance to total being.

Both the French Enlightenment narrative and the German knowledge narrative are what Lyotard calls meta-narratives or grand-narratives, big stories, stories of mythic propositions – that claim to be able to account for, explain are subordinate all lesser, little, local narratives. Some other meta-narratives are philosophies of Marxism or the narrative of Christian salvation. Lyotard's claim is that all these meta-narratives – natural science and philosophic science – are supposed as they are objective and impartial, which is not the reality.

"Science alone, however, cannot provide the whole of the meta-narratives." [161]

According to Lyotard, the first problem with modernity is that it limits the knowledge only up to the sphere of science, and secondly, it insists to accept that knowledge as ultimate. This is the reason why Lyotard is not ready to accept the modern Enlightenment development. Accordingly, all those knowledge, which is not legitimized, is not knowledge in real sense of the term. In fact, there would never be any ultimate knowledge, which can be applied fully upon the society. Hence, Lyotard suggests:

> It is philosophy rather than science as such which decides what is to be classed as 'real' science and what is to be stigmatized as 'mere' narrative; it is philosophy which exists to inform us of what the true essence and end points of the story of human progress and knowledge are; and it is philosophy which judges what counts as true and what does not.[162]

Thus, it is clear that the modernist conception of knowledge, which features such a cozy partnership between the pursuit of science and the legitimating discourse of philosophy, should be abandoned completely. Instead of pursuing the truth, we should openly embrace the postmodern condition of uncertainty and 'agonistic' (i.e., rhetorical jousting). To understand this uncertainty, according to Lyotard, our focus must be towards language. He says, "The social subject itself seems to dissolve in [this] dissemination of language games. The social bond is linguistic, but is not woven with a single thread. It is a fabric formed by the intersection of at lest (and in reality an indeterminate number of) language games, obeying different rules."[163] Lyotard further says:

> ... the aim to define the postmodern condition becomes a linguistic project on language games, narratives and meta-narratives. The fragmentation and the loss of shared values, characteristic of postmodernity, becomes the incommensurability of language games and the disbelief in meta-narratives.[164]

According to Lyotard, the fragmented postmodernist society is based on linguistic discourse. Those are a good relationship between narratives and sciences, which is called as 'language game' by Lyotard. His aim is to show that these narratives allow us to define rule-governed practices that coincide with the fields of science, literature and the arts and many others. The narrative on truth, norms and goals defines how the 'game' of art or science should be played. Hence, Lyotard's profound interest in borrowing Ludwig Wittgenstein's term 'language game'.[165]

> ... the postmodern condition is first described in terms of a multiplicity of language games where language games are linguistic practices defined by particular rules. There are many different

> language games and these enter into conflict with one another over what proper practice is in given cases. In a language games, various categories of utterance can be defined in terms of rules specifying their properties and uses to which they can be put – exactly the same way as the game of chess is define by a set of rules determining the properties of each of the pieces, in other words, the proper way to move them.[166]

These language games, which are not subservient to one overarching principle or universal language, together constitute the socio-cultural formation that Lyotard calls postmodernity. He argues there is no unity of language, but rather *islets* of language, each governed by a system of rules untranslatable into those of others.[167]

That is, truth and meaning are constituted by their place in specific local language games and cannot be universal in character. Knowledge is specific to language games. Consequently, postmodern philosophy embraces local, plural and heterogeneous knowledge, rejecting grand narratives or big totalizing explanatory stories. In Lyotard's interpretation, this implies the 'incommensurability' or untranslatability of languages and cultures. From this follows the celebration of difference and 'local' knowledge regimes.

Even, Richard Rorty,[168] influenced by Wittgenstein,[169] argues that we should see language as a practice, which utilizes skills. Though exact translation of knowledges or culture is not feasible, we can learn the skills of language to make cross-cultural communication possible.

For Rorty, human beings use noises and marks, which we call language, to coordinate and to adapt to the environment. Here, Rorty makes Wittgensteinan point that language is a tool used by a human organism and that pairing off the marks and noises it makes with those we make will prove a useful tactic in predicting and controlling its future behaviour.[170] In this view, the relationship between language and the rest of the material universe is one of causality and not of adequacy of representation or expression. That is, we can usefully try to explain how human organisms come to act or speak in particular ways, which have casual relationships, but we cannot usefully see language as representing the world in ways which more or less correspond to the material world.

Further, Rorty by making addition says that "no linguistic items represent any non-linguistic items".[171] That is, no chunks of language line up with or correspond to chunks of reality. There is no

Archimedean place where one could independently verify the truth of a particular description of the world (if truth taken to be the correspondence between the world and language). There is no God-like vantage point from which to survey the world and language separately in order to establish the relationship between them, for we cannot escape using language itself if we try to establish such a relationship. While we can describe this or that discourse, chunk of language as being more or less useful and as having more or less desirable consequences, we cannot do so by reference to its correspondence with an independent reality, but only in relationship to our values. It shows that meaning of language would be depended only on local context, and not on universal.

Why these postmodernist thinkers focus too much on language? Lyotard says that it is the language through which individuals develop relationship among each other. In its absence, we cannot think about society or about our social relationship. In the absence of language, the whole society would be a silent one. Hence, Lyotard further says that it is the language game, which develops the society and individual's personality in real sense of the term. While discussing about the nature of the language game, Lyotard raises the question of legitimacy of knowledge. He says:

> A language game that doubles as such a *petit recit* ('little narrative') may serve to regulate and implicitly to legitimate a whole culture – it may contain 'denotic statements prescribing what should be done with respect to kinship, the difference between the sexes, children, neighbours, foreigners, etc. – but that legitimation is always immanent: 'Narratives ... define what has the right to be said and done in the culture in question, and since they themselves are part of that culture, they are legitimated by the simple fact that they do what they do'.[172]

Knowledge must be legitimized, and then only it can be called as an authentic knowledge. Knowledge, by nature, must be authenticated or legitimized by the members of society. Meta-narratives are not the legitimized knowledge, that is why, they are loosing attraction. In the postmodern society, knowledge came down into the sphere of market economy. Thus, the whole society gets changed.

According to Lyotard, knowledge is concerned with signs and symbols. How to lead life, how to learn, how to perform – all these are statements of knowledge, which in fact tell us that the knowledge based on languages is directly or indirectly linked with traditions and customary rules. Actually, these rules provide legitimacy to language. Hence, locality gets importance while providing legitimacy to language games.

Jean Jacques Derrida is another profounder thinker of postmodernist philosophy. He also accepts localism as the basic feature of the postmodernist society. If Lyotard has rejected the universal meta-narratives with the help of an interesting concept of language game, then Derrida does the same exercise with the help of a unique principle of deconstruction.

In fact, deconstruction is associated with Derrida's 'undoing' of the binaries of the western philosophy and its extension into the fields of literature and postcolonial theory. To deconstruct is to take apart, to undo, in order to seek out display the assumption of a text. In particular, deconstruction involves the dismantling of hierarchical conceptual oppositions, such as man/woman, black/white, reality/appearance, nature/culture, reason/madness etc., which serves to guarantee truth by excluding the inferior part of the binary. Thus, speech prevails over writing, reality over appearance, man over woman, and the like.

The purpose of deconstruction is not simply to reverse the order of binaries but to show that they are implicated in each other. Deconstruction seeks to expose the blind spots of texts, the unacknowledged assumptions upon which they operate. This includes the places where a text's rhetorical strategies work against the logic of its own arguments, that is, the tension between what a text mean to say and what it is constrain to mean.

One of the central problems of deconstruction is that it must use the very conceptual language it seeks to undo. For example, to deconstruct western philosophy is to use the very language of the western philosophy. To mark this tension, Derrida places his concepts under erasure. To place a word under erasure is to first write the word and then to cross it out, leaving both the word and its crossed-out version. As Spivak explains, "Since the word is inaccurate, it is crossed out, since it is necessary, it remains legible."[173]

The use 'under erasure' of accustomed and known concepts is intended to destabilized the familiar, making it as useful, necessary, inaccurate and mistaken. Thus, Derrida does seek to illuminate the undecidability of meaning.

Accordingly, in postmodernist society, the philosophy of deconstructionism has great importance because of its faith in local and contextual meaning. Hugh J. Silverman writes:

> What would postmodernism be without deconstruction? And what would deconstruction be without Jacques Derrida? Postmodernism-or at least postmodern thought-operated in tandem with deconstruction as its operative theoretical strategy. To think postmodernism without deconstruction is to think heterotopias, multicultural sites, juxtaposition, marginalities, and the very relation of the modem to the postmodern with the risk of the misguided claim that in the postmodern 'anything goes'. The postmodern (which is not necessarily the same as postmodernism) is carefully motivated.[174]

The postmodern places the modern in question by asking how the modern marks its own limits and margins. If this relation between the modern and the postmodern were to be inverted, the new dominance of the postmodern would take place by unfolding the differences between the modern and postmodern. That is why Derrida rejects any tendency of localism of the modern western tendencies, which follows the norm of metaphysics.

Derrida takes an axiomatic Saussure's claim (which he argues Saussure himself contradicts) that language is always a system of differential signs, which generate meaning through difference rather than by correspondence with fixed transcendental meanings or referents to the 'real'. Consequently, "From the moment that there is meaning there are nothing but signs. We think only in signs".[175] There is no original meaning outside of signs, which are a form of graphic 'representation', so that writing is in at the origins of meaning. We cannot think about knowledge, truth and culture without signs, that is, writing. For Derrida, writing is a permanent trace which always exists before perception or conscious self. Thus, Derrida deconstructs the idea that speech provides an identity between signs and meaning.

Derrida points out that nature is already a concept in language (i.e., culture) and not a pure state of being beyond signs. Christianity is said to be based on the transcendental truth of the word of God. Yet, the word of God is available only through the unstable signs of writing, that is, the Bible. Ultimately, Derrida argues, the very idea of literal meaning is based on the idea of the 'letter', which is writing. Literal meaning is thus underpinned by metaphor – its apparent opposite. As Derrida puts it:

> All that functions as metaphor in these discourses confirms the privilege of the *logos* and founds the 'literal' meaning then given to writing: a sign signifying itself signifying an eternal *logos*.[176]

Actually, Derrida critiques what he calls the '*logocentrism*' and '*phonocentrism*' of western philosophy. By 'logocentrism', Derrida means the reliance on fixed a priori transcendental meanings. That is, universal meanings, concepts and forms of logic which exist within human reason before any other kind of thinking occurs, for example a universal conception of reason or beauty. By 'phonocentrism', Derrida means the priority given to sounds and speech over writing. Derrida says:

> ... a text is not a line of words releasing a single 'theological' meaning (the 'message' of the Author – God) but a multi-dimensional space in which a variety of writings, none of them original, blend and clash. The text is a tissue of quotations drawn from the innumerable centers of culture- we cannot think about knowledge, truth and culture without signs, that is writing.[177]

In other words, textual meaning is unstable and cannot be confide to single words, sentences or particular texts. Meaning has no single originatory source, but is the outcome of relationships between texts, that is, intertextuality. According to Derrida, Socrates held speeches to be direct from the heart of truth and self while writing was regarded as a form of sophistry and rhetoric. For Derrida, this signals Socrates' attempt to find wisdom and truth through reason unmediated by signification. This privileging of speech, argues Derrida, allows philosophers to regard the formation of subjectivity as unmediated agency with "the unique experience of the signified producing itself spontaneously from within".[178] This, Derrida argues, is the search for a universal transcendental truth that grounds itself as a source of the self, which is pure and spontaneity. Derrida argues that the privileging of speech relies on the untenable idea that there is direct access to truth and stable meaning. This idea is fallacious because, in representing a truth, which is argued to exist outside of representation, one must be re-representing it. That is, there can be no truth or meaning outside of representation. There is nothing but the signs.

For Derrida, since meaning is generated through the play of signifiers, and not by reference to an independent object world, it can never be fixed. Words carry multiple meanings, including the ethos and traces of other contexts. Languages are non-representational and meanings an inherently unstable so that it constantly slides away. Thus, by difference, the key Derridean concept is meant 'difference and deferral'. The production of meaning in the process of signification is continually deferred and supplemented in the play of more than one. Derrida writes:

> Meaning is no longer fixed outside any textual location or spoken utterance and is always in relation to other textual locations in which the signifier has appeared on other occasions. Every articulation of a signifier bears a trace of its previous articulations. There is no fixed transcendental signified, since the meaning of concepts is constantly referred, via the network of traces, to their articulations in other discourses: fixed meaning is constantly deferred.[179]

Meaning is always displaced and deferred. The continual supplementary of meaning, the continual substitution and adding of meaning through the play of signifiers, challenges the identity of noises and marks with fixed meaning.

Hence, with the principle of deconstruction, Derrida proves it very well that knowledge or truth is not metaphysical, transcendental or universal, rather it is specific to particular context. In other words, the nature of knowledge/truth should be treated as local. By deconstruction, Derrida never tries to suggest that we do have to be 'for' or 'against' the Enlightenment truth/knowledge. Rather, it is question of accepting the Enlightenment thoughts in particular local context. He suggests that readers and critics should study the texts and formulate their meaning through their own individual (subjective) perspective. Hence, Derrida's deconstruction demands a new way for the search of reality/truth. Texts should be analysed both in the implicit as well as explicit contexts. Metaphysics/transcendental norms should be rejected and signs or symbols should be given more importance to develop a new grammatology, which will be oriented not towards universalization but towards localism.

Like Derrida, Michel Foucault (1926–1984), another postmodernist philosopher, also characterized the principle of postmodernism in the context of local culture. He developed his theory of localism through the unique relationship between 'power' and 'knowledge'. Accordingly, knowledge, discourse and power are the keywords through which postmodernist society develops. Foucault says:

> Postmodernism swims, even wallows, in the fragmentary and the chaotic currents of change as if that is all there is.[180]

Foucault instructs us to develop action, thought and desires by proliferation, juxtaposition and disjunction and to refer what is positive and multiple, difference over uniformity, flows over units and mobile arrangements over system. Believe that what is productive is not sedentary but nomadic. To the degree that it does try to legitimate itself by reference to the past, therefore, postmodernism typically shares back to that wings of thought.

In Foucault's thought postmodernist society is one which is very much disinterested in nature. In this postmodernist society we can see the lots of diversities in actions, thoughts and desires. This postmodernist society accepts differences, disintegration, fragmentation and plurality instead of universality/similarity, interaction and unification. All the actions of postmodernist society move towards instabilities rather than stability.

Foucault tries to elaborate the basic features of postmodernist society in context of power and knowledge relations. By explaining the nature of knowledge, Foucault says, "Knowledge is not metaphysical, transcendental or universal. Rather it is specific to particular times and spaces".[181]

In fact, Foucault's thinking breaks with the premises of 'classical' Enlightenment thought where he talks not of truth *per se,* but of 'regimes of truth', that is, the configuration of knowledge that 'count as truth', under determinate historical condition. Foucault clearly says:

> Knowledge is perspectival in character. There can be no one totalizing knowledge which is able to grasp the 'objective' character of the world. Rather, we both have required multiple viewpoints or truth by which to interpret a complex heterogeneous human existence.[182]

For Foucault, knowledge is not regarded as a pure or neutral way of understanding. It is implicated in regimes of power. Foucault breaks with the central Enlightenment metaphor of 'depth'. He argues against interpretative or hermeneutic methods, which seek to disclose the hidden meanings of language. Foucault is concerned with the description and analysis of the surfaces of discourse and their effect under determinate material and historical conditions.

Foucault casts doubt on the Enlightenment understanding of progress. Knowledge as discourse does not unfold as an even historical evolution but is discontinuous. That is, Foucault identifies significant epistemological breaks in knowledge across time ,and rejects any notion of *telos* or the inevitable direction of human history. He was of the opinion that any knowledge can never be applied universally throughout the globe. Knowledge, in fact, is subjective not objective in nature:

> It is now impossible to believe that in the rending of the veil, truth remains truthful; we have lived long enough not to be taken in.

> Truth is undoubtly the sort of error that cannot be refuted because it was hardened into an unalterable form in the long backing process of history.[183]

Foucault tries to explain his concept of local knowledge with the help of a new concept of 'discourse'. Explaining the meaning of discourse, Foucault says:

> ... discourse 'unites' both language and practice and refers to the production of knowledge which gives meaning to material objects and social practices. Though material objects and social practices 'exist' outside of language, they are given meaning or 'brought into view' by language and are thus discursively formed. Discourse constructs, defines and produces the object of knowledge in an 'intelligible way while excluding other forms of reasoning as unintelligible'.[184]

Foucault argues against formalist theories of language which conceive of it as an autonomous system with its own rules and functions (i.e., structuralist semiotics). He also opposes interpretative or hermeneutic methods, which seek to disclose the 'hidden' meanings of language. Instead, he is concerned with the description and analysis of the surfaces of discourse and their effects. Foucault is determined historical in his insistence that language develops and generates meaning under specific material and historical conditions. He explores the particular and determinate historical conditions under which statements are combined and regulated to form and define a distinct field of knowledge/objects requiring a particular set of concepts and delimiting a specific 'regime of truth'. Foucault attempts to identify the historical conditions and determining rules of formation of regulated ways of speaking about objects. And he calls this unique methodology of knowing truth as the *'Archaeology of Knowledge'*.

Foucault argues that in the transition from one era to another the social world is no longer perceived, described, classified and known in the same way. That is, discourse is *discontinuous*, it is marked by historical breaks in understanding, and changes in the way objects are conceptualized and understood. Different historical eras are marked by different *episteme*, or configurations of knowledge that shape the social practices and social order of particular historical periods.[185] For example, Foucault points to rupture in the understanding of madness wherein modern reason breaks off its dialogue with madness and seeks to set up oppositions between madness and reason, the sane and the insane. History is not to be explained in terms of connections across historical periods (though breaks are never complete and are to be understood on the basis of that which already exists), nor in terms of the inevitable movement of history from locatable origins towards a predetermined destiny. Thus, Foucault's stress on discontinuity is an aspect of his questioning of the modern themes of genesis, teleology, continuity, totality and unified subjects. [186]

Archaeology is a branch of knowledge, wherein the deteriorated things, monuments etc. are studied through scientific methods, to know about the society of the past. Foucault's intention was to know the discourse of knowledge with the help of archaeology. Have a intervene look of a particular thing, i.e., monument, building etc., and try to find out the particular discourse behind the construction. It is the content where Foucault is explaining the process of discursive formation.

> Where discourses provide ways of talking about a particular topic in similar ways with repeated motifs or cluster of ideas, practices and forms of knowledge across a range of sites of activity, we may speak of a *discursive formation*. A discursive formation is a pattern of discursive events which refer to, or being into being, a common object àcross a number of sites. They are regulated maps of meaning or ways of speaking through which objects and practices acquire meaning.[187]

Foucault's intention was not only to discuss about discourse and its formation but he was also intended to elaborate and explain the relationship between power and knowledge with the help of a methodological approach described as archaeology. Foucault argues that discourse regulates not only what can be said under determinate social and cultural conditions, but who can speak, when and where. Thus, much of his work is concerned with the historical investigation of power.

For Foucault, power is distributed throughout sociai relation and is not to be reduced to centralized economic forms and determinations nor to its legal or juridical character. Rather, power forms a dispersed capillary woven into the fabric of the entire social order. Foucault writes:

> The relation between power and knowledge is there a central theme. But Foucault breaks with the notion that power is ultimately located within the state, and abjures us to 'conduct an ascending analysis of power, starting, that is, from its infinite mechanisms, which each have their own history, their own trajectory, their own techniques and tactics, and then see how these mechanisms of power have been – and continued to be – invested, colonized, utilized, transformed, displaced, extended etc. by even more general mechanisms and by

> forms of global domination. Close scrutiny of the micro-politics of power relations in different localities, contexts and social situations leads him to conclude that there is an intimate relation between the system of knowledge ('discourses') which codify techniques and practices for the exercise of social control and domination within particular localized context. The prison, the asylum, the hospital, the university, the school, the psychiatrist's office, are all examples of sites where a dispersed and piecemeal organization of power is build up independently of any systematic strategy of class domination.[188]

The above lines make it clear that power is not simply repressive but is *productive*; it brings subjects into being. Power is implicated in "generating forces, making them grow, and ordering them, rather than one dedicated to impeding them, making them submit or destroying them".[189] For example, Foucault argues against the 'repressive hypothesis' that there has been an 'incitement to discourse', a proliferation of discourses about sex in, amongst other medicine, Christianity and population studies. These discourses about sex analyse, classify and regulate sexuality in ways which produce sexed subjects, making sexuality a cornerstone of subjectivity.

Foucault establishes a mutually constituting relationship between power and knowledge so that knowledge is indissociable from regimes of power. Knowledge is formed within the practices of power and is constitutive of the development, refinement and proliferation of new techniques of power. For example, psychiatry emerges through the practices of trying to understand and control 'madness' at the same time that it classifies madness, thereby bringing new forms of discipline and new kinds of subject into being. Hence, the analytic term 'power/knowledge'.[190]

Foucault always looks at the concept of power as a micro-politics. Power cannot exist separately. It always finds in social relationships. It is very much neutral in nature. Like force or capacity it is functioning.[191] For Foucault bodies are 'subject to' the regulatory power of discourse by which they become 'subjects for' themselves and others. Here, Foucault is concerned with subjectivity as formed within the subject positions of discourse. The speaking subject is not the author or originator of statement but depends on the prior existence of the discursive positions which "can be filled by virtually any individual when he formulates the statement; and in so far as one and the same individual may occupy, in turn, in the same series of statements, different positions, assume the role of different subjects."[192]

Thus, Foucault provides us with useful tools for understanding the way the social order is constituted by discourse of power, which produce subjects fit into, constitute and reproduce that order. In this power and knowledge discourse Foucault treats the knowledge as subjective rather than objective and concludes that knowledge is not only represented by an individual but also by family, class, caste and community. And, if the scope of knowledge is not centralized, the nature of power gained by knowledge can never be centralized. Hence, any study of power and knowledge should necessarily be based on context or local or cultural rather than universal or metaphysical concepts.

In this way postmodernist thinkers open a new regime of knowledge and conclude that postmodernist society is a local society. Postmodernist society believes that sources of knowledge must be local, contextual, situational, fragmented or deconstructed, rather than being universal or global.

Rejection of Rationalism

The second main feature of postmodernist philosophy is rejection of the reason. The modernists' belief that reason is the ultimate source of knowledge and truth, is forcefully rejected by postmodernist thinkers. Accordingly, truth cannot be defined rationally and there is not any particular rational source, i.e., mind/reason, to know about truth.

> Postmodernists ... reject foundationalism, the attempt to justify realist knowledge through recourse to 'basic' or fundamental or incorrigible cognition. In this denial postmodernists are not alone; many other recent philosophical movements like pragmatism and ordinary language philosophy, have likewise denied presence or immediacy. Postmodernists are more radically anti-foundationalist than others, however, in denying the legitimacy of the whole enterprise of epistemology or the attempt to justify human knowledge. They are utterly sceptical of the three great Western sources of cognitive norms: God, Nature and Reason.[193]

Foucault, who was hardly influenced by structuralism and Marxism, rejected rationality in the early 1960s because of its totalizing nature. As a historian, he set out to uncover the necessary links between, on the one hand, disciplines or forms of knowledge, and on the other, oppressive institutions and their practices, which subjects the individual.[194] In Foucault's words:

> ... Any discourse takes place within a historically, socially and institutionally structure of statements, terms, categories and beliefs and

> against this background meanings are contested and power relations are determined. Moreover, one exercises power and control knowledge and meaning not only through writings but also through professional institutions. Therefore, the false power of hegemonic knowledge can only be challenged by counter hegemonic discourses which offer alternative explanations of reality.[195]

Accordingly, reason is not the only instrument through which the ultimate truth or reality can be discovered. According to Foucault, the so-called modern truth is nothing else but a kind of false-consciousness. Nature of truth or knowledge can never be universal; instead, it is partial, local or very much particular according to the context. What is truth? Its answer should not be discovered only by the universal vision, but local or cultural contexts should also be studied or highlighted. If we are not accepting these aspects, it means, we are recognizing partial truth as an absolute truth or as an absolute knowledge. It further means, we are accepting the truth under the domination of reason. It also means that we are highlighting only instrumental knowledge and disregarding substantial or intuitive knowledge.

This is the reason why all the postmodernist scholars talk about writing in terms of 'discourse'. As per their account, 'statements' or 'discourses' cannot be defined in a particular context. One discourse cannot be explained in the context of the other discourse. According to Foucault:

> ... Discourses are not in themselves true or false, scientific or ideological. Each society has its own regime of truth, its own accepted discourses which function as true its own mechanism and procedures for deciding what counts as true.[196]

Foucault rejects all those epistemologies as wrong, which accept the nature of truth or knowledge as universal or certain. He argues that knowledge is there within the discourse and discourses regulate not only what can be said under determinate social and cultural conditions but who can speak, when and where. According to Foucault, discourses are neither wrong nor right, but any attempt to prove them as an absolute truth or universal truth, is wrong. For Foucault, different historical eras are marked by different *epistemes,* or configurations of knowledge that shape the social practices and social orders of particular historical periods. That is, *discourse* is discontinuous, it is marked by historical breaks in understanding, and charges in the way objects are conceptualized and understood. Foucault argues that in the transition from one historical era to another the social world is no longer perceived, described, classified and known in the same way. Every society has its own ideal/truth or conception of knowledge at particular time on the basis of which discourses are created. So, it (truth) would be relevant only for that particular society of that particular time. Foucault writes:

> ... the analysis of form of knowledge or 'discursive formations' can not be carried out from the point of view of epistemology, that is to say, the question whether discourses are true or false, ideological or scientific, rational or irrational, is no longer relevant.[197]

Foucault argues that we do not have to be 'for' or 'against' the Enlightenment. It is question not of accepting or rejecting rationality but of asking: What is this reason that we use. What are its historical effects? What are its limits, and what are its dangers? Philosophy has a function within critical thought, it is precisely to accept this sort of spiral, this sort of revolving door of rationality that refers us to its necessity, to its indispensability, and at the same time to its intrinsic dangers.

Foucault dismisses 'reason' as a fiction and sees 'truth' simply a partial, localized version of 'reality', transform into a fixed form in the long process of history. According to him:

> ... subjects are not the producers of discourse but rather 'position' in discourse, which can be occupied by individuals. The subject is not the speaking consciousness nor the author of the formulations but a position which may be filled in certain conditions by various individuals. The subject is, rather, shaped by power through his/her body rather than through his/her consciousness. [Therefore], we should try to grasp subjection in its material instance as a constitution of subjects.[198]

Foucault says that the modern concept of reason was very much partial in nature because it tried to see the truth only as reason-centric. But, the fact is that 'discourses' or 'discursive formations' are based on the principle of 'fragmentation' where other aspects of human consciousness are also adhered.

In a similar way, even Jean Jacques Derrida talks about the rejection of reason. He emphasizes on the concept of 'deconstruction of texts'. If other postmodernist scholars reject reason with the help of language or discourse formation, Derrida focuses on writing.

By writing, Derrida means not simply text on a page but what he calls *arch-writing* in which there is no 'outside' of the text. Writing is always already part of the outside of texts and texts are constitutive of their outsides. It is in this sense that there is nothing outside of texts or nothing but texts (by which is not meant that there is no external material world), so that texts are constitutive of practices.

Writing plays an important part in Derrida's work. First, writing is seen not as secondary to speech (as self-present meaning) but a necessary part of speech and meaning. Not only is writing always already inside speech but, since writing is a 'sign of a sign', then the meaning of words cannot be stable and identical with a fixed concept but must be deferred by dint of the traces of other words. Second, the meaning and truth claims of philosophy (and of any other forms of knowledge) are always dependent on writing and subject to the rhetorical claims, metaphors and strategies of writing. Truth is not outside of a writing which tries to express them; rather, the strategies of writing are constitutive of any truth claims and can be deconstructed in terms of those strategies.

For Derrida, language is always a system of differential signs, which generate meaning through difference rather than by correspondence with fixed transcendental meanings or referents to the 'real'. Consequently, "from the moment that there is meaning there are nothing but signs. We think only in signs."[199] There is no original meaning outside of signs, which are a form of graphic 'representation', so that writing is in at the origins of meaning. We cannot think about knowledge, truth and culture without signs, that is, writing.

Derrida deconstructs the idea that speech provides an identity between signs and meaning. Derrida rehearses this argument in a number of places.

Derrida argues even Socrates' concept of truth was related with speech to be held direct from the heart of truth and the self while writing was regarded as a form of sophistry and rhetoric. This privileging of speech, argues Derrida, allows philosophers to regard the formation of subjectivity as unmediated agency with "the unique experience of the signified producing itself spontaneously from within itself".[200] This, Derrida argues, is the search for a universal transcendental truth which grounds itself as a source of the self, which is pure spontaneity. Derrida argues that the privileging of speech relies on the untenable idea that there is direct access to truth and stable meaning. This idea is fallacious because, in representing a truth which is argued to exist outside of representation, one must be re-representing it. That is, there can be no truth or meaning outside of representation. There is nothing but the signs. Thus, Derrida is demanding for the generation of meaning where reliance should be towards the play of signifiers not by reference to an independent object world, it can never be fixed. Derrida writes,

... the idea of 'true' meaning or communications is displaced for meanings circulate without any absolutely authorized source or destination. Reason is unable to permanently fix and define the meaning of concepts.[201]

Thus, all the reason-oriented concepts are partial in nature and they should be deconstructed. The Derridean principle of deconstruction never tries to see the western universal reason-centric-ideological philosophy as the ultimate basis of truth; within the deconstructionist philosophy all are equal, i.e., reason and intuition, language and science.

Similar to Derrida, Lyotard and Foucault, Barry Hindess and Paul Hirst also argue for the end of epistemology:

> The entities referred to in discourse are constituted solely in and through the forms of discourse in which they are specified. Objects of discourse cannot be specified extra-discursively ... There is no question here of whether *objects* of *discourse* exist independently of discourses which specify them. Objects of discourse do not exist at all in that sense: they are constituted in and through the discourses, which refer to them.[202]

By criticizing the classical notion of Marxist ideology, Hindess and Hirst say that fanaticism and fundamentalism are the main problems of modern epistemology. And, this is because of its more inclination towards objectivity. This tendency of knowledge is usually trying to present the truth only in the context of reason. They write:

> Every epistemology assumes that there is a level of discourse which serves as the absolute standard against which all claims to knowledge are evaluated. Within this absolute yardstick, epistemology assesses the degree of correspondence between knowledge and objective reality achieved by other discourses. But this privileged form of discourse is not itself rationally demonstrable 'except by means of forms of discourse that are themselves held to be privileged.[203]

According to Hindess and Hirst, every kind of knowledge is originated by social practices, which do not follow any fixed or permanent process. Even, the result of every practice or behaviour is not same because it depends on the particular time and space. Thus, knowledge, alike its source, is dynamic and spontaneous in nature. It is impossible to define all the social behaviour only from a particular perspective of reason-centric epistemology. That is why, Hindess and

Hirst claim about the end of epistemology or escape from epistemology. Further, by suggesting the way of rejection of rationalism, Hindess and Hirst say:

> The only way of escaping epistemology is to reaffirm that each discourse specifies its own objects. It follows that discourses can only be judged in terms of their own internal consistency. If this is so, then no discourse can be said to 'represent' or 'misrepresent' an external reality.[204]

Accordingly, we should try to accept the reality that discourses can be analysed only within their own paradigm, within their own context. The meaning of a particular discourse can be produced within specific time and space. The discourses cannot be judged on the basis of any prior existing universal truth. For Hindess and Hirst, truth is not so much found as made. We should always try to study one discourse in the context of another but not to find out any particular or fixed transcendental truth or universal reason. In fact, any approach to protect a knowledge, on the basis of reason, would be anti-progressive or non-futuristic or destructive in nature.

Hindess and Hirst's critique of modern epistemology inevitably leads to relativism and to an even more entrenched dogmatism than the one they claim to fight against. They refuse to privilege any particular form of discourse, but then, by contrast, they must privilege all discourses. Every discourse becomes a closed world, which creates its own objects, its own logic and its own truth. Because discourses cannot be measured against any external yardstick, they cannot be properly compared to one another, nor can they be disproved. Discourses become incommensurable and there cannot be any rational discussion between them.[205]

Similarly, under the influence of Foucault, E. Laclau and C. Mouffe have also rejected the reason-centric universalism or universe-centric rationalism. They are critical of universal reason and argue that all progressive values must be defined within the pragmatic context of particular moral traditions without appeal to absolute standards of legitimation. The formulation of what is equitable involves for the recovery of modern political ideas of democracy, justice, tolerance, solidarity and freedom.[206]

Laclau and Mouffe argue that the 'social' is to be thought of not as a totality but as a set of contingently related aggregates of difference articulated or 'sutured' together. They write:

> The identity and unity of a discourse is purely relational and does not depend on a founding subject; rather, diverse subject positions

> appear dispersed within a discursive formation but these subject position can neither be permanently fixed nor enter into permanently fixed relations.[207]

Laclau and Mouffe are particularly critical of the essentialism, foundationalism and reductionism of Marxism. They reject the idea that there are any essential, universal concepts (such as class, history, mode of production) which refer to unchanging entities in the world. Further, discursive concepts are not to be reduced to or explained solely in terms of the economic base as in reductionist form of Marxism. Instead, Laclau and Mouffe argue, along with Foucault, that discourse constitutes the objects of its knowledge. Consequently, they analyse the 'social' (a concept they reject as being not a proper object of analysis) in terms of the discursive construction of reality. For them, 'society' is an unstable system of discursive differences in which socio-political identities represent the open and contingent articulation of cultural and political categories. They write:

> In a discourse no relation or identity is necessary or ever fully constituted. There can only be partial fixations of meaning or 'nodal points' which are constructed by a practice of articulation. As subject positions are constructed within discourse, they cannot be totally fixed, nor can they have fixed relations. Hence, articulatory practices are essentially contingent and have no necessary articulating subject. All that is required for a process of hegemonic articulation to take place is 'the presence of antagonistic forces and the instability of frontiers which separates them.[208]

Accordingly, there is no essential subject, no necessity, and no guarantee of success in any struggle. Socialism is, of course, an important dimension of the struggle for a radical and plural democracy, but by no means the only one or the most important. From the fact that socialism may succeed in destroying inegalitarian relations of production, it does not follow that it will cure other inequalities too. Socialism must cease to be a discourse of the universal. For Laclau and Mouffe, there are no subjects, which can be specified extra-discursively, no fixed identities, no essential interests, no determining conditions, no necessary contradictions and struggles, no necessary relations. Everything in society is infinity variable and contingent because it is discursively constructed and, in a discourse, there can only be partial and temporary fixations of meaning. In fact, they criticize not only partial classical approach to study history, but also reject the modern rational approach through which a study goes on towards its destination. For Laclau and Mouffe the modern reason-centric methodology depicts only a picture of socio-reality, which is very much substantive and intuitive or irrational in nature.

Hence, the above discussion on 'rejection of rationalism' has explained it very well that the modern reason-based development was very much partial in nature and postmodernist scholars are not ready to accept it as the ultimate source of knowledge. They are of the view that along with reason we should also consider the other sources of knowledge. As contextual and cultural codes, signs/symbols also have their meanings, and play important role in the formation of meaning and construction of knowledge and truth.

Anti-essentialism

Essentialism assumes that words have stable referents and social categories reflect an essential underlying identity. By this token there would be stable truths to be found. However, for postmodernism, there can be no truths, subjects or identities outside of language – a language which does not have stable referents and is therefore unable to represent fixed truths or identities. Truth or identities are not fixed universal things but descriptions in language which through social convention come to be "what counts as truth" (i.e., the temporary stabilization of meaning). For a postmodernist, a person or subject is not a stable universal entity but an effect of language which constructs an 'I' in grammar. The speaking subject is dependent on the prior existence of discursive subject positions, empty spaces or functions in discourse from which to comprehend the world. Living persons are required to 'take up' subject positions in discourse in order to make sense of the world and to appear coherent to others.

Anti-essentialism does not mean that we cannot speak of truth or identity. Rather, it points to them as being not universals of nature but productions of culture in specific times and places. The speaking subject is dependent on the prior existence of discursive positions. Truth is not so much found as made and identities are discursive constructions. Instead of the scientific certainty of structuralism, post-structuralism offers us irony, an awareness of the contingent, constructed character of our beliefs and understandings which lack firm universal foundations. It has been argued here that identity is cultural "all the way down", being specific to particular times and places. This suggests that forms of identity are changeable and related to definite social and cultural conjunctures. The idea that identity is plastic is underpinned by arguments referred to as anti-essentialism. Here words are not taken as having referents with essential or universal qualities, for language 'makes' rather than 'finds'. Identity is not a thing but a description in language. Identities are discursive constructions, which change their meanings according to time, place and usage.

The core idea of anti-essentialism can be analysed here from two perspectives: firstly, the perspective, through which an individual's identity would be studied within cultural and local context; and secondly, from the feminist perspective.

For postmodernist anti-essentialist thinkers, we are constituted as individuals in a social process using socially shared materials. This is commonly understood as socialization or acculturalization. Without acculturalization we would not be persons as we understood that notion in our everyday lives. Without language the very concept of personhood and identity would be unintelligible to us. There are no transcendental or a-historical elements to what it is to be a person. Identity is wholly social and cultural.

The postmodern subject assumes different identities at different times – identities which are not unified around a coherent 'self'. Within us there are contradictory identities, pulling in different directions, so that our identifications are continually being shifted about. If we feel that we have a unified identity from birth to death, it is only because we construct a confronting story or "narrative of the self" about ourselves.[209] S. Hall writes:

> ... the inner core of the subject was not autonomous and self-sufficient, but was formed in relation to 'significant others', who mediated to the subject the values, meanings and symbols – the culture - of the worlds he/she inhabited.[210]

By enlarging their arguments, postmodernist philosophers say that the resources that form the material for an identity project, namely, language and cultural practices, are social in character. Consequently, what it means to be a woman, a child, Asian or elderly is formed different in different cultural contexts.

In this very context, according to Michel Foucault the essential similarity about which modernist philosophy talks, is the perspective of the selected (elite) people of the society. These are those powerful people who have control over all the sources of power. Though the postmodernist philosophy believes that knowledge is the source of all power, thus those who are having expert knowledge or control over means of communication or information-technology should be assumed as the most powerful. They are the actual mentors, builders or constructors of the society, through which an individual gets identity.

Foucault also concentrates on the issues of discourse, discipline and power. Subjects are understood as discursive constructions and the products of power, where discourse regulates what can be said about person under determinate social and cultural conditions. Specifically, the 'regime of truth' (what counts as truth) of modernity involves relations of power/knowledge whereby knowledge is a form of power implicated in the production of subjectivity. As such, Foucault provides us with useful tool for understanding the connection between subjectivity/identity and social order.

Similarly, Gayatri Chakravorty Spivak, influenced by Antonio Gramsci, says that identity of a society depends on specific elite groups. Other groups or members of societies generally depend on them. These elite groups may belong to the same group or same time that may also be a colonial or imperialist power. In such an elite-dominated society, subaltern can never raise their voices. Chakrovorty Spivak writes:

> The first part of my proposition – that the phased development – of the subaltern is complicated by collection of individuals who may be called the 'subaltern studies' group. They must ask, can the subaltern speak? [211]

In Indian context, Ranjit Guha says, "the historiography of Indian nationalism has for a long time been dominated by elitism- colonialist elitism and bourgeois-nationalism elitism ... [shar]ing the prejudice that the making of the Indian nation and the development of the consciousness – nationalism – which conformed this process were exclusively or predominantly elite achievements."[212]

For a long period of time Indian continent was not only dominated by imperialist or colonial power, but also directed by imperialist cultural trades. Consequently, subaltern groups lose the importance of their own cultural and local practices. In a view to create Euro-centric world scenario, elite groups develop the universal and essential perspective, within which subaltern cultures were greatly ignored.

The concept of essentialism was also criticized by feminist scholars. Although, interestingly initially all the feminist scholars worked together along with the essentialism. Modern feminist scholars have founded on the belief that throughout the world women, have shared common interests. They have assumed that women either belonging to North or South, because they have the same biological connection, their interests must also be same.

However, very soon, a new group of feminist scholars emerged and raised the voice against this conception of global feminism. These feminist scholars were called postmodern feminist thinkers. They claim that it is difficult to see, on the basis of biology, women could form a politics of common interests. It does not follow that because women have similar bodies, they share common cultural or political interests. They asked how can there be a universal or global feminism when there is an unbridgeable difference between the African, American, British and Asian women. They assumed that there may appear to be no agreed rules for coming to agreement as to what would constitute justice or women's rights and interests. By implication, universal women's right are either impossible, or if declared, another version of the imperialist representation of western categories as applicable at all times and in all places. Postmodernist feminist scholars criticize the modern biological essentialism and argue, that Women are divided by class, ethnicity, nationality and other cultural forms and practices.[213]

These postmodernist feminists assumed that since all knowledge is positional or culture-bound, cultural and political discourses can in the abstract be said to be incommensurable, there being no meta-language of translation. Feminism cannot bridge cultures but must be satisfied with being specific to users.

L. Nicholson, a famous postmodernist feminist scholar, goes on to argue that we should regard the meaning of the word 'women' not in the singular but as a part of a language game of different and overlapping meanings. Consequently, feminism is conceived of as a coalition politics formed amongst women who come to believe that they share particular interests in specific contexts. The meaning of 'woman' in feminist politics has to be forged rather than taken as a given. The politics of identity has to be made rather than found. Nicholson says:

> In this view the body does not disappear from feminist theory. Rather, it becomes a variable rather than a constant, no longer able to ground claims about the male/female distinction across large sweeps of history but still there is always a potentially important element in how the male/female distinction gets played out in any specific society.[214]

According to Nicholson, though the modern feminist scholars have accepted the biological differences between male and female, yet within this dissimilarity another discourse of differentiation is always needed. Because sex is defined by nature, but gender is a social construction where differentiation of time and space has its own importance. That is why, Nicholson makes voice against any universal concept of feminism.

Another feminist scholar Judith Butler argues, discourse and materiality of bodies are indissoluble. Not only is discourse the means by which we understand what bodies are, but discourse brings bodies into view in particular ways: "In other words, 'sex' is an ideal construct which is forcibly materialized through time. It is not a specific fact or static condition of a body, but a process whereby regulatory norms materialize 'sex' and achieve this materialization through a forcible reiteration of those norms." [215]

Similarly, Julia Kristeva while deconstructing sexual identity argues that to believe that one "is a woman" is almost as absurd and obscurantist as to believe that one "is a man". While we may identify with gendered identities and find it necessary for political reasons to continue to campaign as women (i.e., strategic essentialism) one cannot be a woman. Sexual identities as opposites can only come into being after entry into the symbolic order, that is, sexual identity is not an essence but a matter of representation.

In fact, feminity is a condition or subject position of marginality which some men can also occupy. Indeed, it is the patriarchal symbolic order that tries to fix all women as feminine and all men as masculine, rendering women as the 'second sex'. Kristeva advocates:

> The very dichotomy man/women as an opposition between rival entities may be understood as belonging to *metaphysics*. What can 'identity', even 'sexual identity', mean in a new theoretical and scientific space where the very notion of identity is challenged? ... What I mean is, first of all, the demassification of the problematic of *difference* ... in order that the struggle, the implacable difference, the violence be conceived in the very place where it operates with the maximum intransigence, in other words, in the personal and sexual identity itself, so as to make it disintegrate in its very nucleus.[216]

Kristeva suggests that the struggle over sexual identities takes place within each individual. Rather than a conflict between two opposing male-female masses, sexual identity concerns the balance of masculinity and feminity with specific men and women. This struggle, she suggests, could result in the deconstruction of sexual and gendered identities. She contends that the time has perhaps come to emphasize the multiplicity of female expressions and preoccupations.

Another postmodernist feminist scholar Francoise Lionnet has also contributed to this debate on anti-essentialism or anti-foundationalism. Francoise stood against all the universal legal provisions like universal women's rights etc., which see the women and the other related issues throughout the world with similar glass. Lionnet argues, since our behaviour is in accordance with deeply held socio-cultural and religious beliefs, how can a universal law would be applied? Further, the increasing diversity and plurality has given rise to cultural conflicts that forcing a re-examination of the principles of universal democracy and natural rights that had theoretically been taken for granted for the modern feminist scholars. Suggesting an approach for postmodernist feminist movement, Francoise says:

> The approach we propose would not take the individual subject as its point of departure, but would look at the human being as a member of a diversified community. This would avoid the resource to either the pure cultural relativism that undermines the unity of the human race of the total pseudo-universalism that would refuse the right to difference and lead to the negation of all cultural and religious identity, in keeping with 'the modern' individualist configuration of values.[217]

In fact, the concept of universalism, which is not able to resist its temptation to convert the whole world into a singular framework, must adhere the value of cultural context also. It may be possible that women throughout this globe have similar problem like wife battering, sexual harassment, etc., but as far as their solutions are concerned one has to look at the cultural and societal differences. On the one hand it requires a deep understanding of cultural traditions, of their evolutions, of their transformation and on the other hand it has to have a critical look at the notion of identity as to avoid the falling into the trap of ethno-centricism.

It means, according to postmodernist conception, sex is a construction, but an indispensable one which forms subjects and governs the materialization of bodies. Therefore, the cross-cultural environment must be given importance while building any discourse like feminism.

Chandra Talpade Mohanty criticizes the modern universal feminist viewpoints from Third World perspective. Mohanty says:

> I would like to suggest that the feminist writing I analyse here discursively colonizes the material and historical heterogeneities of the lives of women in the third world, thereby producing/

> representing a composite, singular third world women' – an image which appears arbitrarily constructed but nevertheless carries with it the authorising signature of western humanist discourse.[218]

The above statement by Chandra Mohanty shows that through the universal or global concept of feminism, modern feminists are trying to colonized the feminist folk in the Third World countries. The women in Third World countries have their own cultural and historical contexts. We have to accept these historical backgrounds, traditional norms and cultural' differences. Chandra Mohanty argues that assumptions of privilege and ethnocentric universality, on the one hand, and inadequate self-consciousness about the effect of Western scholarship on the Third World system dominated by the West, on the other, characterize a sizeable extent of western feminist work on women in Third World. [219]

In fact, feminism does not need essentialism at all. What it required is a 'new language' in which the claims of women do not sound crazy but come to be accepted as 'true' (in sense of social commendation). Feminism involves not less distorted perspective but a language with consequences, which serve particular values and purposes. Further, the emergence of such language is not the discovery of universal truth but part of an evolutionary struggle, which has no immanent teleology, that is, no future predetermined destiny to which it must evolve.

To sum up, we can say that postmodernist anti-essentialist thinkers reject any concept of universal or cultural essentialism. Each and every individual is the product of certain cultural historical context. That is why, postmodernist thinkers are asking for localism by criticizing any notion of universalism or essentialism.

Critical Analysis

Very soon a new group of scholars emerged and raised voice against the core idea of post modernism, which is basically against the modernist norms of rationalism, universalism and essentialism. The new groups of scholars are coming from the Marxist family as well as from the eastern countries. All these critics argue that postmodernism as a concept, is a new ideology of imperialism. Accordingly, the deconstructed society about which these postmodernist scholars talk is a new form of imperialism, came to us earlier in economic form and now it is coming via culture. It means culture has become new instrument of production and exploitation.

One of the most outspoken critics of postmodern theory has been the German philosopher, Jurgen Habermas. Reacting specifically to the argument about a *legitimation* crisis (the collapse of our grand narratives) in Lyotard's philosophical critique of Enlightenment, Habermas' most frequently cited critique of postmodernism, 'Modernity: An Incomplete Project', initiates one of the most prominent debates about the politics of postmodernism.[220]

Habermas defines himself as the defender of the 'project of modernity' against the 'anti-modern' sentiments of a line of French post-structuralist thinkers running "from Bateille to Derrida by way of Foucault". Habermas' argument is that modernity has yet to be fulfilled as a social and political enterprise, and that to proclaim its demise is actually a neo-conservative reactionary argument, which ignores its democratic and liberatory potential. He takes the 'modern' to be akin to the Enlightenment, and hence seeks to defend many of those principles which perceive individual freedom emerging from shared communicative rationality and aesthetic creativity between several people.[221]

Further, by criticizing the Derridian deconstructionist principle, Habermas said that deconstruction understood language as a series of signs, which create a set of relations, which we mistakenly take to be putative things, but which is in fact nothing more than a chain of infinite references to other signs, thus forestalling the possibility of a definite interpretation of a text. Habermas, on the contrary, develops a theory based on rational consensus, which opposes the positive position (truth based upon scientific, empirical, objective observation), but which does not resort to the radical *textuality* of postmodernism (where the text is understood as an open-ended, infinite *process of disruptive signification).* Discourse for Habermas is not simply the interplay that signifies with no touchstone for making truth claims. Habermas has sought to defend many of the same principles, while making a more detailed critique of the ideas of postmodernist theorists in *The Philosophical Discourse of Modernity.*[222]

Further, Lyotard's *The Postmodern Condition* directly challenges the two great Hegelian meta-narratives allegedly underlying the philosophical position of Habermas, namely, the goal of the ultimate emancipation of humanity and the speculative aim of achieving a unity of knowledge. Lyotard's assault on the concept of 'totality' and the notion of sovereignty, which underpins the autonomous, rational subject, confronts Habermas' notion of a rational society modelled on communicational processes. Habermas urges a 'universal pragmatics', through which he aims to identify and reconstruct the universal conditions of possible understanding in the context of specific validity claims like comprehensibility, truthfulness and rightness. Searching for the general conditions of communication between two or more people, this model offers a deep structure embedded in all societies and is known as the 'theory of communicative action'. Habermas responds to Lyotard's charges by focusing on the alleged conservatism of the post-structuralist position. His initial lecture in 1980, 'Modernity versus Postmodernity' (*New German Critique*, 22, 1981: 3–22), is deliberately framed within a binary opposition which is the hallmark of classical reason.

Like that of Habermas, Frederic Jameson also criticizes the theory of postmodernism from the Leftist perspective. He argues that postmodernism ought to be thought of as the apologetic or justificatory cultural discourse of the third stage of capitalism, namely, late or multinational capitalism. In fact, Jameson periodizes capitalism into various phases.

He suggests that the first two phases are classical capitalism and high capitalism. Each new phase of capitalism has brought with it a concomitant distancing of the social. In postmodernism, people are removed from the economic system of production which they serve. Postmodernism in Jameson's view ought to be understood as a 'cultural dominant' rather than a single style, as modes rather than a genre. Jameson uses the term 'cultural dominant' to ensure that his historical period is not understood as the presence and coexistence of a variety of alternative, competing features. In other words, not everything is postmodern, but postmodernity acts as "the force field in which very different kinds of cultural impulses ... must make their way".[223]

According to Jameson, the principal characteristics of this discourse of postmodernism are that it is a new kind of flatness or depthlessness, a new kind of superficiality in the most literal sense – perhaps the supreme formal feature of all the postmodernisms.[224]

The effacement of a personal, unique style and a sense of history itself, and their replacement by *pastiche* (not parody, but the rewriting or transcoding of typical modernist idioms into jargon, badges and other decorative codes) and nostalgia, thereby instituting a celebration of surfaces which denies the hermeneutics of depth.[225]

Further, Jameson says that postmodernism is something where the fragmentation of artistic text after the model of schizophrenic *ecriture,* which specifically takes the form of colarge governed by a logic of "differentiation rather than unification". This is an attempt to resist the obliteration of differences, the effort to make unlike things the same, and the imposition of an overall identity on radically dissimilar concepts, ideas, or persons. Further, the 'hysterical sublime', a theme developed by Lyotard, in which the 'other' of human life, what lies beyond our powers of understanding, surpasses our power to represent it and pitches us into a sort of Gothic rapture.[226]

For Jameson, in postmodernist society, 'culture' becomes a commodity. Like other consumer goods cultures are also producing and discriminating by new kind of capitalist groups in this market economy. Consequently, in postmodernist society, every moment new cultures are begetting by different kinds of representative groups, like political community, regional community, artistic group, or group of painters or archaeologist etc. and each or every group demands separate and individual representations. In such a situation clashes of civilization are very much natural.

Further, by criticizing the depthless and historyless nature of postmodernist culture, Jameson says that postmodernist society is a society of 'simulacrum' or 'hyper-reality' (as Jean Baudrillard said). There is not anything original. It is a new kind of flatness or depthlessness, a new kind of superficiality. Due to this superficiality, there is a great tendency of alienation.[227]

Further, Jameson also criticizes another facets of postmodernist society, i.e., end of history. Jameson contrasted postmodern 'pastiche' with modernist conception of parody. He suggests:

> Parody, plays on the uniqueness of a style; it, seizes on[its] idiosyncrasies and eccentricities to produce on imitation which mocks the original ... Pastiche, on the other hand, whilst sharing many of these features, is a neutral practice. It lacks parody's 'ulterior motive', its satirical impulse, and any sense of a norm against which the original is to be compared ... postmodern pastiche is symptomatic, contends Jameson, of a general loss of historicity and our incapacity to achieve aesthetic representations of our own current experience.[228]

Similarly, postmodernist technology and distribution and production relationship, which is emerging there in the postmodernist society is also criticized by Jameson. He argues that during the modern days the technology was oriented towards production according to the demand of the society; on the contrary, in the postmodernist society, technologies are increasing the demands of the society. Market is not directed by individuals, but individuals are controlled by markets. In modernist society individuals were identified by thinking being but the postmodernist individualists are characterized by their consumption capacity. Modernist Descartes says, 'I think, therefore I am.' But postmodernist Baudrillard says, 'I consume, therefore I am'. "There has been a significant decline ... in our sense of history, narrative and memory and simultaneously an erosion of aesthetic depth and classical distance. This experience finds aesthetic representation through the related concepts of pastiche and schizophrenic temporality."[229]

Marx has described the concept of capitalism in relation to means and modes of production. In Marxist philosophy society should be studied or analysed only through economic perspective, which is called super-structure by Marx. On the contrary, Jameson represented it as a partial concept. Capitalism is not simplistic in nature. A form of capitalism would always be there in every society. In postmodernist society the tendency of capitalism is coming in the form of culture. Culture now is becoming an accessory of production. Signs, symbols, idioms etc. are now new means of production in this market society. This tendency of capitalism is called as 'late-capitalism' by Jameson. The commodification of culture and language is affecting each and every aspect of our life. Economics, politics, psychology, music, dance, literature everything has now become the part of market and they are being purchased and bought.

In order to combat this cultural deterioration, Jameson proposes, in a sonorous phrase, "an aesthetic of cognitive mapping" as a remedy. 'Cognitive mapping' is a reorientation of our experience of time and space in an era where the opportunity to place ourselves into a definable time-space location (viz., a place with a unique, individual identity) has become systematically challenged by the culture of global capitalism, which, for example, replicates the same chain stores, fast food outlets, theme pubs and shopping malls, in every high street across the land. This is Jameson's 'cure' for the fragmented alienation of subjects in postmodern culture. Yet, in the final analysis, although Jameson utilizes modernist Marxism to combat what he feels to be the alienating and deliberating effects of postmodernist logic, he appears to harbour a grudging penchant for many of the cultural artifacts of postmodern culture.

Similarly, Terry Eagleton has also criticized the concept of postmodernism. He argues against the notion of binary oppositions. According to Eagleton, postmodern theory often operates with quite rigid binary oppositions, with 'difference', 'plurality' and allied terms lined up bravely on one side of the theoretical fence as unequivocally positive, and whatever their antithesis might be (unity, identity, totality, universality) ranged balefully on the other.[230] He further says:

> One may, by and large, speak of human culture but not human nature, gender but not class, the body but not biology, *jouissance* but not justice, postcolonialism but not the petty bourgeoisie. It is a thoroughly orthodox heterodoxy, which like any imaginary form of identity needs its bogeymen and straw targets in order to stay in business. It is not, on the whole, comfortable with producing statements like 'liberal humanism' ...[231]

Further, like Jameson, even Eagleton criticizes the postmodernist notion of 'end of history'. For Eagleton, postmodernist thinkers reject the concept of history because they have to criticize any universal or meta/grand narratives. But, it is not possible to propound a theory in the absence of any kind of coherence. According to Eagleton, by nature, history is a dynamic subject. It is based on differences and plurality. Thus, one cannot say that here history has lost its importance. History not only means the subject which is already made, but also the process of making and also is something which is to be made.

Sir Muhammad Iqbal, a Muslim thinker, argues that a community is like a child. A child acquires a sense of its worth when it learns to remember and link tomorrow with its yesterday, and hence "createth its own history". It is the personal history of the child that opens its "being's eye": "so his memory maketh him aware of his own 'self'". Similarly, it is its memory, its living history, its tradition, that makes a community 'self-aware'; and only through self-awareness can a group of individuals actually becomes a community. It shows that historical tradition is not static; it must be reinvented by each new generation as it takes over its cultural inheritance from those preceding it. Only through the interweaving of past and present can change attain a meaningful form.

For Oriental thinkers, postmodernism celebrates egoism – and it is the ego that ultimately leads to the demonization of the Other and the ensuring conflict. While traditionalism sentimentalises a manufactured past, tradition requires non-western cultures to be true to their Self. But this Self is not the 'I' of western individualism, what is known in Islamic parlance as *nafs*: subservience to *nafs* leads to selfishness, greed, perpetual desire and cynicism. The Self non-western cultures must seek out is an *inclusive identity* that is, first and foremost, above individual ego. What all Others share today is What separates them from and impels their resistance to postmodernism. Each non-western tradition has to recover the Self that enables it to begin making its present and future anew within the continuity of its own history. This is not an isolated or lonely struggle: culturally alive non-western writers, academics and activists share many premises in their struggle for cultural renewal, though the cultural premises they draw from are different for each, according to the tradition from which they come. It is not a homogenization of all Others that one is talking about, but a kind of solidarity through difference, a compatibility through plurality, which can strengthen them in their contest with the massed forces of postmodernism. The cultures of resistance that the non-West must seek to create are not about eradicating the individual in the search to re-establish the community as a viable thriving entity. It is rather the rejection of notion that human beings can find and are fulfilled through the existential loneliness and angst of postmodern existence. The quest is to find a new dispensation, their own multiple and diverse cultural means beyond the straitjacket of western modernity and postmodernism where individual and community form a symbiotic whole.

According to famous Islamic thinker, Iqbal, the moral and ethical framework of values, origin and purpose endures self and by implication, community must be created, striven for, reforged in each generation. Islam has never been interested in that quintessentially western concept of the good citizen; the whole focus of Islamic discourse on politics, society and the individual concerns how to foster the holistic conception of the 'moral human being': only a good society can generate good people, while good people cannot be fulfilled without exerting themselves to achieve a good community.[232]

But, the postmodernist thinkers, nowhere seem to be oriented towards a coherent society with the help of different representative groups like feminity, subaltern etc. Actually, these postmodernist thinkers, by rejecting the ideas of history and traditions, try to dominate the Oriental or non-western countries where history or tradition has its own relevance or importance. Ziauddin Sardar writes:

> ... postmodernism in fact dismembers Other cultures by attaching their immune system: eradicating identity, erasing history and tradition, reducing everything that makes sense of life for non-secular cultures into meaninglessness. It places the inhuman and degrading on a par with the humane and ethical.[233]

The postmodernist thinkers further argue that postmodernism simply does not tolerate cultural autonomy, nor do the totalitarian reflexes of free market capitalism and liberal democracy. Creating the space, resources and empowerment needed to nurture the cultural autonomy that will permit cultural authenticity to mature will be hard. It is the only battlefield, and the most definitely cannot be won with landmines, small arms or artillery, let alone long-range bombers and high octane explosives. It is a work of imaginative reconstruction.[234]

By declaring that there is no truth and no morality, that all is meaningless and that life itself is a meaningless problem; by announcing that religion and philosophy, history and tradition are symptoms of will of power and symbols of decadence; by raising doubt, cynicism and ambivalence to an arch value; by its acceptance of barbarism and embrace of evil and hence legitimation of every act of cruelty, neglect and intolerance; by appropriating the knowledge, history and cultural products of the Others; by embarking on a crusade to transform Other cultures into ahistorical, identityless masses and perpetual consumers of its cultural products; by isolating and further marginalizing Other cultures by irony and ridicule; by attempting to subsume Other cultures into the grand narrative of bourgeois liberalism, free market capitalism and secularism; by giving a new life to the old tools of colonial domination and subjugation – by all these means, postmodernism has declared a war on non-western cultures and societies.[235]

Similarly, Ron Shaprio argues that the concept of postmodernism is not very much clear. He says:

> ... the postmodern is a mode which results in a disconnection from the cultural world, and which displays a kind of nostalgia for the past, ... our inability to look directly at the real world of either the present or the past which remains 'forever out of reach'. In this sense of human disconnectedness one can of course also discern important parallels with Derrida's deconstructive notion that linguistic meaning also remains forever out of reach, or endlessly deferred.[236]

For Shaprio, on the one hand, postmodernism discusses its life through the notion of hyper-reality or the concept of simulacra, and on the other, it demands for the end of history. Again, on the one side, it is against the concept of structuralism, and on the other it demands for the end of any kind of uniformity. But, it is not possible at all, arguing Shaprio, even to think about any society in the absence of coherent principle.

Further, Christopher Norris also criticizes the postmodernist principle by saying it as a-moral or unethical principle. He says that in fact the concept of postmodernism cannot be actualized in the real sense of the term. The postmodernist philosophers propose an 'abstract theory' because there is neither any history nor any real or actual present world order. Norris warns that the Lyotard's or Rorty's language discourses are an extremist principle and thus not going to do any good for the society. He writes:

> ... the extreme forms of 'discursive anarchy' released on the world by radical postmodernist like Rorty and Lyotard, a species of cognitive and ethico-political relativism pushed to the point where criticism is powerless against those same (nowadays resurgent) dogmatic truth-claims. Such, after all, is the lesson often derived from Wittgenstein, Lyotard, and other proponents of the view that every language-game (or discourse) disposes of its own *sui generic* criteria, so that the best we can do – in the interest of justice – is acknowledged this open multiplicity of the life- from and given up the attempt to criticize 'truth' or values different from our own. And this (be it noted) at a time when fundamentalist creeds of various description – Christian, Islamic, Nationalist, free-market capitalist, and so forth- are vigorously asserting their claim to supersede not only the secular discourse of Enlightenment but also its associated values of participant democracy, liberty of conscience, social welfare, and egalitarian reform.[237]

Similarly, David Simpson, by criticizing postmodernism, says that nothing can be true but everything can be false, so that "the mission of theoretical discourse thus becomes a kind of search and destroy operation and stigmatized, in the hope that a theoretical discourse negative and critical enough will not itself become the target of such linguistic demystification in its truth".[238]

Thus, the whole critical analysis of the postmodernist philosophy depicts that it is an illusionary concept. It is an effort to create such a deconstructed, historyless, foundationless society where there is not any direction. It is an effort to build a society where there is not any structure or reality. Hence, it is an abstract concept. That is why, the Marxist philosophers and the philosophers from the Third World countries say that it is a new kind of ideology of domination. It is not possible to live in a deconstructed divided society at all. Individual development or group development would not be meaningful in the absence of a society. Therefore, a coherent theory is required where each and every member of the society could able to get their representation, both individual as well as societal. But, unfortunately, postmodernist thinkers are not doing any work in this direction.

Notes

1. John Johnson (ed.) (1936) *Oxford English Dictionary*, New York, Oxford University Press, p. 523.
2. Edwin R.A. Seligman and Alvin Johnson (eds) (1937) *Encyclopedia of Social Sciences*, Vol. IX-X, New York, Macmillan Publication, p. 564.
3. Roger Scruton (1984) *A Dictionary of Political Thought*, New York, Macmillan Press.
4. Neil J. Smelser and Paul B. Baltes (eds) (2001) *International Encyclopedia of the Social and Behavioral Sciences*, Cambridge, Cambridge University Press, p. 9955.
5. Lawrence Cahoone (ed.) (2003) *From Modernity to Post-modernity: An Anthology*, Oxford, Blackwell Publishers, p. 8.

   "The term 'modern' derives from the late fifth century Latin term *modenus* which was used to distinguish an official Christian present from a Roman pagan past. Thereafter the terms employed to situate the present in relation to the past of antiquity, appearing and reappearing exactly during those periods in Europe when the consciousness of a new epoch formed itself through a renewed relationship to the ancients."

   Also see, Byran S. Turner (ed.) (1990) *Theories of Modernity and Post-modernity*, London, Sage Publications, pp. 16–17.
6. Mike Featherstone (1992) *Consumer Culture and Post-modernism*, London, Sage Publications, p. 3.
7. Edward Shills *Tradition* in Rajendra Pandey, (1988) *Modernisation and Social Change*, New Delhi, Criterion Publication, pp. 19–20.
8. Stuart Hall and Bram Gieben (eds) (2001) *Formations of Modernity*, Cambridge, Polity Press, p. 31.
9. Krishna Kumar (1988) *The Rise of Modern Society: Aspect of the Social and Political Development of the West*, Oxford, Basil Blackwell Publishers, Chapter 1, p. 3.
10. Ibid., pp. 3–4.
11. Mark Soloman (1973) *Modernization in Society Today*, California, CRM Books, 2nd ed., pp. 497–511.
12. Rajendra Pandey (1988) *Modernization and Social Change*, New Delhi, Criterion Publication, p. 22.
13. John Naisbitt and Patrica Aburdence (1990) *The New Directions for the 1990s*, New York, William M., p. 298.
14. Talcott Parsons (1964) "Evolutionary Universals in Society", *American Sociological Review*, pp. 339–57.
15. Ralf Dahrendorf (1979) *Life Chances*, Chicago, University of Chicago Press.
16. Stuart Hall, David Held and Tony McGrew (eds) (1992) *Modernity and its Future*, Cambridge, Polity Press, p. 3.
17. Stuart Hall and Bram Gieben (eds) (2001) *Formations of Modernity*, Cambridge, Polity Press, p. 21.

18. G.H. Sabine (1973) *A History of Political Theory*, Oxford, Oxford Publication, pp. 271–310.
19. See, Rene Descartes (1931) *Discourses on Method*, trans. by Haldon and Ross, Cambridge, Cambridge University Press.
20. J.H. Hallowell (1950) *Main Currents in Modern Political Thought*, Durham, North Carolina, p. 38.
21. Stuart Hall and Bram Gieben (eds) (2001) *Formations of Modernity*, London, Polity Press, p. 21.
22. Rene Descartes (1931) *Discourses on Method*, trans. by Haldon and Ross, Cambridge, Cambridge University Press.
23. Rene Descartes (1931) *The Philosophical Works of Descartes*, trans. by Haldane and Ross, Cambridge, Cambridge University Press, p. 221.
24. J.H. Hallowell op. cit., p. 58.
25. N. Machiavelli *Discourse*, Book III, Chapter 41.
26. N. Machiavelli (1949) *The Prince*, London, Oxford University Press, pp. 77–79.
27. J.H. Hallowell (1950) op. cit., pp. 60–61.
28. Erlangen (ed.) *Martin Luther Works*, Vol. XII, p. 15.
29. Martin Luther (1913) *Reformation*, Vol. I, 3rd ed., New York, p. 443.
30. J.H. Hallowell op. cit., p. 61.
31. Ibid.
32. See, Thomas Hobbes (1968) *Leviathan*, Harmondsworth, Penguin.
33. Thomas Hobbes (1947) *Leviathan*, edited with an Introduction by Michael Oakeshott, New York, Oxford University Press, p. 5.
34. Ibid., p. 94.
35. J.H. Hallowell (1950) op. cit., p. 94.
36. John Locke (1967) *An Essay Concerning Human Understanding* Book IV, Chapter I, Secs. 1–2.
37. Hugo Grotius (1625) *The Law of War and Peace*, Sec. 28 Oxford, Clarendon Press.
38. Ibid., Sec. 92.
39. Hugo Grotious (1625) *The Law of War and Peace*, Ch. 1, Sec. X, Para I, Oxford, Clarendon Press.
40. In the article on "Enlightenment" in the *Encyclopedia of Social Sciences* (1937), Vol. 5.
41. See, C.L. Montesquieu (1899) *The Spirit of the Laws*, trans. by T. Nugent, New York, Oxford University Press.
42. Ibid., pp. 4–5.
43. Ibid., p. 6.
44. John Wise (1717) *Vindication of the Government of New England Churches*, Boston, Bostonpul, pp. 54–55.
45. Jean Jacques Rousseau (1968) *The Social Contract*, Harmondsworth, Penguin, p. 152.

46. See, Carl Becker (1942) *The Declaration of Independence*, New York, Macmillan.
47. Stuart Hall and Bram Gieben (eds) (2001) *Formations of Modernity*, Cambridge, Polity Press, p. 22.
48. C.H. McIlwain (1932) *The Growth of Political Thought in the West*, New York, Macmillan Press, p. 162.
49. Niccolo Machiavelli (1949) *The Prince*, London, Oxford University Press, Chapter XVIII, p. 77.
50. Thomas Hobbes (1968) *Leviathan*, p. 32.
51. Ibid., Part I, Chapter 13, p. 32.
52. Ibid., p. 83.
53. Ibid., p. 84.
54. Ibid., Chapter 17.
55. Ibid., Chapter 21, p. 142.
56. John Locke (1946) *The Second Treaties of Civil Government*, edited by J.W. Cough, Chapter 8, New York, Oxford.
57. Ibid., p. 48.
58. C.L. Montesquieu (1899) *The Spirit of Laws*, trans. by T. Nugent, New York, Oxford University Press, pp. 151–152.
59. Jeremy Bentham (1879) *An Introduction to the Principles of Morals and Legislation*, Cambridge, Oxford University Press.
60. Ibid.
61. Jeremy Bentham and F.C. Montague (eds) (1931) *A Fragment on Government*, trans. and edited by F.C. Montague, Oxford, p. 137.
62. See, J.S. Mill (1957) "Considerations on Representative Government", in B. Action (ed.) *Utilitarianism, Liberty and Representative Government*, London, Dent.
63. Herbert Spencer (1884) *Men versus the State*, New York, Oxford.
64. Stuart Hall and Bram Gieben (eds) *Formations of Modernity*, Cambridge, Polity Press, Vol. I, p. 22.
65. G.H. Sabine (1973) *History of Political Theory*, New Delhi, Oxford.
66. J.H. Hallowell (1950) op. cit., pp. 16–17.
67. G.H. Sabine (1973) p. 152.
68. See, G.H. Sabine (1973).
69. J.H. Hallowell (1950) pp. 21–22.
70. "The great impact of the achievements of science, and specially the work of Newton, led the philosophy to believe that scientific method might be applied to society, and that science could become the basis of future social values, which could be selected rationally in relation to predetermined goals." Stuart Hall and Bram Gieben (eds) *Formations of Modernity*, p. 30.
71. Niccolo Machiavelli (1950) *The Prince and the Discourses*, Book I, Vol. II, New York, Random House, p. 217.
72. See, Thomas Hobbes, *Leviathan*, (Introduction).
73. J.H. Hallowell (1950) p. 89.

74. C.H. McIlwain (1932) *The Growth of Political Thought in the West*, New York, Macmillan Press, pp. 370–371.
75. Ibid., pp. 370–371.
76. Ibid., p. 1.
77. John Wise (1860) *Vindication of the Government of New England Churches*, Boston, Bostonpul, p. 153.
78. Jeremy Bentham (1962) "An Introduction to the Principles of Morals and Legislation", J. Bowring (ed.) *The Works of Jeremy Bentham (1838–1843)*, II Vols. New York, Russell & Russell.
79. See, J.S. Mill (1957) "Considerations of Representative Government", in B. Acton (ed.) *Utilitarianism Liberty and Representative Government*, London, Dent.
80. J.H. Hallowell (1950) p. 522.
81. R.S. Woodworth (1948) *Contemporary School of Psychology*, New York, Ronald Press, p. 255.
82. William McDougall (1908) *Introductions to Social Psychology*, Cambridge, London, p. 44.
83. William McDougall (1920) *The Group Mind*, New York, p. 6.
84. Ibid., p. 20.
85. Ibid., p. 78.
86. Ibid., p. 53.
87. R.S. Woodworth (1948) *Contemporary School of Psychology*, New York, Ronald Press, p. 255.
88. "The unconscious motives do not lie dormant. Form time to time at least they become urgent and seek to emerge into conscious behaviour. But they are not pretty pleasant motives. When they threaten to emerge they awaken anxiety, shame, and a guilty feeling in the conscious self, which therefore resists and try to hold them down." R.S. Woodworth, *Contemporary School of Psychology*, p. 255.
89. Max Weber (1964) *The Theory of Social and Economic Organisation*, London, Macmillan Press. Also see Talcott Parsons (1951) *The Social System*, London, Routledge and Kegan Paul.
90. Vilfredo Pareto (1935) *The Mind and Society*, New York, Harcourt and Brace, Vol. III, p. 1401.
91. William James (1928) *Pragmatism*, New York, Longman, p. 8.
92. Ibid., p. 8.
93. William James (1937) *The Will to Believe*, New York.
94. F.W. Nietzsche (1968) *The Will to Power*, New York, Vintage Books, Sec. 537, p. 291.
95. Ibid., Sec. 584, pp. 314–15.
96. Ibid.
97. Jorge Larrians (1985) *Ideology and Cultural Identity: Modernity and the Third World Presence*, Cambridge, Pluto Press, p. 40.

98. S. Best and D. Kellner (1991) *Post-modern Theory: Critical Interrogations*, London, Macmillan Publishers.
99. Jurgen Habermas (1985) "Modernity: An Incomplete Project" in H. Foster (ed.) *Postmodern Culture*, London, Pluto Press, pp. 8–15.
100. Ibid.
101. Jurgen Habermas (1968) *Knowledge and Human Interests*, Cambridge, Polity Press, pp. 310–11.
102. Ibid.
103. Jurgen Habermas (1991) *The Theory of Communicative Action*, Vol. I, "Reason and Rationalisation of Society", Cambridge, Polity Press, (originally in German 1981), pp. 1–141.
104. Ibid., p. 236ff.
105. Jurgen Habermas (1989) *Communication*, Cambridge, Polity Press (originally published in German in 1991), pp. 1–59.
106. Ibid., pp. 59–68.
107. Jurgen Habermas (1976) *Legitimation Crisis*, Cambridge, Polity Press, pp. 68–92.
108. Jurgen Habermas (1987) *The Theory of Communicative Action*, Vol. II, "Life-world and System: A Critique of Functionalist Reason", Cambridge, Polity Press, pp. 332–73.
109. See, Anthony Giddens (1990) *The Consequences of Modernity*, Cambridge. Polity Press.
110. See, Anthony Giddens (1994) "Living in a Post-traditional Society", in U. Beck, A. Giddens and C. Lash (eds), *Reflexive Modernisation*, Cambridge, Polity Press.
111. Anthony Giddens (1991) *Modernity and Self-identity*, Cambridge, Polity Press, p. 244.
112. See, Erich Fromm (1950) *The Fear of Freedom*, London, Routledge & Paul.
113. See, Karl R. Popper (1971) *The Open Society and its Enemies*, Vol. I, Princeton, Princeton University Press.
114. See, Karl R. Popper (1952) *The Logic of Scientific Discovery*, London, Hutchinson Publication.
115. Alasdair MacIntyre (1981) *After Virtue*, Notre Dame, University of Notre Dame Press, p. 205.
116. Ibid., p. 53.
117. Charles Taylor (1996) "Sources of Self", in *Liberals and Communitarians*, Stephen Mulhul and Adam Smith (eds) Oxford, Blackwell Publishers, p. 112.
118. Micheal Walzer (1986) "Spheres of Justice", in Stephen Munhall and Adam Smith (eds) *Liberals and Communitarians*, Oxford, Blackwell Publishers, p. 127.
119. Robert Mayer and Michael Walzer (2001) "Industrial Democracy and Complex Equality", *Political Theory: An International Journal of Political Philosophy*, Sage Publications, Vol. 29, No. 2, pp. 237–261.
120. Rudolf Pannwitz (1917) *Die Krisis der Europaeishen Kulture*, Numberg: Hans Carl, p. 64.

121. See, Federico de Onis (1934) *Antologia de la Posia espandae hispanomericana: 1882–1932*, Madrid, pp. XVII-XIX. Note: For the best historical discussion of the term postmodernism see, Margaret Ross, *The Postmodern and the Postindustrial: A Critical Analysis,* Cambridge, Cambridge University Press, 1991.
122. See, Bernard Iddings Bell (1939) *Religion for Living: A Book for Postmodernists*, London, The Religious Book Club.
123. Arnold Toynbee (1939) *A Study of History*, London, Oxford University, Vol. 5, p. 43. Toynbee referred to postmodernism again in Vol. 8, published in 1954, p. 338.
124. Tim Woods (1999) *Beginning Postmodernism*, Manchester, Manchester University Press, p. 49.
125. Terry Eagleton (1996) *The Illusion of Postmodernism*, Oxford, Blackwell Publishers.
126. Tim Woods (1999) *Beginning Postmodernism*, Manchester, Manchester University Press, p. 95. Also see, Robert Venturi (1966) *Complexity and Contradiction in Architecture*, pt.1988. David Harvey (1990) *The Condition of Post-modernity*, Oxford, Blackwell Publishers. Charles Jenks (1991) *The Language of Postmodern Architecture,* London, Academy Edition. Charles Jenks (1995) *The Architecture of Lumping Universe*, London, Academy Edition.
127. Lawrence Cahoone (2003) *From Modernism to Postmodernism*, Oxford, Blackwell Publishers, pp. 2–3.
128. See Denial Bell (1973) *The Coming of the Post-industrial Society*, New York, Basic Books.
129. J. Allen (1992) "Post-industrialism and Post-fordism", in S. Hall and T. McGrew (eds) *Modernity and its Future*, Cambridge, Polity Press. Also see, J. Burnham (1941) *The Marginal Revolution*, New York, Doubleday.
130. See, A. Touraine (1971) *The Post-industrial Society*, New York, Random House.
131. Ibid.
132. Lawrence Cahoone (2003) *From Modernism to Postmodernism*, Oxford, Blackwell Publishers, p. 3.
133. For some of this theory, see Vincent Descombes (1980) *Modern French Philosophy*, trans. by L. Schoott Fox and J.M. Harding, New York, Cambridge University.
134. In the 1960s and 1970s, however, their critique had a patently political meaning. It served to undermine the claims to legitimate by academic authorities and the state and was connected to the critique of western imperialism and rationalism, especially American involvement in Indo-China, and eventually to the feminist critique of male power as well.
135. See, Christopher Lasch (1991) *The True and Only Heaven: Progress and its Critics*, New York, Norton.
136. Joe Doherty, Elspeth Graham and Mo Malck (eds) (1992) *Postmodernism and the Social Sciences*, Basingstock, Macmillan Press, p. 12.
137. "... positivism believes that facts are out there waiting to be discovered and that only reliable way to be achieve this knowledge is to follow methods based on the natural sciences ... (but) the model of natural sciences as paradigm for

knowledge began to be rejected because people increasingly saw it as a part of a larger, corrupting, techno-scientific cultural imperative. Consequently, a crisis of methodology and representation emerged, as the aims and goals of modernist social analysis gradually fell into disrepute offering indeterminacy instead of determinacy, diversity instead of unity, difference over synthesis, complexity in the place of simplification, and inter-textuality relations rather then causality, postmodernist social sciences appear to be 'locate' meaning rather than 'discover' it."

Steve Smith, Ken Booth and Marysia Zalewski (eds) (1996) *International Theory: Positivism and Beyond*, Cambridge, Cambridge University Press, pp. 11–44 and p. 15.

138. Thomas Kuhns (1962) *The Structure of Scientific Revolution*, Chicago, University of Chicago Press.
139. Irving Howe (1970) "Mass Society and Postmodern Fiction", in *The Decline of the New*, New York, Harcourt, Brace and World, pp. 190–207.
140. The term had been used in architecture by Joseph Hudunt in the 1940s to mean extreme – or ultra-modern architecture. See his "The Postmodern House", *Architectural Record*, Vol. 97, May 1945, pp. 70–75. Charles Jenks, in the 1970s, was the first architectural writer to use the word to mean 'the end of or transformation' of modernism.
141. Jane Jacobs (1961) *The Death and Life of Great American Cities*, New York, Vintage Books.
142. Jean-François Lyotard (1984) *The Post-modern Condition: A Report on Knowledge*, Manchester, Manchester University Press, pp. xxiii-xxv and 3–11.
143. Jean Baudrillard (1993) *Symbolic Exchange and Death*, London, Sage Publications, p. 8.
144. Ibid., p. 10.
145. Ibid., p. 19ff.
146. Ibid., p. 31ff.
147. For detailed discussion please see, Jean Baudrillard (1993) *From Symbolic Exchange to Death*, trans. by H. Grant, Chapter 1, London, Sage Publications, pp. 6–12.
148. See, Jean Baudrillard (1981) *For a Critique of the Political Economy of the Sign*, St. Louis, Telos Press.
149. Hans Bertens and Joseph Natoli (eds) (2002) *Postmodernism: The Key Figures*, Oxford, Blackwell Publishers, pp. 50–53.
150. Fredric Jameson (1991) *Postmodernism Or The Cultural Logic of Late Capitalism*, London, Verso Publications.
151. Fredric Jameson (1991) *Postmodernism Or the Cultural Logic of Late Capitalism*, London, Verso Publications.
152. See, Michel Foucault (1980) *Power/Knowledge*, (Selected Interview and Other Writings, 1972–1977, Colin Edition), New York, Pantheon Books.
153. Michel Foucault (1984) "What is Enlightenment?" in P. Rabinow (ed.). *The Foucault Reader*, New York, Pantheon, p. 249.

154. For details see, Jean Jacques Derrida (1981) *Writing and Deference*, London, Routledge Publishers.
155. For details see, Jean Jacques Derrida (2002) *Of Grammatology*, Delhi, Motilal Banarsidas Publishers, trans. by Gayatri Chakravorty Spivak.
156. Anthony Giddens, (1990) *Consequences of Modernity*, Cambridge, Polity Press. Also see, Anthony Giddens (1991) *Modernity and Self Identity*, Cambridge, Polity Press.
157. Terry Eagleton (1996) *The Illusions of Post-modernism*, Oxford, Blackwell Publishers, p. vii (Preface).
158. Lawrence Cahoone (ed.) (2003) *From Modernism to Postmodernism*, Oxford, Blackwell Publishing, p. 10.
159. See, James Williams (1998) *Lyotard: Towards a Postmodern Philosophy*, Cambridge, Polity Press.
160. Jean-François Lyotard (1984) *The Postmodern Condition: A Report on Knowledge*, Minneapolis, University of Minnesota Press.
161. Stuart Hall, David Held and Toney McGrew (eds) (1992) *Modernity and its Future*, Cambridge, Polity Press, p. 332.
162. Ibid.
163. Steven Seidman (ed.) *The Postmodern Turn: New Perspectives on Social Theory*, Cambridge, Cambridge University Press, pp. 30–31.
164. James Williams (1998) *Lyotard: Towards a Postmodern Philosophy*, Cambridge, Polity Press, p. 27.
165. Ibid.
166. Jean-François Lyotard (1984) *The Postmodern Condition: A Report on Knowledge*, Minneapolis, University of Minnesota Press, p. 10.
167. Ibid., p. 61.
168. Richard Rorty (1991) *Objectivity, Relativism and Truth: Philosophical Papers*, Vol. I, Cambridge, Cambridge University Press.
169. Ludwig Wittgenstein (1953) *Philosophical Investigations*, Oxford, Blackwell Publishers.
170. Richard Rorty (1998) *Contingency, Irony and Solidarity*, Cambridge, Cambridge University Press, p. 52.
171. Richard Rorty (1991) *Objectivity, Relativism and Truth: Philosophical Papers*, Vol. I, Cambridge, Cambridge University Press, p. 2.
172. Hans Bertens and Joseph Natoli (eds) (2002) *Postmodernism: The Key Figures*, Oxford, Blackwell Publishers, p. 247.
173. G.C. Spivak, "Translator's Introduction" in J.J. Derrida (1976) *Of Grammatology*, Baltimore, Johns Hopkins University Press, p. XIV.
174. Hans Bertens and Joseph Natoli (eds) (2002) *Postmodernism: The Key Figures*, Oxford, Blackwell Publishers, p. 110.
175. See, Jean Jacques Derrida (1976) *Of Grammatology*, Baltimore, Johns Hopkins University Press, p. 5.
176. Ibid., p. 15.

177. Chris Barker (2000) *Cultural Studies: Theory and Practices*, London, Sage Publications, pp. 72–73.
178. Jean Jacques Derrida (1976) *Of Grammatology*, Baltimore, Johns Hopkins University Press, p. 20.
179. S. Hall, D. Hobson, A. Lowe and P. Will (eds) (1980) *Culture, Media and Language*, London, Hutchinson, p. 199.
180. Michel Foucault (1984) *The Foucault Reader*, edited by P. Rabinow, Harmondsworth, p. XII.
181. Michel Foucault (1984) "What is Enlightenment?" in Rabinow (ed.) *The Foucault Reader*, New Delhi, Pantheon, p. 249.
182. Ibid.
183. Lawrence Cahoone (2003) *From Modernism to Postmodernism*, Oxford, Black wall Publishers, pp. 242–243.
184. Michel Foucault (1972) *The Archaeology of Knowledge*, trans. by A. M. Sheridan Smith, London, Tavistock Publication, pp. 31–39.
185. See, Michel Foucault (1972) *The Archaeology of Knowledge*, trans. by A.M. Sheridan Smith, London, Tavistock Publication.
186. See, Michel Foucault (1973) *The Birth of the Clinic*, trans. by A.M. Sheridan Smith, London, Tavistock Publication.
187. Michel Foucault (1972) *The Archaeology of Knowledge*, trans. by A.M. Sheridan Smith, London, Tavistock Publication, pp. 31–39.
188. Stuart Hall, David Held and Tony McGrew (1992) *Modernity and its Future*, Oxford, Polity Press, p. 259.
189. Michel Foucault (1980) *Power/Knowledge*, New York, Pantheon, p. 136.
190. See, Michel Foucault (1980) *Power/Knowledge*, New York, Pantheon.
191. See, Alan Sheridan (1984) *Michel Foucault: The Will to Truth*, New York, Routledge.
192. Michel Foucault (1972) *The Archaeology of Knowledge*, trans. by A.M. Sheridan Smith, London, Tavistock Publishers, p. 94.
193. Lawrence Cahoone (2003) *From Modernism to Postmodernism*, Oxford, Blackwell Publishers, p. 10.
194. See, Jorge Larrian (1994) *Ideology and Cultural Identity: Modernity and the Third World Presence*, Cambridge, Polity Press.
195. Michel Foucault (1972) *The Archaeology of Knowledge*, London, Tavistock, pp. 31–39.
196. Michel Foucault, "Truth and Power", in C. Gordon (ed.) (1980) *Michel Foucault: Power/Knowledge*, (Selected Interviews and Other Writings, 1972–1977), Brighton, Harvester Press, p. 114.
197. Ibid.
198. Michel Foucault (1977) *The Archaeology of Knowledge*, London, Tavistock Publication, p. 97.
199. Jean Jacques Derrida (1976) *Of Grammatology*, Baltimore, Johns Hopkins University Press, p. 50.
200. Ibid., p. 20.

201. See, Jacques Derrida (1980) *Le Carte Postal*, Chicago, University of Chicago Press.
202. A. Culter et al. (1997) *Marx's Capitalism and Capitalism Today,* London, Routledge and Kegan Paul, Vol. I, pp. 216– 217.
203. B. Hindess and P. Hirst (1977) *Mode of Production and Social Formation: An Auto-Critique of Pre-capitalist Mode of Production*, London, Macmillan, pp. 13–14.
204. Jorge Larrian (1994) *Ideology and Cultural Identity: Modernity and the Third World Presence*, Cambridge, Polity Press, p. 98.
205. Ibid., pp. 98–99.
206. Chris Barker (2000) *Cultural Studies: Theory and Practice*, Landon, Sage Publishers, p. 82.
207. E. Laclau and C. Mouffe (1985) *Hegemony and Socialist Strategy,* London, Verso Publications, p. 109.
208 Ibid., p. 136.
209. S. Hall (1992) "The Question of Cultural Identity", in S. Hall, David Held and Toney McGrew (eds), *Modernity and its Futures*, Cambridge, Polity Press, p. 277.
210. Ibid., p. 275.
211. Gayatri Chakravorty Spivak, "Can Subaltern Speak?" in Cary Nelson and Lawrence Grossberg (eds) (1988) *Marxism and the Interpretation of Culture*, Cambridge, Unit Illinois Press, pp. 279– 289.
212. See, Ranjit Guha (ed.) (1982) *Subaltern Studies I: Writing on South Asian History and Society*, Delhi, Oxford University Press.
213. See, Reina Lewis and Sara Mills (eds) (2003) *Feminist Postcolonial Theory: A Reader*, Edinburgh, Edinburgh University Press.
214. See, L. Nicholson (1995) "Interpreting Gender", in L. Nicholson and S. Seidman (eds) *Social Postmodernism*, Cambridge, Cambridge University Press.
215. Judith Butler (1993) *Bodies that Matter*, London and New York, Routledge Publications, pp. 1–2.
216. J. Kristeva (1986) "Women's Time", in T. Moi (ed.) *The Kristeva Reader*, Oxford, Blackwell Publishers, p. 209.
217. See, Francoise Lionnet (1992) *Feminisms and Universalisms, Universal Rights and the Legal Debate around the Practice of Female Excision in France*, Vol. 6, pp. 97–113.
218. Chandra Talpade Mohanty (1980) "Under Western Eyes, Feminist Scholarship and Colonial Discourse", in *Feminist Review*, pp. 65–88.
219. Ibid., pp. 65–88.
220. See, Thomas Docherty (ed.) (1993) *Postmodernism: A Reader*, Brighton, Harvester Wheatsheaf.
221. Tim Woods (1999) *Beginning Postmodernism,* Manchester, Manchester University Press, pp. 34–35.
222. See, Jurgen Habermas (1987) *The Philosophical Discourse of Modernity,* Cambridge MA, MIT Press.

223. F. Jameson (1991) *Postmodernism or the Cultural Logic of Late Capitalism*, London, Verso Publications, p. 57.
224. Ibid., p. 61.
225. Ibid, pp. 64–65.
226. Ibid., p. 76.
227. Jean Baudrillard (1994) *Simulacra and Simulation*, Ann Arbor, University of Michigan Press.

     "... modern societies are organized around the production and consumption of commodities, while postmodern societies are organized around simulation and the play of images and signs, denoting a situation in which codes, models and signs are the organizing principles of a new social order where simulation rules. In the society of simulation, identity are constructed by the appropriation of images and codes and models determine how individuals perceive themselves and relates to other people. Economics, politics, social life and culture are all governed by the logic of simulation, whereby codes and models determine how goods are consumed and used, politics unfold, culture is produced and consumed and everyday life is lived."
228. Hans Berterns and Joseph Natoli (eds) (2002) *Postmodernism: The Key Figures*, Oxford, Blackwell Publishers, p. 182.
229. Fredric Jameson (1985) "Postmodernism and Consumer Society", in H. Foster (ed.) *Postmodern Culture*, London, Pluto Press, pp. 111–125.
230. Terry Eagleton (1996) *The Illusions of Postmodernism*, Oxford, Blackwell Publishers, pp. 25–26.
231. Ibid., p. 26.
232. Ziauddin Sardar (1998) *Postmodernism and the Other: The New Imperialism of Western Culture*, London, Pluto Press, p. 275.
233. Ibid., p. 279.
234. Ibid., p. 282.
235. Ibid., p. 291.
236. Ron Shaprio (1998) *Surviving Postmodernism*, New Delhi, Prestige Books, p. 22.
237. Christopher Norris (1994) *Truth and Ethics of Criticism, Knowledge and Human Interest*, Manchester, Manchester University Press, pp. 25–26.
238. David Simpson (1995) *The Academic Postmodern and the Rule of Literature: A Report on Half Knowledge*, Chicago, University of Chicago Press, p. 161.

2

Gandhi's Critique of Modernism

Like the postmodernists, Gandhi also criticized the modernism, particularly its facets – rationalism, universalism and individualism. The objective of this chapter is to present the Gandhi's critique of modernism by placing the Gandhian thought and modernism face to face. A comparative analysis of both of these shows that both have shared their views on rationalism. Like modernist thinkers Gandhi does not deny the importance of reason. However, he said that this is the one way of organizing ideas and, in some cases, not the most important one. For him, Hindu cosmology provides an account of the organization of the world, its fixity and feudality, and the relationship of human beings to the cosmos as well as each other. For Gandhi, this provides a grouping for reason but is not something the unaided reason can discover by itself.[1] Throughout his life, Gandhi raised his voice against the irrational or inhuman social practices in the name of tradition or religion like child marriage, untouchability etc. For Gandhi:

> Rationalism is a hideous monster when it claims for itself omnipotence. Attribution of omnipotence to reason is as bad a piece of idolatry as is worship of stock and stone believing it to be God. I plead not for the suppression of reason, but [an appreciation of its inherent limits].[2]

According to Gandhi, reason is not the only faculty through which you get knowledge; intuition, love, forgiveness etc., are also the instruments of knowledge. For modern rationalists all these aspects of human personality do not play any role as far as the knowledge (instrumental one) is concerned. Contrary to this, Gandhi thought that the role of emotions has its own importance for knowledge, which we gained through experience. Ronald J. Terchek writes:

> Our love, trust, forgiveness and generosity do not flow primarily from reason. Indeed, for some rationalists these feelings may be misplaced; but not for Gandhi. He sees these dispositions and actions that flow from them embodying the best in human beings. He also knows that the opposition of these dispositions is not always reason. When love and trust is involved, the choice is not invariably between them and reason but between love and hate or trust and suspicion. To assume that reason should always be the arbiter is to misunderstand both its strengths and limitations. Reason can speak to an impulse to love, for example, but after a while reason is exhausted and has nothing more to say. We love or we do not. Gandhi wants to unite love, trust and forgiveness from calculation and join them to the developmental capacities of everyone.[3]

For Gandhi, a watertight compartmentalization is not at all possible between mind and heart, rationality and morality etc. According to him, rationality can prove untruth, but truth is beyond these kinds of mental exercises. In fact, an individual's comprehensive personality depends on both rationality and intuition. Thus, we should not accept only one aspect as a whole, as that would be a partial perspective. In Gandhi's words:

> I have come to the conclusion that if you want something really important to be done, you not merely satisfy the reason, you must move the heart also. The appeal of reason is more important to the head.[4]

In fact, Gandhi was not against the reason or rationality at all but he did not favour the dominative and hegemonic nature of modern instrumental rationality. For him, this modern hegemonic rationality and its basic tenets can be seen in different aspects of modern lifestyle. Gandhi criticized each of these features one by one, in this chapter.

For Gandhi, machine and technology, which is the fundamental feature of modern civilization, is responsible for the destruction in human life. A cursory glance at the history of human civilization shows that in every era, human beings had been using different types of machines and after the industrial and technological revolution of the eighteenth century these machineries have come in a more sophisticated manner. The whole scenario of human life gets changed or, in other words, can be said to get mechanized. For Gandhi, the mechanization or fetishism of technology was closely tied up with the largest phenomenon of industrialism – another apparently self-propelling and endless process of creating larger and larger industries with no other purpose except to produce cheap consumer goods and maximize profit. He argued that since modern economic life followed an inexorable momentum of its own, it reduced men to its helpless and passive victim and represented a new form of slavery – more comfortable and invidious and hence more dangerous than the earlier one.

The capitalist hunt for profits led to mechanization and industrialism. For Gandhi, machines relieved drudgery, created leisure, increased efficiency and were indispensable when there was a shortage of labour. Their use must therefore be guided by a well-considered moral theory indicating how the new men should live, spend their free time and relate to one another. Since modern economy lacked such a theory and was only propelled by the search for profit, it mechanized production without any regard for its wider moral and cultural consequences.

Replying to the question whether he was against all machinery, Gandhi said:

> How can I be when I know that even this body is a most delicate piece of machinery? The spinning wheel is a machine; a little toothpick is a machine. What I object to is the craze for machinery, not machinery as such. The craze is for what they call labour-saving machinery. Men go on 'saving labour' till thousand are without work and thrown on the open streets to die of starvation. I want to save time and labour not for a fraction of mankind but for all. I want the concentration of wealth, not in the hand of a few, but in the hands of all. Today machinery merely helps a few, but in the backs of millions. The impetus behind it all is not the philanthropy to save labour, but greed. It is against this constitution of things that I am fighting with all might ... the supreme consideration is man. The machine should not tend to atrophy the limbs of man.[5]

It is clear from the above statement that Gandhi was not against the machines and machinery but against its craze. According to Gandhi, machines are loosing the importance of labour. It is propelled by a long chain of continuous wants or greed and thus making the process of production and distribution more crucial. For Gandhi:

> Machinery has its place; it has come to stay. But it must not be allowed to displace necessary human labour. I would welcome every

> improvement in the cottage machine, but I know that it is criminal to displace hand labour by the introduction of power-driven spindles unless one is at the same time ready to give millions of farmers some other occupation in their houses.[6]

In Gandhi's view, in modern era, the increasing use of machinery and technology has created unemployment to a large extent. Men are replaced by machines and thus there is a great scarcity of work. And consequently we are facing the problem of corruption and immorality in economy. Gandhi was intended to provide the minimum basic needs to each and every member of the society. If machine can do so then it is accepted, otherwise it should be regarded as a curse for the society.

In fact, Gandhi had his own perspective towards industrialization. He wanted to restrict the use of machinery at a particular limitation. He explained:

> Granting for the moment that machinery may supply all the needs of humanity, still, it would concentrate production in particular areas, so that you would have to go about in a round about way to regulate distribution; whereas, if there is production and distribution both in the respective areas where things are required, it is automatically regulated, and there is less chance for fraud, none for speculation.[7]

In his famous book *Hind Swaraj*, Gandhi wrote:

> Today machinery merely helps a few to ride on the back of millions. The impetus behind it all is not the philanthropy to save labour, but greed. It is against this constitution of things that I am fighting with all my might ... the supreme consideration is man. The machine should not tend to atrophy the limbs of man.[8]

Men were replaced by machines and thus there is a great scarcity of work in modern society. And consequently we are facing the problem of corruption and immorality in modern economy. Gandhi was intended to provide the minimum basic needs to each and every one. If machines can do so than it is accepted otherwise it should be regarded as a curse for the society. Whether it is machine or anything else ultimate objective must always be to get freedom, freedom from our own blemishes, and freedom from our own flows and imperfections. And Gandhi assumes that even machines must help us in this direction of getting salvation. He says:

> Ideally, I would rule out all machinery, even as I would reject this body, which is not helped to salvation, and seek the liberation of the

> soul. From that point of view I would reject all machinery, but machines will remain because, like the body, they are inevitable. The body itself, as I told you, is the purest piece of mechanism; but if it is a hindrance to the highest fights of the soul, it has to be rejected.[9]

Actually, the ideal society about which Gandhi discussed, is the society where individual is supreme consideration and all the other aspects of the society, either it is machine, industry, production or distribution, evolve around individual. That is why, Gandhi said that healthy soul and body along with healthy relations would be the basic tenets of '*swaraj*'. For Gandhi, science is equal to spirituality; both should mean the same thing. One is more concerned with the outer aspect of the world and other with the inner aspect, and if both are combined, they will give us the whole world in ourselves. So, science and spirituality should go together and it is the only way to liberate not only India but the whole world and there can be kingdom of heaven on this earth, otherwise if science goes alone, it would destroy the whole world.

Thus, Gandhi was in favour of controlled and balanced development founded by humanity and morality. But, a body-centric or materialist view of man attributed two basic properties to him and regarded them as natural and legitimate, namely, 'selfishness' and an 'infinite multiplicity of wants'.[10] Gandhi went on to say:

> Modern man spent most of his energy trying to steady himself in a holistic and unsteady environment. He had neither the inclination nor the ability to show down the tempo of his life, relax, compose himself, and reflect on his pattern of life and nurture the inner springs of energy. He lived outside himself and exhausted himself physically and spiritually. Predictably he needed to depend on such ultimately debilitating sources of instant energy an intoxicating spirits, tea and coffee, in order constantly to whip him into action. *Inwardly empty* and frightened to be alone with himself, he was always busy, turning to one activity after another, easily bored and feverishly looking for new sources of amusement.[11]

Gandhi thought that modern civilization had a depressing air of 'futility' and 'madness' about it and was likely to destroy itself before long. As per Gopinath Dhawan, "So long as we act as machine, there can be no question of morality. If we want to call an action moral, it should have been done consciously and as a matter of duty."[12] It shows that the Gandhian philosophy emphasizes the importance of morality and dignity of man. Although he accepts the utility of machines, yet he knows that it should not be accepted on the cost of human beings. For Gandhi, man is the supreme consideration and he must always be adhered.

After criticizing the mechanical aspect of modernism, Gandhi also attacked the profession of doctors or lawyers. For Gandhi, a civilization properly so-called placed man at its centre and measured its greatness in terms of its ability to produce men and women possessing such distinctively human powers as self-determination, autonomy, self-knowledge, self-discipline and social cooperation. Modern civilization did the opposite. By encouraging them to alienate their powers to large organizations run by experts, it rendered men passive, helpless and heteronymous. Gandhi took the example of medical science. Ideally, it should aim at two things. First, it should help people acquire a greater understanding and control of their bodies by explaining to them the causes and axiology of their ailment, how to represent them and they were integrally related to their ways of life. Second, since the body was not an inert machine but a living organism with its own rhythm and built-in intelligence, medical science should mobilize its internal resources and wisely activate them where necessary by external help. Modern medicine did neither.

In Gandhi's words:

> Doctors have almost unhinged us. Sometimes I think that quacks are better than highly qualified doctors. Let us consider: the business of a doctor is to take care of the body, or, properly speaking, not even that. Their business is really to rid the body of diseases that may afflict it. How do these diseases arise? Surely by our negligence or indulgence. I overeat, I have indigestion, I go to a doctor, he gives me medicine. I am cured. I overeat again, I take his pills again. Had I not taken the pills in the first instance, I would have suffered the punishment deserved by me and I would not have overeaten again. The doctor intervened and helped me to indulge myself. My body thereby certainly felt more at ease; by my mind became weakened. A continuance of a course of medicine must, therefore, result in loss of control over the mind.[13]

Gandhi further said:

> I have indulged in vice, I contract a disease, a doctor cures me, the odds are that I shall repeat the vice. Had the doctor not intervened, nature would have done its work, and I would have acquired mastery over myself, would have been freed from vice and would have become happy.[14]

From both the above statements it is very much clear that Gandhi was against the tendency of profit and money-making professions like medicine. Doctor's job is to save the body but Gandhi's ultimate aim was to save even the soul, along with, the body. Accordingly, let the nature to do its own work, because it will make the body comparatively healthy and controlled one.

Bhikhu Parekh, one of famous Gandhian scholars, said that modern civilization also involved an egregious amount of violence against nature, which was largely seen as man's property to do with it what he liked. Its resources were ruthlessly exploited and its rhythm and balance distributed, and animals were freely killed or tortured for food, sport, fancy clothes and medical experiments. In Gandhi's view violence oozed from every pore of modern society and had so much become a way of life that modern man could not cope with his relations with himself or other men without translating them into the military language of conflict, struggle, mastery, subjugation, domination, victory and defeat. Deeply rooted in violence man felt suffocated in its absence. Medical science also showed little respect for the integrity of the body and was suffused with the spirit of violence characteristic of modern civilization. It did not see the aliment as the overworked and undisciplined body's plea for rest and discipline, but rather as an unacceptable interference with its hectic routine, requiring an immediate and effective response. The body was not allowed to cope with illness at its own pace and by means of its own judiciously activated resources; instead its sluggish rhythm was aggressively manipulated by bombarding it with powerful chemical agents which ended up doing it grave long-term harm.

> ... like the other form of violence, medical violence too was subjected to an inflationary spiral. Once the 'enemies' invading the body developed 'defenses' against one set of drugs, more potent ones were invented doing yet greater violence to it and to the animals on whom they were first tried out. The poor body become a battle field where powerful armies fought out a deadly contest in which it was itself often the first casualty.[15]

Modern medical science also represents the form of violence. Criticizing the modern methodology of medical profession, Gandhi writes:

> European doctors are worst of all. For the sake of a mistaken care of the human body, they kill annually thousands of animals. They

practice dissection. No religion sanctions this. All say that it is not necessary to take so many lives for the sake of our bodies.[16]

Another tenet of modernism, which is harshly criticized by Gandhi, was the profession of law. He said:

> Modernity which has all the characteristics of inhuman, brutal, barbarous or unfeeling or feelingness, law played its important role in destroying the community and family faith among men. The profession of law teaches immorality: it is exposed to temptation from which few are saved.[17]

Accordingly, the profession of law in modern era is intended to corrupt the human values, which are playing an important role as far as family and community link, are concerned. In Gandhi's own words:

> Lawyers are also men, and there is something good in every man. Whenever instances of lawyers having done good can be brought forward, it will be found that the good is due to them as men rather than as lawyers. All I am concerned with is to show you that the profession teaches immorality; it is exposed to temptation from which few are saved.[18]

Men were intelligent and moral beings capable of resolving their differences by discussing them in the spirit of charity and good will or by seeking the arbitration of widely respected men and women in their community. Explaining his views, Gandhi said:

> The *Hindu* and the *Mohomedans* have quarrelled. An ordinary man will ask them to forget all about it; he will tell them both must be more or less at fault, and will advise them no longer to quarrel. But they go to lawyers. The latter's duty is to side with their clients to which they (the clients) are often strangers. If they do not do so they will be considered to have degraded their profession. The lawyers, therefore, will, as a rule, advance quarrels instead of repress them. Moreover, men take up that profession not in order to help others out of their miseries, but to enrich them. It is one of the avenues of becoming wealthy and their interest exists in multiplying disputes.[19]

According to Gandhi, it was within Gandhi's knowledge that lawyer were glad when men had disputes ... lazy people, in order to indulge in luxuries, take up such professions. This is a true statement. Any other argument is a mere pretension. It is the lawyers who have discovered that theirs is an honourable profession. They frame laws as they frame their own praises. They decide what fees they will charge and they put on so much side that poor almost consider them to be heaven-born.

Gandhi was of the opinion that the institution of law is a sign of slavery. "If I ask a third party to decide between you and me? Surely, the decision of the third party is not always right. The parties alone know who is right. We, in our simplicity and ignorance, imagine that a stranger, by taking our money, gives us justice."[20]

For Gandhi, the institution of law is only an external institution to settle the dispute but the ultimate aim is to change the heart. Thus, for family and community feeling we have to expand our love and trust and tendencies of forgiveness to the larger extent. The modern legal system did little to develop and mobilize man's moral impulses and capacities for reflection and introspection. Instead, it required him to alienate them to a central agency telling him how to run his life and conduct his relations with others, including his own neighbours, wife, ex-wife and children. Bhikhu Parekh writes that Gandhi found it strange that modern man, who talked so much about his self-respect and dignity, did not find all this deeply humiliating. Thus, Gandhi said that the professions of lawyers and doctors are corrupting the moral and human influences in the modern society. And, he added, whatever he told while criticizing these professions, the point which he raised was not original one. In fact, even western writers have used stronger language regarding both lawyers and doctors. One writer has linked the whole modern system to the *Upas* tree. Its branches are represented by parasitical professions, including those of law and medicine, and over the trunk has been raised the axe of true religion. Immorality is the root of the tree.

Actually, the main hurdle of modernism is its too much reliance on rationality. Hence, reason is dominated and it is supposed to be the most important factor. For Gandhi, except reason, so many other factors are also there in human personality like love, trust, emotion, intuitions, consciousness etc. But, for modern rationalists, these factors have not their importance in human life. For Gandhi, it is very difficult to compartmentalize human personality between head and heart, rationality and humanity. With the help of head (reason) we can prove the authenticity of untruth but to propound the importance of truth we often bound to go with heart (irrationality). Both of these aspects are inherent in human nature. There, if we are accepting the dominance of one factor, it means we are accepting the overdue importance to the partial theory.

Similarly, by rejecting the second feature of modernism, i.e., universalism, Gandhi favoured local and *swadeshi* elements in a larger manner. He was against any form of centralized tendency of modernism. He argued that the highly centralized and bureaucratic modern state enjoying and jealously guarding its monopoly of political power is a by product of modern civilization.

> The state represents violence in concentrated and organized form. The individual has a soul, but as the state is soulless machine, it can never be weaned from violence to which it owns its very existence.[21]

Accordingly, modern states are structured in such a way that they encourage exploitation and violence discovering the importance of individual and his/her local recognitions. That is why, Gandhi usually said that the state dehumanized its citizens in more or less the same way as the medical, legal and other institutions do. It had a vested institutional interest in monopolizing all initiatives and fostering a state-centred political culture. The more its citizens become 'addicted' to it and the more they feel helpless without it, the safer it feels. Accordingly, it systematically nurtured the illusion that the problems of society were too complex and intractable to be solved by ordinary citizens acting individually or collectively, and were best left to the state and its official agencies. It felt threatened by active and independent-minded citizens determined to participate in the conduct of their affairs and worried lest they should be morally compromised by what it did in their name. It, therefore, denied them access to vital information and opportunities for political participation, and discouraged independent and vibrant local communities capable of challenging its decisions.[22] Thus, Gandhi was totally opposed to the state organized by violence and based on the tendencies of exploitation.

A well-known Gandhian philosopher Gopinath Dhavan writes in this context:

> Gandhi sincerely believed that the state represented an organization based on force. It manifested its coercive power through compulsion and exploitation of the individuals in the society. Gandhi held the view that any action of the individuals in the state which was immoral, since in his scheme of thinking every action was judged from the touchstone of ethical priority. He argued that "no action which is not voluntary can be called moral ... if we want to call an action moral, it should have been done consciously and as a matter of duty.[23]

Gandhi wanted to convince the politicians to accept the institution of state and power not as an end in itself but as an instrument. Accordingly, state should be regarded as a servant of the society and all its deeds should be guided by the same, then only it would be able to do humanitarian works in real sense of the term. In fact, Gandhi looked upon an increase in the power of the state with the greatest fear, because although while apparently doing well by minimizing exploitation, it does the greatest harm to mankind destroying individuality, which lies at the root of all progress.[24]

> Destroying individuality means exploitation led to violence. Therefore, to avoid violence and to ensure maximum flowing of human personality, decentralization of political power must become an end of a progressive and welfare oriented society.[25]

For Gandhi, politics should be treated only as means through which, an individual could flourish his/her inherent personality. Thus, state should decentralize its power. As much powers would be dispersed, the state would be non-violent and thus an individual can utilize the importance of his rights. According to Gandhi, rights are not the claim but it is a kind of social value through which an individual will move on the path of self-realization and, thus could able to establish his/her relation with the other members of the society.

According to Gandhi, "if an individual is embedded with the moral and human values, then automatically he/she will achieve rights to actualize his/her humanitarian deeds. Then, the importance of the institution of state, as law provider institution, would be automatically withered away. There is then a state of enlightened anarchy. In such a state sovereignty vests in everyone, who is his own ruler. He governs himself in a manner that he represents the freedom of his neighbours and in all such activity there is no political power because there is no state."[26] But, not a single trait of all these features is found in the modern system of state.

Contrary to these, Gandhian *Ramrajya* does not accept any concept of state. For him, *Swaraj* is to be obtained by educating the masses to an extent of their capacity to regulate and control authority. He said, this *Swaraj* would be of each and every individuals, whosoever are residing there inside the state by accepting the importance of differences of caste, community, society and the different cultural and historical backgrounds. Because there are factors through which an individual gets his/her recognition. Thus, Gandhi criticized universalistic tendency of modernism. As per Ronald J. Terchek:

> Gandhi sees the universalizing impulse of modernity as inhospitable of plurality. In its search for general rules, modern reason seeks to identify relevant verities and discards superfluous one what remains outside of the realm of the verifiable is unimportant

> to the enterprise replicated with the same result by distant, neutral strangers.[27]

According to Gandhi, on the one hand, modernism accepts the universalizing tenets, but it does not all accept the absolute power or ultimate eternal truth, which is really universal in nature. It shows that for modernity accepting only those factors as universal which can be proved by reason. And rationally those universal norms can be applied throughout the world. Gandhi says, the notion of rational universalism or instrumental universalism is continuously corrupting the human life and human values in modern society. Logico-enlighted universalist modern society is not only discouraging the traditional values, but also defining the meaning of the terms rationalism and universalism in a very restricted and limited sense. What we are getting from modern science is that only those happenings are 'truth' which can be proved by the scientists through their fixed rationalistic mathematical equation. Contrary to these, for Gandhi, the nature of truth is very much dynamic. One truth or argument can be truthful for one person at particular space and time, but it would be totally untruth for a person who is residing at different place. If science can evolve a methodology where different truths can be amalgamated, then it would be more relative and more moral. But, there is not any space for 'difference' in modern science. For Gandhi, modern science is wholly inadequate to serve as the epistemological arbiter of how the discrete parts should be joined together.[28] Terchek says:

> Universalizing impulse of modernity threatens diversity as well as enervates the quest for moral judgments, and it does this with its emphasis on procedures that requires detachment and indifference. Such modern claims represent the antithesis of everything. Gandhi deserves morality in his accounts, is no more revealed through the scientific method than through a blind faith in a sacred text.[29]

Thus, Gandhi sees the universalizing impulse of modernity as inhospitable of plurality. In its search for general rules, modern reason seeks to identify relevant variables and discard superfluous ones that carry no explanatory weight. What remains outside the realm of verifiable is important to the enterprise that seeks to generate theory that can be replicated with the same result by distant, neutral strangers. Gandhi fears that such an outlook decentres not only traditional morality but also common sense and reason, and ultimately self, which becomes a reminder. For her part, Arendt argues that science has taught us not to trust our sense and reason. She is particularly troubled with the claim that "faculty of reasoning can only happen to be the same in everybody."[30]

Gandhi was of the opinion that truth can be absolute or universal in nature but at the moment an individual states to regulate his/her life, he/she has to pass through many experiences, which cannot be predefined and forecasted by any branch of modern science. For Gandhi, since these life experiences are different for each one, truth would be different for everyone. That is why, he accepts the 'relative nature' of truth. In his own words:

> Truth was moral; unified, unchanging, and transcendental. It was not an object of critical inquiry or physical speculation. It could only be found in the experience of one's life, by unflinching practice of moral living. It could never be correctly expressed within the terms of rational theoretical discourse; its only true expression was lyrical and poetic.[31]

Though, for Gandhi, the 'absolute truth' is the ultimate truth, he used to say, "as long as I have not realized this Absolute Truth, so long must I hold by the Relative truth as I have conceived it. That relative truth must, meanwhile, be my beacon, my shield and buckler."[32]

That is why, Gandhi accepts the theory of *advaita* (non-duality) in fullest sense of the term. Interpreting Gandhi in this context, Terchek says, "In his (Gandhi) view, plurality simultaneously requires distinctiveness and unity, individual integrity and cooperation." In fact, Gandhi never tried to accept any partial perspective whether it would be *advaita* of metaphysics or logico-metarialism of scientific knowledge of modern day. He wanted a comprehensive or balanced perspective of science, society and spirituality.

The third feature of modernism is individualism. Since modern era is assumed to be developed by modern rationalistic man, all the modern developments are inclined only towards the individual self. In this modern society, traditional laws and customary practices, which cannot be proved by individual's reason, would not be accepted. Thus, reason becomes the foremost important factor and since man is the master of this reason, all the developments and norms of development stand moving around the individual only. Gandhi was strongly against this individualistic notion of modernism.

Though Gandhi was the defender of the individual's freedom and individual autonomy and his ultimate advice was:

> If the individual ceases to count what is a society? Individual freedom alone can make man voluntarily surrender himself completely to the service of society. If it is wrested from him he becomes an automation and the society is ruined, no society can possibly be built on a denial of individual freedom.[33]

But, by making his point more clear, he said:

> And one discovery I have made is that there is no distribution whatever between individual growth and corporate growth, that corporate growth is therefore entirely dependent on individual growth and hence that beautiful proverb in the English language that "a chain is no stronger than weakest link in it.[34]

Gandhi claims, "the individual is the one supreme consideration".[35] However, it turns out that his celebration of freedom is very different from conventional liberal ones. He encumbers agents with duties, assigning them responsibilities to lead a moral life and attend to the good of their community. Moreover, he champions those at the periphery, emphasizing the basic rights of untouchables, women, the unemployed and others, who have been the objects of domination, exploitation and humiliation. The idea of rights he has in mind, however, are not exhausted with the usual list of liberal rights but he seeks to the rights of individuals to meet their basic needs in dignity. Gandhi also departs from standard expressions of rights when he holds that freedom should not be taken to mean that an individual should be left alone to make their way in the world. Rather, he wants them to have the freedom to cultivate the love and service which he believes the best feature of human nature. In his own words:

> Unrestricted individualism is the law of the beast, of the jungle. We have learnt to strike the mean between individual freedom and social restraint. Willing submission to social restraint for the sake of well-being of the whole society enriches both the individual and the society of which one is a member.[36]

But, in modern mechanistic and rationalistic society, individual freedom stands for an abstract individual. Here liberty means absence of any kind of social or traditional restraints. Because an individual's happiness is not complementary, but it is contradictory to social development. The harsh reality is that in this highly mechanized and industrialized society, an individual is also becoming a commodity. In such a situation, the foundational values of the society are getting affected. Gandhi said:

> Our purpose to life today becomes increasingly mechanical. Our main aim is to produce things, and in the process of this idolatry of things we transform ourselves into commodities. People are treated as numbers. The question here is not whether they are treated nicely and are well fed (things too can be treated nicely): the question is whether people are things or living beings. People love mechanical gadgets more than living beings. The approach to man is intellectual-abstract. One is interested in people as objects, in their common properties, in the statistical rules of mass behaviour, not in living individuals.[37]

Gandhian philosophy is the critique of this individualistic nature of modern life. In fact, there is not any dichotomy between individual and society in Gandhian philosophy. In his ideal state of *Ramrajya,* both individual and society develop in parallel lines. Both are interdependent, intermingled and complementary. In modern society competition plays much more important role whereas in Gandhi's *Ramrajya* cooperation is the fundamental feature of the society.

In fact, Gandhi favours the non-dual or spiritual development of the whole societal set-up. He said:

> I do not believe ... that an individual may gain spiritually and those who surround him suffer. I believe in *advaita* (non-duality), I believe in the essential unity of man and for that matter of all that lives. Therefore, I believe that if one man gain spiritually, the whole world gains with him and if one man falls, the whole world falls to that extent.[38]

Gandhi's idea towards collectivism and egalitarianism are beautifully expressed in the following words: "A drop torn from the ocean perishes without doing any good. If it remains a part of the ocean, it shares the glory of carrying on its bosom a fleet of mighty ships."[39]

Thus, in Gandhian philosophy individual and society are not different and contradictory to each other but they are essentially complementary to each other. The mutual development of both will serve the purpose in real sense of the term.

Notes

1. Ronald J. Terchek (1998) *Gandhi: Struggling for Autonomy*, New Delhi, Vistaar Publication, p. 98.
2. *Young India*, 27–6–1939.

3. Ronald J. Terchek (1998) *Gandhi: Struggling for Autonomy*, New Delhi, Vistaar Publication, p. 80.
4. *Young India*, 3–11–1913.
5. M.K. Gandhi (1998) *Hind Swaraj or Indian Home Rule*, Ahmedabad, Navajivan Publishing House, pp. 7–8.
6. *Young India*, 5–11–1925.
7. *Harijan*, 2–11–1934.
8. M.K. Gandhi (1998) *Hind Swaraj or Indian Home Rule*, Ahmedabad, Navajivan Publishing House, pp. 7–8.
9. See, M.K. Gandhi, *Hind Swaraj*, p. 9.
10. Raghavan N. Iyer (ed.) (1986) *The Moral and Political Writings of Mahatma Gandhi*, Oxford, Clarendon Press, Vol. 11, p. 328.
11. Bhikhu Parekh (1989) *Gandhi's Political Philosophy: A Critical Examination*, London, Macmillan Press, p. 25.
12. Gopinath Dhavan (1962) *The Political Philosophy of Mahatma Gandhi*, Ahmedabad, Navjivan Publication, p. 282.
13. *Hind Swaraj*, p. 53.
14. Ibid.
15. Bhikhu Parekh (1998) *Gandhi's Political Philosophy: A Critical Examination*, London, Macmillan Press, p. 27.
16. *Hind Swaraj*, p. 53.
17. Ibid., p. 80.
18. Ibid., p. 50.
19. Ibid.
20. Ibid., p. 51.
21. *The Modern India Review*, 1935, p. 413.
22. Bhikhu Parekh (1998) *Gandhi's Political Philosophy: A Critical Examination*, London, Macmillan Press, p. 28.
23. Gopinath Dhavan (1946) *The Political Philosophy of Mahatma Gandhi*, Ahmedabad, Navajivan Publications, p. 282.
24. *The Modern India Review*, October 1935, p. 143.
25. Gopinath Dhavan (1946) *The Political Philosophy of Mahatma Gandhi*, Ahmedabad, Navajivan Publications, p. 323.
26. *Young India*, 26–3–1937.
27. Ronald J. Terchek (1998) *Gandhi: Struggling for Autonomy*, New Delhi, Vistaar Publication, p. 90.
28. Ibid., p. 91.
29. Ibid.
30. Hannah Arendt (1958) *The Human Condition*, Chicago, University of Chicago Press, p. 277.
31. Partha Chatterjee (1986) *Nationalist Thought and The Colonial World: A Derivative Discourse*, Delhi, Oxford University Press, p. 97.

32. M.K. Gandhi (2001) *An Autobiography: My Experiments with Truth*, p. XI (Introduction), Ahmedabad, Navajivan Publishing House.
33. *Harijan*, 1–02–1924.
34. *The Collected Works of Mahatma Gandhi*, 1934, p. 505.
35. *Young India*, 13–11–1924.
36. *Harijan*, 27–05–1939.
37. Erich Fromm (1964) *The Heart of Man*, New York, Harper Row, p. 57.
38. *Young India*, 4–12–1912, p. 398.
39. *Harijan*, 23–3–1947, p. 78.

3

Contemporary Debate on Gandhian Philosophy as Pre-modern, Modern or Postmodern Philosophy

The postmodernist winds, which have been blowing since 1920s, are influencing every branch of knowledge. As a result, now, we have postmodern art and architecture, postmodern music and dance, postmodern philosophy and science and so on and so forth. Gandhian thinkers are also equally keen to evaluate their philosophy in this changing postmodernist scenario. Several new works in the field of Gandhian thought have emerged; for example, Nicholas F. Gier's article, "Gandhi: premodern, modern or postmodern?"[1], Ronald J. Terchek's "Problematizing modernity: Gandhi's decentring impulse"[2], L.I. Rudolph and S.H. Rudolph's book *Postmodern Gandhi*[3] and many others.

Before evaluating the Gandhian philosophy as postmodern, it is essential to know that Gandhi's thoughts were highly influenced by both western and eastern philosophies. His thoughts and philosophies were so multifarious and multidimensional in nature that sometimes it seems very difficult to categorize them under any particular category. Sometimes it appears like pre-modernist thought, sometimes as modernist and sometimes as postmodernist. A group of the thinkers, who assume his philosophy as pre-modernist, argue that throughout his life Gandhi used to criticize various aspects of modernity and tried to give due respect to the traditional and spiritual values, thus his thoughts must be regarded as the pre-modernist.

Another group of the thinkers, for whom Gandhian philosophy is strongly modernist in nature, are of the view that, since Gandhi gave more importance to the individual's rationality and autonomy against the irrational-inhuman social practices and he also raised voice for individual's emancipation and liberty like any other modernist thinker, his thoughts must be acknowledged as modernist thoughts.

Contrary to both of these perspectives, a new group of thinkers also emerged, for whom Gandhian philosophy may be categorized as the postmodernist. For these thinkers, as all the basic modern philosophical facets, i.e., universalism, rationalism and individualism are relegating towards down in postmodernist changing scenario, in Gandhian philosophy too one can easily see these postmodernist tendencies. For Gandhi, *Swadeshi* and *Swaraj* play more important role than universality in making an individual's identity. Like postmodernists, even Gandhi gave importance to historical and cultural contexts. He wrote in his autobiography that 'relativity of truth' must be accepted as a shield in the way of self-realization. Thus, he is a postmodernist thinker.

Hence, it shows that a very interesting debate is going on among the contemporary scholars on Gandhian philosophy. For some, it is pre-modern. For others, it is modern and for so many, it could be postmodern. Actually, Gandhian philosophy is so flexible that it can attain shape of any bowl. However, at the same time, it appears so firm like solid that it is very difficult to categorize it under any particular class in its strict sense of the term. Its nature is unique. It is both static as well as dynamic. In fact, it is beyond every kind of categorizations. The present chapter shall try to deal with the same debate at length. The author has tried her best to be as neutral as possible throughout the debate.

Gandhian Philosophy as a Pre-modern Philosophy

The groups of the thinkers, who assume Gandhi as the pre-modernist, raise their claims on the basis of the fact that the core idea of Gandhian philosophy revolve around the spirituality. Originally, Gandhi is a religious man and influenced by all the religions of the world. Whether it is Hindus' *Gita, Ramayana, Mahabharata*; or Jains' *Jind-avesta*; or Christians' holy the *Bible*, all these had its great influence on Gandhi. At the same time, thinkers like John Ruskin, Tolstoy, Thorough, Majini, Max Nadeero, Dadabhai Naroji, Ramesh Chandra Dutta, Adolf Dutte etc. influenced him greatly that his perspective became religion-centric or spiritual-centric.[4] As per Ramjiee Singh:

> Gandhi's personality is incarnation of spirituality ... if Gandhi is described by Prof. D.D. Ranade as 'auto-mystic', by Dr R.R. Diwakar as 'the spiritual seeker', by Prof. N.A. Nikam as 'Discoverer of Religion', he is also characterized as 'A Sage in Revolt' by Pran Chopra, as a great 'Social Technocrat', by Arnold Toynbee as a prophet, statesman, economist and educationist of the highest order by Prof. Tsurmi.[5]

Actually, while criticizing or rejecting modernity, Gandhi presents traditional, spiritual and cultural values as a solution. He said:

> The tendency of the Indian civilization is to elevate the moral being that of the western civilization is to propagate immorality. The latter is godless; the former is based on a belief in God. So understanding and so believing, it behaves every lover of India to cling to the old Indian civilization even as a child clings to the mother's breast.[6]

Accordingly, India is more inclined to enrich or strengthen its roots of morality. To Gandhi, traditional and moral values are the essential part of any civilization. In his *Ramrajya* all the aspects of society, i.e., politics, economics, education etc. were essentially inclined towards moral or spiritual values. That is why, he is frequently regarded as a pre-modernist thinker. In his own words:

> I haven't propounded a new philosophy. I only try to do experiments with those universal or ultimate truths, which are related with our daily life.[7]

Actually, he never gave us any new philosophy but only actualized age-old philosophies in his day-to-day life. The modern theory construction requires essential cause and effect relationship, which is absent in Gandhi's philosophy. He never took any interest in formulation of theories and philosophies. In fact, whatever is called universal or absolute truth, Gandhi learnt all through senses and sages. Whatever seems to him acceptable, he accepts from our traditions. Hence, Gandhi can never be recognized as a trained philosopher.

For modernists the centre of study is individual. Although, Gandhi too accepts individual, God or *Brahma* is core of his philosophy. Like an ancient thinker, he too was influenced by the notion that the universe is governed by a mysterious power and men are only a part of it. In his own words:

> There is an indefinable mysterious power that pervades everything. I feel it, though I do not see it. It is this unseen Power which makes itself felt and yet defies all proof, because it is so unlike all that I perceive through my sense. It transcends the senses.[8]

In fact, Gandhian philosophy tries to prove that an ultimate power is prevailed everywhere. We can realize this power through our senses, but it cannot be seen through the bare eyes. For Gandhi, this invisible power is God. He says:

> Man's ultimate aim is the realization of God, and all his activities, political, social and religious, have to be guided by the ultimate aim of the vision of God. The immediate service of all human beings becomes a necessary part of the endeavour simply because the only way to find God is to see Him in His creation and be one with it. This can only be done by service of all. And this cannot be done except through one's country. I am a part and parcel of the whole, and I cannot find Him apart from the rest of the humanity.[9]

Although, like modernist thinkers, Gandhi also believes in a universal system but his universalism is not rationalistic (instrumental); rather, it is spiritual or religious in nature. For Gandhi, the essence of life lies in following these universal spiritual principles in our day-to-day life. Like *Bhagavad Gita,* a religious text of Hindu community, Gandhi also believes that there is a central truth and we are compelled to accept its absoluteness and this ultimate reality is God. We have to accept it that God is our father. That is why, we are influenced by everyone and at the same time each and every person around us is influenced by us. Gandhi says:

> I do not believe ... that an individual may gain spiritually and those who surround him suffer. I believe in *advita* (non-duality), I believe in the essential unity of man and, for that matter, of all that lives. Therefore, I believe that if one man gains spiritually, the whole world gains with him and, if one man falls, the whole world falls to that extent.[10]

Since, we all are sons of the same God, we all are eternally attached to each other. Directly or indirectly we are getting influenced by our fellow beings and also influencing them. That is why, Gandhi believes in the principle of non-duality. In his own words:

> The *atman* was the same in all men and could not provide the principle of individuation. Although separate and distinct human bodies were so many different anatomical configurations of the

> identical material substance, were subject to the same laws, displayed the same basic properties and functioned in the same way. The body was the seat of particularity not individuality, a principle of numerical not substantive or essential differentiation.[11]

Like the ancient thinkers Gandhi also believes that we all are the part of the same soul. Though all of us are having different outlook physically, yet spiritually the essence of our life is one. God is the primary source of all our activities. It is only this spiritual force through which we are bounded. That was the reason why Gandhi accepted the power of spirituality in the life.

Actually, Gandhi's approach is slightly different from that of the philosophical approach. Not man but cosmos was his starting point. The cosmos consisted of different orders of ranging from the material to the human, each autonomous and standing in a complete pattern of relationship with the rest within a larger framework. It was polycentric and without a dominant centre to which the rest of the universe could be instrumentally related. Since, man represented only one order of being, obviously he could not be the centre of the universe. And, since Gandhi conceived the cosmic spirit as a principle of order and not a creator, it too lacked the separateness, transcendence and independence necessary to continue one. Man was an integral part of the cosmos, tied to it by a million bonds and incomprehensible outside of it. Since he was internally and necessarily related to the rest of its members, Gandhi saw him not as a bearer of properties but as a world of relationships, a whole, and a member of such increasingly wider wholes as the family, the caste, the community, mankind, the sentient world, the material world – all encompassing cosmos. Each whole was self-contained but not self-sufficient, and both autonomous and pointing to the larger whole of which it was a part. In Gandhi's favourite metaphor the cosmos was not a pyramid of which the so-called nature or material world was the basis, and man the apex, but a series of ever-widening circle.[12] This is the reason why he used to say:

> The purpose of life is undoubtedly to know oneself. We cannot do this unless we learn to identify ourselves with all that lives. The sum total of that life is God. Hence, the necessity of realizing God living within every one of us.[13]

The above statement of Gandhi tells us clearly that for him the ultimate aim of human life is to gain spirituality and that is why his social, political, economic etc. ideas are God-centric. Gandhi always suggests us that the service of mankind is a religious task because man is the creation of God. In his words:

> Man's ultimate aim is the realization of God, and all his activities, social, political and religious, have to be guided by the ultimate aim of the vision of God. The immediate service of all human beings becomes a necessary part of the endeavour simply because the only to find God is to see Him in His creation and be one with it. This can only be done by service of all. And this can not be done except through one's own country. I am a part and parcel of the whole, and I cannot find Him apart from the rest of the humanity.[14]

Gandhi was also of the view that each individual is a unique combination of good and bad habits. It is the social system of our surrounding through which we are getting influenced. If we really want to survive on this earth, we have to ignore the bad practices and should try to incorporate good behaviour into our life. And, the service of human being is the best way through which we can realize the charisma of God. Thus, self-realization or self-actualization would only be fulfilled by the service which we are contributing for the welfare of the society.

For Gandhi, though man is a combination of good and bad behaviour, yet the ultimate truth is that all men are good in nature. But, the modern soulless mechanical surroundings are courting the influences. Gandhi says:

> The more I observe, the greater is the dissatisfaction with the modern life. I see nothing good in it. Men are good. But they are poor victims making themselves miserable under the false belief that they are doing good. I am aware that there is fallacy underneath this. I who claim to examine what is around me may be a deluded foal. This risk all of us have to take. The fact is that we are all bound to do what we feel is right. And with me I feel that the modern life is not right. The greater the conviction, the bolder my experiments.[15]

For Gandhi, modern civilization is corrupting the moral and spiritual spirits. Western civilization is more inclined towards materi-alistic or comfortable life and they are doing this with the help of science and technology. That is why, Gandhi's philosophy always tries to define the development from ethical and moral perspectives. And, morality in life will be achieved only by following truth and non-violence. If one really wants to achieve this destitute position, he/she has to be very positive towards his/her family and relatives. Gandhi believes that those eternal or good aspects of human behaviour can be actualized in this earth only. He says:

I am endeavouring to see God through service of humanity, for I know that God is in heaven, nor down below, but in every one.[16]

Like a pre-modernist philosopher, Gandhi says that to me 'To realize God', 'To realize the Self' and 'To realize Truth' are three expressions for the same development. 'To realize God' is another expression for 'To become like God' and 'To face God'. The identification of development with that of self-realization is clearly stated in Gandhi's highly interesting and original interpretation of the *Bhagavad Gita:*

> Man is not at peace with himself till he has become like unto God. The endeavour to reach this state is the supreme, the only ambition worth having. And this is self-realization. This self-realization is the subject of *Gita,* as it is of all scriptures. But its author surely did not write it to establish that doctrine. The object of the Gita appears to one to be that of showing the most excellent way to attains self-realization. That which is to be found, more or less clearly, spread out here and there in Hindu religious books, has been brought out in the clearest possible language in the *Gita* even at the risk of repetition.[17]

Gandhi believes that religion of self or truth or God is possible only through service of humanity. Contrary to the self-centric materialistic, instrumental modern civilization, Gandhi holds that when an individual does duty without any passion of gain or reward, then only he could actualize the nature of God or truth in real sense of the term. Accordingly, God, truth and love mean nothing but service and morality. He says, "To me God is Truth and Love, God is ethics and morality."[18]

For Gandhi, it is impossible to reach God, that is truth, except through love. Love can only be expressed fully when man reduces himself to a cipher. This process of reduction to cipher is the highest effort a man or a woman is capable of making. It is the only effort worth making, and it is possible only through ever-increasing self-restraint. That is why, Gandhi said that the seeker after truth should be humbler than the dust. The world crushes the dust under its feet, but the seeker after truth should be so humble himself that even the dust could crush him. Only then, and not till then, will he have a glimpse of truth.

Hence, contrary to the modern materialistic or self-centric society, Gandhi wanted to build a society based on the fundamental values like love and humanity. As a result, he seems to be a pre-modern philosopher. Like Jesus Christ, he used to say "kill to sin, not the sinner".[19]

By propounding his philosophy on essentially good human nature, Gandhi was intended to reject the modern concept of individual-centric state. For him, the ultimate objective of all political institutions is to flourish an individual's inherent qualities. That is why, the state must work like servant, not as a master.

Further Gandhi's politics was aimed to realize God or self, it was never separated from religion. Gandhi used to say:

> For me, politics bereft of religion are absolute dirt, ever to be shunned. Politics concern nations and that which concerns the welfare of nations must be one of the concerns of a man who is religiously inclined, in other words, a seeker after God and Truth. For me, God and Truth are convertible terms, and if anyone told me that God was a God of untruth or a God of torture, I would decline to worship Him. Therefore, in politics also, we have to establish the Kingdom of Heaven.[20]

Actually, like a pre-modernist thinker, Gandhi attaches all aspects of life with religion or spirituality. He himself wrote for so many times that "spirituality is not a matter of knowing scriptures and engaging in philosophical discussions. It is a matter of heart-culture of immeasurable strength. We often prate about spirituality as if it has nothing to do with the ordinary affairs of life and has been reserved for anchorites lost in the Himalayan caves."[21] For Gandhi, spirituality is an all-pervading factor. Our social, political as well as economic life is continuously influenced by this spirituality. He says:

> I must confess that I do not draw a sharp or any distinction between economies and ethics. Economics thus hurt the moral well-being of an individual or a nation is immoral and, therefore sinful. Thus, the other is immoral. It is sinful to buy and use article made by sweated labour.[22]

The above statement shows that for Gandhi, even economics is also a part of ethics. Accordingly, the ultimate aim of all the activities, which we are doing at social, economic or political spheres, is to uplift an individual being for which the ethical laws are required to be followed in a strict manner. For Gandhi, true economics never militates against the highest ethical standard, just as all true ethics to be worth its name must at the same time be also good economics. In his words, "true economics, on the other hand, stands for social justice; it promotes the good of all equally, including the weakest, and is indispensable for decent life".

Where modern economics is intended to earn more and more profit, Gandhian economics talks about ethical norms within the process of production, distribution and consumption. In Gandhian philosophy economics is oriented towards the welfare of all because its ultimate aim is to realize the God, to attain self-realization. That is why, Gandhi talks about economics in terms of spirituality or ethics. As a result, he is classified as a pre-modernist philosopher.

Further, Gandhian conception of economy is based on the principle like equality, and here he developed his unique 'theory of trusteeship'. Actually, the theory of trusteeship " ... is not only a theory of property but of every human faculty which goes to enrich society as a whole. Viewed from this perspective, not only all property should be held in trust for the good of the society, but also the talents, the skill, the creative faculty of individual; because it is these qualities of the individual also which become the source of inequality within society. Trusteeship, therefore, is posited as means to achieve equality in so far as man's material existence is concerned. Its emphasis, although primarily on property, is also on inherent inequality in talents, creativity etc."[23] Gandhi never believes that equality will be prevailed in the society through law and constitutions; contrary to this, he argues that it is possible only in a non-violent society, where actual and active love flows freely. He says:

> The real implication of equal distribution is that each man shall have thee wherewithal to supply all his material needs and no more ... the economic equality is the master key to non-violent independence. Working for economic equality means abolishing the eternal conflict between capital and labour. It means the levelling down of the few rich in whose hands is concentrated the bulk of the nation's wealth on the one hand, and a levelling up of the semi-starved naked millions on the other.[24]

By explaining the other aspect of the concept to economic equality, Gandhi said, "I wanted to bring about an equalization of status. The working classes have all these centuries been isolated and relegated to a lower status. They have been *shoodras,* and the word has been interpreted to mean an inferior status. I want to allow no differentiation between the son of a weaver, of an agriculturist and of a school master."[25]

In this way, by adopting the principles of equality, non-possession, trusteeship etc., Gandhi wants to convert the whole economic scenario. He says:

> Man has been conversant with violence from the animal in his nature. It was only when he rose from the state of a quadruped (animal) to that of a biped (man) that the knowledge of the strength of *Ahimsa* entered into his soul. This knowledge has grown within slowly but surely. This knowledge were to penetrate to and spread amongst the poor, they would become strong and would learn how to free themselves by means of non-violence from the crushing inequalities which have brought them to the verge of starvation.[26]

Where modern economic system is revolving around selfishness, profit-making etc., Gandhian philosophy argues about development of all or *Sarvodaya*. This is the reason, why he must be as regarded as pre-modernist thinker.

Further, his idea on *Gram Swarajya* also makes him a pre-modernist thinker. Criticizing the mad craze behind the modern urbanization, Gandhi said:

> It is only when the cities realize the duty of making an adequate return to the village for the strength and sustenance, which they deserve from them, instead of selfishly exploiting them, that a healthy and moral relationship between the two will spring up. And if the city children are to play their part in this great and noble work of social reconstruction, the vocation through which they are to receive their education ought to be directly related to the requirements of the villages.[27]

Thus, Gandhi was in favour of returning towards villages, and this classifies him as a pre-modernist thinker. According to Nicholas F. Gier:

> When Gandhi says that in order to restore India to its pristine condition, we have to return to it [village communities], most commentators have taken this to mean that Gandhi has joined the premodernist revolt against modernism. The pristine India was for him the village communities, where a vast majority of Indian still live today. In the village Gandhi found people who overflowed with faith and where wisdom was boundless. Because of his confidence in these people he called for a dismantling of centralized state authority and a return to what he called village republicanism.[28]

The basic reason behind this call for returning back to village is to build a society based on the fundamental principles of truth and non-violence. And Gandhi thought that it is the simplicity or the purity of the villages when an individual and along with him the whole society may flourish his personality in the fullest manner. It was believed by Gandhi that Indian civilization can be identified only by the village itself. He writes:

> It is profitless to find out whether the villages of India were always what they are today. If they were never better it is reflection upon the ancient culture in which we take so much pride. But if they were never better, how is it possible that they have survived centuries of decay which we see going on around us ... the task before every lover of the country is how to prevent the decay or, which is the same thing, how to reconstruct the village of India, so that it may be as easy for anyone to live in them as it is supposed to be in the cities. Indeed, it is the task before every patriot. It may be that the villages are beyond redemption, that rural civilization has had it's allay and that the seven hundred well-ordered cities supporting a population not of three hundred millions but thirty. If such is to be India's fate, even that wont comes in a day. It must take time to wipe out a number of villages and villagers and transform the remainder into cities and citizens.[29]

Thus, for Gandhi, protection of villages is necessary if we want to protect the culture of India. According to him, the concept of *Swaraj* is not only limited up to economic and the political spheres, but it must also be seen from social and cultural perspectives. And it will be achieved through the non-violent and truthful *Gram Swaraj*. The people, who are living in the self-sufficient and the self-controlled village, are much disciplined ones; they have lots of the chances to fulfil their social responsibility.

Further, thinkers say that Gandhi's faith in truth or non-violence is also responsible to call him as a pre-modernist thinker. All of Gandhian philosophy is based on the concepts of truth and non-violence. Truth is the end of his life, which would be achieved by *Ahimsa*. Gandhi explains the meaning of truth in terms of God. Sometimes he called upon truth as God and sometimes God as truth. He says:

> If it is possible for the human tongue to give the fullest description of God, I have come to the conclusion that God is Truth. Two years ago I went a step further and said that truth is God.[30]

Whatever the attempt Gandhi ever made to define truth, it could never be separated either from God, spirituality. Even the process through which Gandhi wanted to achieve that truth was religious. To be a truthful person, in Gandhian way, one must take inspiration from Hindu ethical philosophy. He further says:

> ... truth is the sovereign principle, which includes numerous other principles. This truth is not only truthfulness in word, but truthfulness in thought also, and not only the relative truth of our conception but the Absolute Truth, the eternal principle that is God. There are innumerable definitions of God, because His manifestations are innumerable. They overwhelm me with wonder and awe and for a moment stun me. But I worship God as Truth only. [31]

The above definition of truth in the context of God also makes Gandhi a pre-modernist thinker.[32]

Actually, Gandhi expects a lot of positive qualities into the person who is called *Satyagrahi*, a seeker of truth. For Gandhi, passive resistance is a method of securing rights by personal suffering. It is the reverse of resistance by arms. When I refuse to do a thing that is repugnant to my conscious, I use soul force. For instance, the government of the day has passed a law which is applicable to me. I do not like it. If by using violence I forces government to repeal the law, I am employing what may be termed body force. If I do not obey the law and accept the penalty for its breach, I use soul force. It involves sacrifice of self.[33] It revel the truth that contrary to the modern civilization where each and everyone want to resist and dominate other, the Gandhian philosophy is asking for soul force, self-sacrifice or suffering. Thus, Gandhian philosophy is pre-modern in the real sense of the term.

Further, the concept of *Ahimsa* or non-violence in Gandhian philosophy is also influenced by the ancient Indian tradition. For Gandhi non-violence not only means to not to do harm to any living creature, but also in its broader sense, it means active love. To avoid every possibility of hate, selfishness, reaction is called *Ahimsa* in its actual sense. According to Gandhi:

> Identification with everything that lives are impossible without self-purification, the observance of the law of *Ahimsa* must remain an empty dream. God can never be realized by one who is not pure of heart. Self-purification, therefore, must mean purification in all walks of life. And purification being necessary leads to the purification of one's surroundings.[34]

Gandhi added that this path of self-purification is hard and steep. To attain to perfect purity, one has to become absolutely passion-free in thought, speech and action; and also to rise above the opposing currents of love and hatred, attachment and repulsion.

In this way, one can say that all these definitions of truth and *Ahimsa* in Gandhian philosophy place more space to morality, spirituality, humanity and ethics. Gandhi was of the opinion that in every individual God resides and to realize this God is the ultimate objective of human life. Only an individual's efforts can actualize this end. Thus, Gandhi's truthful and non-violent world order is in fact God-centred religious society. Hence, the claim of thinkers that the Gandhian philosophy is pre-modernist, proves true.

Gandhian Philosophy as a Modern Philosophy

Although Gandhi had his fundamental faith in value-orientated teaching of old Indian tradition, yet his insistence for individual freedom, rational adaptability of traditional practices and universal principles of *Sarvodaya* and *Satyagraha* categorizes his philosophy as modern. In the words of Ronald J. Terchek:

> ... Gandhi is a defender and champion of a reformed, traditional Hinduism is clear. And it is obvious that he offers a wide-ranging indictment of modern rationality, science and technology. For some, these positions show Gandhi to be inflexible and blind to the positive aspect of modernity. For others, Gandhi borrows more from modernity than is usually acknowledged.[35]

Although the Gandhian philosophy was altogether influenced by traditional values and norms which are written in sacred scriptures, yet he always tried his best to re-evaluate those age-old principles in contemporary times. He said:

> Even today, as far as the people are in general concerned, I am putting before them for practice what you call my old ideas. At the same time, for myself, as I have said, I have been deeply influenced by modern thought.[36]

As a modernist philosopher, the first and the foremost important feature of the Gandhian philosophy was that he gave more and more importance to individual.[37] For Gandhi no society can evolve by ignoring an individual's freedom. In his own words:

> If individual ceases to count, what is left of a society? Individual freedom alone can make man voluntarily surrender himself completely to the service of society. If it is wrested from him he becomes automation and society is ruined. No society can possibly be

> built on a denial of individual freedom. It is contrary to the very nature of man. Just as a man will not grow horns or tail, so he will not exist a man if he has no mind of his own. In reality even those who do not believe in the liberty of the individuals believe in their own.[38]

That is why, Gandhi used to say that the country must rid itself not only of British rule but also traditional form of domination, such as untouchability, as well as tame the forces of modernity and modernization which, he believes, leave millions of Indians unemployed and destitute. For Gandhi, the ultimate objective of human life is to attain the path of perfection and it is possible only in a free society so that an individual can flourish his natural-inherent capabilities in the fullest manner. Like the modernist thinker, Gandhi was of the view that it is good to swim in the waters of tradition but to sink in them is suicide. Accordingly, man is a rational being, thus, he should adopt only those traditions which are rationally right. In fact, the ultimate aim of every kind of education is only to create such a kind of atmosphere where an individual can identify his inherent in-born qualities.[39]

The foundation of the Gandhian philosophy of *Ramrajya* and *Swarajya* is an individual. By acknowledging the importance of individual's sovereignty and an individual autonomous dignity, Gandhi defines the meaning of *Swaraj* as rule of self (*Sw+Raj*). "Real home rule (*Swaraj*) is self-rule or self-control."[40] Accordingly, "Man is the maker of his own destiny in the sense that he has freedom of choice as to the manner in which he uses that freedom."[41] And for Gandhi only a self-disciplined and self-controlled mind can be a free person:

> Civilization is that mode of conduct which points out to man the path of duty. Performance of duty and observance of morality are convertible terms. To observe morality is to attain mastery over our mind and our passions. So doing, we know ourselves.[42]

For Gandhi, freedom means not only freedom from the external material world order but also from own internal weaknesses. Like a modernist, Gandhi was of the opinion that a limited or restricted atmosphere may create problem or hurdle in the way of development so that any kind of imposed rule or imposed administrative orders would not be accepted to him at all. Within that kind of bounded society an individual would not be able to get proper opportunity to improve his personality in fullest manner. According to Gandhi, restricted atmosphere makes individual's liberty not very much conscious or alert. He further says:

> How I can compel anyone to perform even a good act? Has not a well known Englishman said that to make mistake as a free man is better than being in bondage in order to avoid them? I believe in the truth of this. The reason is obvious. The mind of a man who remains good under compulsion cannot improve, in fact it worsens. And when compulsion is removed all the defects well up to the surface with even greater force.[43]

According to Gandhi, the fear of restriction cannot improve an individual's natural and inherent qualities in the fullest manner. Only a free society can produce a free individual in real sense of the term by whom the modern society gets its representation. In this manner, the Gandhian philosophy of individual's freedom or an individual's emancipation may be categorized as the modernist philosophy.[44]

Further, by defining truth, Gandhi's ultimate objective is to gain an individual's liberty. Accordingly, it is impossible to define the meaning of truth with a fixed terminology. Whatever your inner voice says at a particular time will be called as truth. Gandhi says:

> What ... is Truth? A difficult question; but I have solved it for myself by saying that it is what the voice within tells you. How then, you ask, different people think of different and contrary truths? Well, seeing that the human mind works through innumerable media and that the evolutions of the human mind is not the same for all, it follows that what may be truth for me may be untruth for another, and hence those who have made these experiments have come to the conclusion that there are certain conditions to be observed in making those experiments ... It is because we have at the present moment everybody claiming the right of conscience without going through any discipline whatsoever that there is so much untruth being delivered to a bewildered world.[45]

In the above definition of truth by Gandhi, he can be regarded as modernist philosopher from two points of views. Firstly, by defining the truth as an inner voice, he actually accepts an individual's autonomy. And, secondly, his conception of an individual's autonomy is not limited up to a single individual's autonomy but here there is a space for each and every individual's inner voice. It means, it is more liberal and thus more modern. This concept of truth would be changed automatically by changing time and place. By defining truth in this manner, Gandhi automatically comes among the family of modernist philosophers. Raghavan N. Iyer is of the opinion that none of the modernist philosopher is so vocal and blunt in the matter of individual liberty as Gandhi.[46]

While giving recognition and importance to an individual's autonomy Gandhi becomes a modernist philosopher because in this manner he has propounded the concept of equality within his unique norm of individual's freedom. For Gandhi, "Unlike western political thinkers who emphasize the isolated, separated, autonomous individual, I maintained that the self is a relational self, that there is no political self without its internal positive and negative relations with the other, and that the non-social, independent, autonomous, modern, individual self is largely a social, economic, political and cultural construction."[47]

Thus, we are bound to accept different meaning, definitions and conceptions of truth. That would be more comprehensive and balanced. Like modernist philosophers, Gandhi was great champion for the cause of individual's equality. Accordingly, " ... There is no such thing as inherent or required superiority ... I believe implicitly that all men are born equal."[48] All individuals are free to fulfil their basic needs. Neither any traditional, societal, philosophical norms nor any political, bureaucratic power can impose any kind of restriction. For Gandhi, ".. Every human being has a right to live and therefore to find the wherewithal to feed himself and ... to cloth and house himself." [49]

Just as in modern society, in Gandhian *Ramrajya* also, there are no differences on the basis of class, caste, creed, colour etc. He says, "The *Swaraj* of my ... our ... dreams recognizes no race or religious distinctions. Nor is it to be the monopoly of the lettered persons nor yet of moneyed men. *Swaraj* is to be for all, including the farmer but emphatically including the maimed, the blind, the starving toiling millions."[50]

Similarly, Gandhi's philosophy of *advita* is also seen by philosophers as a modernist concept. By seeing the whole world through *advita* perspective Gandhi wants to wipe out all kinds of differences and differentiations. He says, "I believe in *advita* (non-duality), I believe in the essential unity of man, and for that matter, of all that lives."[51]

Gandhi was of the opinion, since naturally all men are equal, hence socially and politically too they should be accepted as an equal being. All the members of society must be given equal opportunity. In his own words:

> ... [*Swaraj*] is much for the prince as for the peasant, as much for the rich landowner as for the landless tiller of the soil, as much for the Hindus as for the Musalmans, as much for Parsis and Christians as

for the Jains, Jews and Sikhs, irrespective of any distinction of caste or creed or status of life.[52]

By rendering his acceptance and support to the *advita* principle, Gandhi seems to be a modernist philosopher. By presenting this principle of *advita* (non-duality), Gandhi tries to omit every kind of discrimination among human beings. Modern philosophers also claim for equality. They argue that the earth is prevailed by similar kind of individuals. Since, *Ramrajya* also talks about the similar kind of norms and practices, thus, Gandhi is a modernist thinker.

Further, Gandhi's religious doctrine may also be analysed in the similar modernist context. By accepting an individual's autonomous emancipation, Gandhi accepts the fact that religion is an individual's personal affair. For Gandhi, religion does not mean any particular community, but it is a kind of jointing element which improves unity among their citizens. In Gandhi's own words:

> Let me explain what I mean by religion. It is not the Hindu religion which I certainly prize above all other religions but the religion which transcends Hinduism, which changes one's very nature, which blinds one indissolubly to the Truth within and which ever purifies. It is the permanent element in human nature, which counts no cost too great in order to find full expression and which leaves the soul utterly restless until it has found itself, known its Maker and appreciated the true correspondence between the Maker and itself.[53]

It seems, in Gandhi's conception of *Swaraj Dharma*, religion plays an important role. It includes Hinduism, Islam, Christianity etc., but it is superior to them all.[54] In fact, the ultimate objective of Gandhian philosophy is to propound the concept of *Ramrajya* where each and every individual is treated his own maker. The modern conception of religion also accepts the notion of reductionist religion. Gier comments in this context in the following manner:

> ... also modernist is his position that the state should not support religious organizations. But this does not mean that religion should not be integrated into political action as its ethical ground and justification. This was a foundational belief for Gandhi and it was shared by thinkers of the European Enlightenment.[55]

It is obvious that the humanist and moralist aspects of the Gandhian religious philosophy can be categorized as the modernist ones because they are as rational and cosmic as the modernist conception of religion. Gandhi says:

> I reject any religious doctrine that does not appeal to reason and is in conflict with morality. I tolerate unreasonable religious sentiment when it is not immoral.[56]

Further, the Gandhian concept of civil disobedience is sometimes also categorized as a modernist concept. According to Gandhi, Civil disobedience means to tolerate the injustice without any protesting activities. Within these activities, sacrifices of titles, surrendering honorary titles, administrative services, power, politics etc. are included. Gandhi was of the opinion that if the citizen of the state could able to realize the fact that the abolition of the state power is their first and foremost duty or *dharma*, then only, the real enlighten society will emerge.

By rejecting the above-mentioned definition of civil disobedience, Gandhi automatically comes amongst the modernist thinkers. Gandhi, by giving due recognition and consideration to the individual's voice and his rational-logical mind set, accepts the importance of an individual before the state. Thus, Gandhi must be regarded as a modernist philosopher. In the words of Terchek, ".. complete moral autonomy, even if it means civil disobedience was Gandhi's goal and if this is so, then he is fully a modernist thinker."[57]

Accordingly, within the programmes of civil disobedience movement, an individual's autonomy is essentially required. Here, an individual will not accept any imposed kind of administration and power. In this violent struggle, though an individual will not take direct participation but indirectly he will not extend his assistance to the opponent party. By accepting this kind of autonomous personality, Gandhian philosophy seems not less than any other modernist conception.

In the similar context, Gier categorizes the Gandhian philosophy as modernist in the following manner:

> Gandhi's commitment to civil disobedience is intimately related to the issue of Gandhi's preferred anarchism. Gandhi called his village republicanism a form of 'enlightened anarchy' in which everyone is their own ruler.[58]

Gandhi propounded the concept of 'enlightened anarchism' with his concept of *Swaraj*. Accordingly, members of *Swaraj* would be so enlightened and conscious toward's their rights and duties that the relevance of external administration will not be required at all. Individual will be alert towards his fellow beings. State and administrative power will always create hurdle in the way of free development of an individual's personality. Thus, external control must be restricted or criticized. To preserve an individual's liberty in such a manner, Gandhian philosophy may be classified as modernist.

In the similar way, Gandhi's tendency to give due respect for individual's reason is again categorized him as a modernist philosopher. In his own words, "We must reject truth claims, even those of scripture that are repugnant to reason or moral sense."[59]

Actually, Gandhi was very much impressed with Tolstoy's dictum that one must obey reason in the pursuit of the God. That is why, Richard B. Gregg ranked him as a social scientist. Accordingly, Gandhi never accepted the writings of scriptures and religious texts if they are not going to satisfy reason. Human reason is the only way to judge the authenticity of these texts. If the wordings of these texts will be actualized in the rational life then only it would be accepted. In Gandhi's words:

> The stories told in the *Puranas* are some of the most dangerous if we do not know their bearing upon the present conditions. The *Shastras* would be death traps if we were to regulate our conduct according to every detail in them or according to that of the characters therein.[60]

Gandhi accepts only those texts as useful or beneficiary with the help of which an individual's liberty and dignity can be achieved maximally. That is why, Gandhi's life becomes a continuous chain of experiments. In Gregg's words:

> Gandhi is a social scientist because he follows social truth by the scientific method of observance, institutional and intellectual hypothesis and experimental texts.[61]

Gandhi himself for so many times said that firstly we should try to evaluate the lessons of these texts critically, and if those are rational or accepted to our mind, then only we can assume them as beneficiary and useful texts. In his own words:

> I have been a sympathetic student of the western social order, and I have discovered that underlying the fever that fills the soul of the West, there is a restless search of Truth. I value that spirit. Let us study our Eastern institutions in that spirit of scientific inquiry.[62]

Like modernist scientists, Gandhi used to say that he had been deeply influenced by modern thoughts. If anyone admits the necessity and desirability of reform of discarding the old, whenever necessary, and building a new system of ethics and morality suited to the present age, then the question of seeking the permission of others or convincing others does not arise. A reformer cannot afford to wait till others are convinced; he must take the lead and ventured forth alone even in the teeth of universal opposition.[63] And, by accepting the limitation of an individual, he, like pure modernist thinkers, said: "The conclusions I have formed and the conclusions I have arrived at are not final. It may change tomorrow; I have nothing new to teach to the world. Truth and non-violence are as old as the hills. All I have done is to try experiments in both on as vast scale as I could do. In doing so, I have sometimes erred and learnt by my errors. Life and its problems have thus become to me so many experiments in the practice of truth and non-violence."

Gandhian Philosophy as a Postmodern Philosophy

Contrary to both of the above-mentioned perspectives, there is another group of thinkers who categorize Gandhian philosophy as postmodernist. For these thinkers, both of these philosophies are identical to each other. All fundamental principles of modernism are as criticized by postmodernists, as they get their radical robust in Gandhism. As Gandhi has presented his unique perspective, similarly, postmodernist philosophers also discuss about the intact aspects of modern philosophy by adding some more perspectives.

Interestingly, truth seems to play a significant role in Gandhian philosophy just like it is in postmodern philosophy. Gandhi was critical of any fixed definition of truth. Once it was asked to Gandhi:

> What ... is Truth? *[He replied]* A difficult question; but I have solved it for myself by saying that it is what the voice within tells you. How then, you ask, different people think of different and contrary truths? Well, saying that the human mind works through innumerable media and that the evolution of human mind is not the same for all, it follows that what may be truth for one may be untruth for another, and hence those who have made these experiments have come to the conclusion that there are certain conditions to be observed in making those experiments ... . It is because we have at the present moment everybody claiming the right of consciousness without going through any discipline whatsoever that there is so much untruth being delivered to a bewildered world.[64]

It is clear form the above that the best explanation of the truth is the voice of your inner self. But, the condition is that it must be a pure voice. But, again, there is a problem: since everyone is having his own way of living, his own cultural, historical and philosophical background, accordingly, the inner voice would be different to different people. In such a situation, to listen to the voice of each and every member of the society would be the foremost aim of every human being. Gandhi was of the opinion that the truth resides in every human heart, and one has to reach for it there, and to be guided by truth as one sees it. But, no one has a right to coerce others, to act according to his own view of truth.[65]

A parallel study of truth in Gandhian thought and postmodernist thought will tell us that both reject structuralism. Like postmodernists, even Gandhi was critical of any fixed definition of truth. Postmodernists reject foundationalism, the attempt to justify realist knowledge through recourse to 'basic' or 'fundamental' or incorrigible cognition.[66]

And even for Gandhi, one of the greatest evils of modern political and other human relations has been our tendency to absolutize what is necessarily relative. Gandhi's insistence on the relativity of all political, religious and other human perspectives is a justification for Gandhian tolerance and respect for others' relative perspectives to truth and reality. Therefore Douglas Allen writes:

> ... the emphasis in Gandhi's political thinking on the relativity of truth and the tolerance of and respect for multiple voices, diversity, and an enriching pluralism of significant differences is similar to what one finds in various postmodernist political orientation.[67]

For Gandhi, "Truth is the first thing to be sought for, and Beauty and Goodness will then be added unto you. That is what Christ really taught in the Sermon on the Mount. Jesus was to me, a supreme artist because he saw and expressed Truth; and so was Muhammad. The Koran being the most perfect composition in all Arabic literature at any rate, that is what scholars say. It is because both of them strove first for Truth that the grace of expression naturally came in and yet neither Jesus nor Muhammad wrote on Art. That is the Truth and Beauty I crave for, live for and would die for."[68]

In this very context, Gandhi said that in the way of struggle after truth we should try to provide due respect for all other's truth. Such an approach is consistent with Gandhi's own dynamic, open-ended, relative experiments with truth. As a conditioned, temporal, historical, finite, fallible being, Gandhi rejected any human perspective that claimed to experience unconditioned, exclusive, absolute, static, eternal, non-contextualized, political truth. Through concrete praxis, Gandhi continually attempted to move from one relative political truth to another greater relative political truth. And in this way Gandhi could be categorized as postmodernist philosopher.

Further, some of the thinkers also claim the Gandhian philosophy of truth to be the postmodernist philosophy. For example, Huiyun Wang says:

> One could perhaps see the beginnings of Gandhi's postmodern theology in his adaptation of Tolstoy's *The Kingdom of God is within you*. One could also say that the proposition that '*Truth is God*' is an attempt to overcome the modernist critique of religion. Gandhi's postmodern religion is all-encompassing because it includes Truth and virtue, seeking atheist as well as other religious people.[69]

Earlier, Gandhi was of the opinion that God is truth but after his extensive experiment he came to the conclusion that truth is God. Explaining his argument, Gandhi said this change will extend the suitability of the definition of truth. In his own words:

> People say that I have changed my view, that I say today something different from what I said years ago. The fact of the matter is that conditions have changed. I am the same ... . There has been a gradual evolution in my environment and I react to it as a *Satyagrahi*.[70]

For Gandhi, if we accept God as truth, then, the meaning and definition of truth will limit us because atheists will never accept it. But if we accept truth as God, then, its boundary will be expended for all – theist or atheist, religious or non-religious etc.

There are a group of philosophers who accept this conversion as a devaluing the notion of God as postmodernists talk about the death of God.[71] As Gier says:

> What the theology of deconstruction calls for the 'death of God' and the demise of meaning that definitely goes with it, constructive postmodern theology insists that religion and spirituality must recover their positive roles in society. It is again clear that Gandhi belongs with the constructive postmodernist rather than with the French school.[72]

Though, in Gandhian philosophy, truth found its fullest expression in the exposition of God, yet for Gandhi absolute truth is the eternal principle which is God only. And, at the same time, Gandhi also accepts the reality that relative truth is the way to achieve this absolute truth; accordingly, it is impossible to represent the nature of truth via only one religion, community, historical, traditional and philosophical perspective. In *Young India*, Gandhi writes:

> ... all religions are more or less true. All proceed from the same God but all are imperfect because they come down to us through imperfect human instrumentality.[73]

Gandhi argues that each and every caste, community, class culture and civilization have their own understanding on the basis of which they are getting their recognition and identity. But this identity is not complete. It is only partial identity and part of the ultimate or absolute truth. According to Gandhi, the definitions of God are innumerable. In his own words:

> There is an indefinable mysterious Power that pervades everything. I feel it, though I do not see it. It is this unseen Power which makes itself felt and yet defines all proof, because it is not unlike all that I perceive through my senses. It transcends the senses ... I do dimly perceive that whilst everything around me is ever changing, ever dying, there is underlying all that change a living Power that is changeless, that holds all together that creates, dissolves and recreates. That informing power or spirit is God. And since nothing else I see merely through the senses, can or will persist, He alone is.[74]

It shows that, for Gandhi, God and his expressions are innumerable. There is not any fixed and particular definition of God because every one of us have our own perspective, own way of life on the basis of which we define God. This is the reason, why some of the postmodernist thinkers consider that Gandhi belongs of their community. Terchek believes that Gandhian way of exploring or critically evaluating the religious texts and Foucault's approach to archaeology of knowledge are very much similar in nature. According to Gandhi:

> Sacred texts suffers from a process of double distillation. Firstly, they come through a human prophet, and then commentaries of interpretations. Nothing in them comes from God directly.[75]

Like postmodernists, Gandhi too was critical towards religious texts. This is the reason, why he used to say, "... each tradition expresses fragments of the truth in its own vernacular and symbols. But because these are the expressions of human beings, they are subject both to the decay that describes the human condition as well as to the possibilities for renewal and revitalization."[76] Terchek argues, the postmodernist thinkers also study texts in the context of signs and symbols and critical of accepting any meta-narratives or grand-narratives. Thus, Gandhi is a postmodernist thinker.

Further, for Terchek, the postmodernist Gandhi talks about so many revolutions and movement for marginalized and degraded people who were dominated and exploited by centralized powerful elite classes. According to Terchek:

> He employs these strategies in his campaign on behalf of untouchables attempting to open the Vykom Temple Road, in his work with striking textile workers in Ahmedabad, and in his salt *satyagraha*.[77]

As Chandra Talpade Mohanty, Gayatri Chakravorty Spivak and other postmodernists ask for subaltern consciousness and women's empowerment, similarly, Gandhi was also very much serious about these concerns. Terchek says that Gandhi never took religious text as sacrosanct and pure as researcher or seeker after truth:

> His archeological approach does not look at traditional texts or practices as sacrosanct expressions of unchallengeable knowledge. Rather, he wants to move beyond standard readings of traditional practices and expose those that spawn domination.[78]

Gandhian philosophy also seems to be completely as the postmodernist one in the context of women or gender relations. He raised the question against the arbitrary rules of society which our female folk are bound to follow. In this context, Gandhi said:

> The ancient laws were made by seers who were men. The women's experience, therefore, is not represented in them. Strictly speaking, as between man and women, neither should be regarded as superior or inferior.[79]

Accordingly, women have been suppressed under custom and law for which man was responsible and in the shaping of which she had no hand. In a plan of life based on non-violence, women have much right to shape their own destiny as men have to shape their's. But every right in a non-violent society proceeds from the performance of a duty, it follows that rules of social conduct must be framed by mutual co-operation and consultation. They can never be responding from outside. Men have not realized this truth in the fullness in their behaviour towards women. They consider themselves as lords and masters of women instead of considering them as their friends and co-workers. Postmodernist feminist scholars Catherien Mackinnon and Carole Gilligon also talk about the deconstruction of all the historical, structural and hierarchical notions in the society. Actually, postmodernist thinkers are of the opinion that all groups have a right to speak for themselves, in their own voice, and have that voice accepted as authentic and legitimate is essential to the pluralistic stance of postmodernism.[80]

For Gandhi, *Swaraj* does not only mean to political independence, but the real *Swaraj* will come only when the poorest individual will able to get his required space in the society which is badly enrooted in conservative practices and customs. Real *Swaraj* will come not by the acquisition of authority by a few but by the acquisition of the capacity by all to resist authority when it is abused. In other words, *Swaraj* is to be obtained by educating the masses to a sense of their capacity to regulate and control authority.[81] Thus, Gandhian philosophy can be regarded as the postmodernist philosophy.

Further, even to actualize the postmodernist philosophy of decentralization, Gandhi, like postmodernist philosophers, seems to adopt the process of deconstruction. In the context of women's empowerment, Gandhi says that the age-old irrational conservative norms and practices should be abolished:

> ... it is essential for women to refuse to be intimated by traditional practices and to decline to accept an inferior position in the social order that they have been taught is natural.[82]

Terchek explained that Gandhi was of the view that tradition must be accepted as a dynamic concept. It may be possible that the assumptions which we are accepting today in the context of husband-wife relationship would not be accepted tomorrow. At one place, Gandhi says:

> *Draupadi* had five husbands at one time and yet has been called 'Chaste'. This is because in that age, just as a man could marry several wives, a woman (in certain regions) could marry several husbands. The code of marriage changes with time and place.[83]

Like Derrida and Lyotard in the above statement, Gandhi seems to accept the importance of context. Accordingly, as the code of marriage changes with time and place, similarly, the social code of conducts, which has been giving us directions since time immemorial should be changed according to the demand of time and circumstances. Gandhi, often the traditionalist, turns out to be one of the hatred critics of his own tradition as he digs through what he takes to be its decay and rubble in order to find its core.[84] Thus, by criticizing traditional irrational norms, Gandhi seems to be a postmodern philosopher. In words of Susanne and LIoyd Rudolphs:

> We all find the postmodern Gandhi in the "contesting discourse" of the 'counter-culture' voices against modernism that he found in Tolstoy, Ruskin and Thoreau.[85]

According to Rudolphs, whatever the experiments of truth Gandhi did, by giving more importance to discourses and circumstances, are in fact the contextualizing studies about which postmodernist thinkers discuss. For Gandhi, all the local practices, partial identities and relative truths have their own importance. Hence, he could able to acknowledge God in the following manner:

> I worship God as truth only. I have not yet found Him, I am seeking after Him. I am prepared to sacrifice the things dearest to me in pursuit of this quest. Even if the sacrifice demanded be my life, I hope I may be prepared to give it. But as long as I have not realize this Absolute Truth, so long must I hold by the relative truth as I have conceived it. That relative truth must, meanwhile, be my bacon, my shield and buckler.[86]

Postmodernist thinker Derrida also discussed about logocentricism and differences. Thus, like Derrida, Gandhian philosophy may also be categorized as postmodernist.[87] Gier argues that as postmodernist philosophers talk about deconstruction or anti-structuralism, similarly, Gandhi shook the roots of British administrative structure in India:

> Gandhi's experiments with truth can be seen as his way to dislodge and discredit the authority structure of British India and therefore, to 'deconstruct' the modernist, imperialist assumptions of British rule. Gandhi does this without falling back into tradition, for he also, at the same time, was deconstructing the *brahmin*-centered caste system of ancient India.[88]

For Gier, by doing various kinds of experiments with truth, Gandhi comes to the conclusion that every individual and every nation has their own notion of truth, which cannot be declared as untruth and wrong. Therefore, Gandhi asked for abolition of British empire in India. This again ranks Gandhi as a postmodernist philosopher.

In fact, Gandhi was against any kind of power domination. Criticizing the modern centralized state, Gandhi proposed for *Gram Panchayat* or local administration. By replacing the modern structure of state or nation, he propounded the philosophy of *Ramrajya* or *Swaraj* where everyone is his/her own ruler. In such a *Swaraj,* which is a unique accumulation of a number of villages, an individual will get his/her local identity. Any national or unknown universal identity will not be imposed on his/her individuality. It means, all the villages will be self-independent and self-sufficient.[89] To illustrate Gandhian perspective, Terchek says:

> For Gandhi, human beings become autonomous, when they are embedded in a vibrant community which provides them with moral standards to judge themselves as well as networks of co-operation which serves as a source of mutual assistance and respect. For this to occur, Gandhi believes that power must be dispersed and inequalities narrowed.[90]

As we have mentioned earlier, ultimate aim of the Gandhian philosophy is to preserve an individual's liberty. Gandhi assumes that an individual can flourish his/her personality if the atmosphere is free. It was his firm belief that a self-disciplined and self-controlled individual is the outcome of a free society. That is why, like postmodernist philosopher Foucault, Gandhi also talks about dispersion of power or authority.

Further, one can find it clearly that even in Gandhian philosophy rejection of domination of rationalism is there. He said, experience, emotion, intuition etc. are the other aspects of an individual's personality, which are as important as reason. In his own way:

> We must resist the tyranny and domination of the modernist idols of science, rationalism, and 'objectivity.' The Enlightenment gave us narrow, oppressive, hierarchical, reductionist projects of rationalistic and scientific hegemony. But rational scientific discourse is only one of many possible ways that human-beings construct their 'stories about political reality. The scientific narrative does not have exclusive privileged access to political truth. Metaphysical spiritual narratives, as other ways of constructing accounts that shed light on political truth and reality, should not be reduced to scientific, rational, historical and other non-ethical and non-spiritual discourses.[91]

Postmodernist philosophers argue that the Enlightenment has created a rational and logical society, which is very much instrumental in nature. This instrumental rationality is creating a kind of rational imperialism. But Dannis Dalton, along with other thinkers, propound the fact that this is the only one aspect of truth. Science and scientific knowledge have its importance but it does not mean that scientific laws and technological rules are the only regulating principles. For Dalton spirituality is another medium to know about truth, which is not at all attached with reason. Gandhi too has this perspective, when he says:

> I have come to the fundamental conclusion that if you want something really important to be done you must not merely satisfy the reason, you must move the heart also. The appeal of reason is more to the head.[92]

For Gandhi, it is impossible to make a watertight compartmentalization between head and heart, rationality and morality. Accordingly, rational ideas are the instrument to find out what is not right or wrong but to know about truth or to realize truth in the real sense of the term one is bound to go to the heart or irrational discussions.[93] Bhikhu Parekh assumes Gandhi's notion of *satyagraha* as a unique contribution of rationality and emotions. In his own words:

> Gandhi's *satyagraha* involved an ingenious and complex tripartite strategy based on a fascinating blend of rational discussion, self-imposed suffering and political pressure. The first appealed to the head, the second to the heart, the third activated both by influencing the structure of power sustaining the relationship between the parties involved.[94]

Both head and heart have their importance in Gandhian perspective. Any discourse where only one is working will not be accepted to Gandhi. In his own words:

> [This] belief in God has to be based on faith which transcends reason. Indeed, even the so-called realization has at bottom and elimination of faith without which it cannot be sustained.[95]

Gandhi was of the opinion that faith is more important than reason. Faith or belief is the medium through which one may achieve divinity. Its existence cannot be proved merely by rationality. Thus, like postmodernist philosophers, Gandhi also argues for both reason and emotion.

Further, like postmodernist philosophy, the concept of rational self is also found there in Gandhian philosophy.[96] For Gandhi, an individual and his/her independent personality is much more important than the society but it is impossible to flourish an independent and free personality in the absence of society. Gandhi says:

> I do not believe ... that an individual may gain spiritually and those who surround him suffer. I believe in *advaita* (non-duality), I believe in the essential unity of man and for that matter, of all that lives. Therefore, I believe that if one man gain spiritually, the whole world gains with him and, if one man falls, the whole world falls to that extent.[97]

Depicting the real picture of the *Ramrajya* of his dream, Gandhi says in this structure composed of innumerable villages there will be ever-widening, never ascending circles. Life will not be a pyramid with the apex sustained by the bottom. But it will be an Oceanic circle whose centre will be the individual always ready to perish for the village, the latter ready to perish for the circle of villages, till at last the whole becomes one life composed of individuals, never aggressive in their arrogance but ever humble, sharing the majority of the oceanic circle of which they are integral units.[98] Gandhi's attempt to define an individual in context of society insisting Douglas Allen to categorize him as postmodernist thinker. Accordingly, to define an individual's existence in the context of society is an effort to criticize modernist conception of an individual self. Allen writes:

> Gandhi's individual is not the non-social/anti-social individual. For Gandhi the latter is the height of egotism and immorality. Such self/ego-centered and ego-attached tendencies must be restrained, even to the extent of placing primary focus on the needs and welfare of the other and placing your 'self' last. In Gandhi's political approach, it is only when one restrains and overcomes the dominant modern focus on the primary of one's own self/ego and instead establishes a dynamic, social, political self-other relations focusing on the primary of the needs of the other that one beings to experience the deeper true, moral and spiritual self and constitutes a more moral and spiritual political order.[99]

Gier also joins hands with Douglas Allen, while accepting the fact that in Gandhian philosophy one can get a rare combination of individual and society. Hence, the importance of individual and society is both complementary as well as contradictory. Actually, Gier is of the opinion that Gandhi also qualifies his individualism with other constitution, and he definitely joins with [this] postmodern reconstruction of the self.[100]

Thus, all these critical and analytical discussions are quite enough to prove that apparently postmodernism and Gandhism may seem identical to each other. But, before going to make any final conclusion it is quite necessary to go through Gandhi's philosophy threadbare. The next chapter is aimed at the same.

Notes

1. Nicholas F. Gier (1996) "Gandhi's Philosophy: Pre-modern, Modern or Postmodern", *Gandhi Marg*, New Delhi, Gandhi Peace Foundations, , Vol. 18, No. 1.
2. Ronald J. Terchek (2001) "Problematizing Modernity: Gandhi's Decentering Impluse", *Gandhi Marg*, New Delhi, Gandhi Peace Foundation, Vol. 23, No. 1.
3. L.I. Rodulph and S.H. Rudolph (2006) *Postmodern Gandhi and Other Essays: Gandhi in the World and at Home*, Oxford, Oxford University Press.
4. Bhikhu Parekh (1989) *Gandhi's Political Philosophy: A Critical Examination*, London, Macmillan Press, p. 65.

   Also see, Gopinath Dhawan (1951) *The Political Philosophy of Mahatma Gandhi*, Ahmedabad, Navajivan Publication.

   * D.M. Dutta (1953) *The Philosophy of Mahatma Gandhi*, Madison, University of Wisconsin Press.
   * V.V. Raman Murthy (1958) *Non-Violence of Politics: A Study of Gandhian Technique and Thinking*, New Delhi, Frank Bros & Co.
   * V.P. Verma (1965) *Political Philosophy of Mahatma Gandhi and Sarvodaya*, Agra, Lakshmi Narain Agrawal.
   * Surendra Verma (1970) *Metaphysical Foundation of Mahatma Gandhi's Thought*, New Delhi, Orient Longmans.
   * Raghavan N. Iyer (1973) *The Moral and Political Thought of Mahatma Gandhi*, New Delhi, Oxford University Press.
5. Ramjee Singh (1993) *Gandhi and the Twenty First Century*, New Delhi, Peace Publications, p. 29.
6. M.K. Gandhi (1998) *Hind Swaraj*, Ahmedabad, Navajivan Publishing House, p. 57.
7. *Harijan*, 28–03–1937.
8. D.G. Tendulkar (1954) *Mahatma: Life of Mohandas Karamchandra Gandhi*, Bombay, V.K. Jhaveri and D.G. Tendulkar, p. 21.
9. D.G. Tendulkar op. cit., pp. 108–109.

10. Arne Naess (1974) *Gandhi and Group Conflict: An Exploration of Satyagraha. Theoretical Background*, Oslo Universitets forlaget, p. 43.
11. Bhikhu Parekh op. cit., p. 93.
12. Ibid., p. 86.
13. Raghavan N. Iyer (1986) *The Moral and Political Writings of Mahatma Gandhi*, New York, Oxford University Press, p. 28.
14. D.G. Tendulkar op. cit., pp. 108–109.
15. Ibid., p. 16.
16. R.K. Prabhu and U.R. Rao (1945) *The Mind of Mahatma Gandhi*, London, Oxford University Press, p. 24.
17. Arne Naess (1974) *Gandhi and Group Conflict: An Exploration of Satyagraha. Theoretical Background*, Oslo-Bergen-Tromso, Universitets for laget, p. 35.
18. Pyare Lal (1956) *Mahatma Gandhi: The Last Phase*, Ahmedabad, Navajivan Publishing House, Vol. 1, pp. 421–422.
19. *Young India*, 12–11–1931.
20. R.K. Prabhu and V.R. Rao (1945) *The Mind of Mahatma Gandhi*, London, Oxford University Press.
21. N.K. Bose (1948) *Selections from Gandhi*, Ahmedabad, Navajivan Publishing House, p. 270.
22. *Young India*, 13–10–1921.
23. Nageshwar Prasad (ed.) (1990) *Gandhi: Historical and Contemporary Perspective*, New Delhi, Segment Book Distributors, p. 116.
24. *Constructive Programme*, pp. 20–21.
25. *Harijan*, 15–1–1938.
26. Ibid., 25–8–1940.
27. Ibid., 19–10–1937.
28. Nicholas F. Gier op. cit., Vol. 17, No. 3, pp. 261–281.
29. *Harijan*, 7–3–1936.
30. D.G. Tendulkar op. cit., pp. 176–77.
31. M.K. Gandhi (2001) *An Autobiography: My Experiments with Truth*, Ahmedabad, Navajivan Publication Trust, p. XI.
32. Ibid., pp. XI-XII.
33. *Hind Swaraj*, p. 71.
34. M.K. Gandhi (2001) op. cit., p. 420.
35. Ronald J. Terchek (2000) *Gandhi: Struggling for Autonomy*, New Delhi, Vistaar Publication, p. 95. Also see, M.P. Mathai, M.S. John and Siby K. Joseph (eds) (2002) *Meditation on Gandhi*, New Delhi, Concept Publications, pp. 150–151. Thomas Pantham and Kenneth Deutsch (eds) (1980) *Political Thought in Modern India*, New Delhi, Sage Publications, pp. 17–31. Also see, Susane and Lloyd Rudolph (1967) *The Modernity of Tradition*, Chicago, University of Chicago Press.

36. Pyare Lal op. cit., p. 228.
37. "... the country must rid itself not only of British rule but also traditional form of domination, such as untouchability, as well as tame the forces of modernity and modernization which, he believes, leave millions of Indians unemployed and destitute." Ronald J. Terchek (2000) *Gandhi: Struggling for Autonomy*, New Delhi, Vistaar Publication, p. 22.
38. *Harijan*, 1–2–1942.
39. ".. any independence worthy of its names must be comprehensive, not only must the Indian nation be self-governing but also must each of its members ... complete Indian independence means the consciousness in the average villagers that he is the maker of his own destiny". *Young India*, 13–2–1930.

    "I am not interested in freeing India merely from the English yoke. I am bent upon freeing India from any yoke whatsoever." *Young India*, 13–2–1930.

    " Swaraj comes only when Indians learn to rule themselves individually and collectively". *Hind Swaraj*, Chapter 14.
40. *Hind Swaraj*, p. 91.
41. *Harijan*, 23–3–1940.
42. *Hind Swaraj*, p. 55.
43. *Harijan*, 29–9–1946.
44. "Gandhi's autonomous persons, wanting to govern themselves, resist any source of domination, whether in a corrupted tradition or in the modern world. With the former a distorted reading of texts is in control; with the latter, the standard of efficiency and productivity dominate, and people lose control of what is important to them. Working with this understanding, Gandhi holds that no economic progress can claim to possess a truth that displaces the autonomy of individuals."

    Ronald J. Terchek (2000) *Gandhi: Struggling for Autonomy*, New Delhi, Vistaar Publication, p. 42.
45. Krishna Kripalani (ed.) (1958) *All Men are Brothers*, Ahmedabad, Navjivan Publishing House, p. 94
46. Raghavan N. Iyer (1986) *The Moral and Political Writings of Mahatma Gandhi*, Oxford, Clarendon Press, p. 132.
47. Douglas Allen (2000) "Gandhi: Contemporary Political Thinking and Self-other Relations", in B.N. Ray (ed.) *Contemporary Political Thinking*, New Delhi, Kanishka Publishers, p. 154.
48. *Young India*, 29–9–1927.
49. *The Leader*, 25–12–1916.
50. *Young India*, 26–3–1931.
51. Ibid., 4–12–1924.
52. Ibid., 5–3–1931.

53. N.K. Bose (1948) *Selections from Gandhi*, Ahmedabad, Navajivan Publishing House, p. 223.
54. *Harijan*, 2–1–1937.
55. Nicholas F. Gier op. cit., p. 11.
56. Krishna Kripalani op. cit., pp. 72–73.
57. Ronald J. Terchek (1992) "Gandhi and Moral Autonomy", *Gandhi Marg*, New Delhi, Gandhi Peace Foundation, Vol. 13, No. 4, p. 459.
58. *The Collected Works of Mahatma Gandhi*, Vol. 68, p. 265.
59. "Gandhi was very much impressed with Tolstoy's dictum that one must obey reason in the pursuit of the good." M.K. Gandhi (1987) *Hindu Dharma*, New Delhi, Vision Books, p. 8.
60. Ibid., p. 23.
61. Richard B. Gregg, *Gandhi as a Social Scientist*, p. 80.
62. *The Collected Works of Mahatma Gandhi*, Vol. 32, p. 219.
63. Manmohan Choudhari (1989) *Exploring Gandhi*, New Delhi, Gandhi Peace Foundation, p. 277.

    "The orthodox conception of the ninefold wall of protection in regard to brahmacharya is in my opinion inadequate and defective. I have never accepted it for myself."

    Pyare Lal op. cit., p. 228. Also see, M.K. Gandhi (1936) *Harijan*.
64. Krishna Kripalani op. cit., p. 94.
65. R.K. Prabhu and U.R. Rao (1945) *The Mind of Mahatma Gandhi*, London, Oxford University Press, pp. 19–20.
66. Lawerence Cahoone (2003) *From Modernism to Postmodernism*, Oxford, Blackwell Publishers, p. 10.
67. Douglas Allen (2000) "Gandhi, Contemporary Political Thinking and Self-other Relations", in B.N. Ray (ed.) *Contemporary Political Thinking*, New Delhi, Kanishka Publishers, p. 139.
68. R.K. Prabhu and U.R. Rao (1945) *The Mind of Mahatma Gandhi*, London, Oxford University Press, p. 38.
69. Huiyyun Wang (1996) "Gandhi's Alternative to Modernization", in Nicholas F. Gier, *Gandhi's Philosophy: Pre-Modern, Modern or Post-Modern*, Gandhi Marg, Vol. 17, No. 3, pp. 261–281.
70. *Harijan*, 28–01–1939.
71. F.W. Neitzsche (1968) *The Will to Power*, Sec. 584, New York, Vintage Books, pp. 314–315.
72. See, Nicholas F. Gier, op. cit., p. 11.
73. *Young India*, 24.05.1924.
74. *The Collected Works of Mahatma Gandhi*, Vol. 37, pp. 348–349.

75. Ronald J. Terchek (2001) "Problematizing Modernity: Gandhi's Decentering Impulse", *Gandhi Marg*, New Delhi, Gandhi Peace Foundati, Vol. 23, No. 1, p. 19.
76. Ibid., p. 11.
77. Ibid., p. 11.
78. Ronald J. Terchek (2001) "Problematizing Modernity: Gandhi's Decentering Impulse", *Gandhi* Marg, New Delhi, Gandhi Peace Foundation, Vol. 23, No. 1, p. 11.
79. Raghavan N. Iyer op. cit., p. 394.
80. Stuart Hall, David Held and Toney McGrew (eds) (1992) *Modernity and Its Futures*, Cambridge, Polity Press, p. 26.

    "The Enlightenment subject was based on a conception of the human person as a fully centered, unified individual, endowed with the capacities of reason, consciousness and action, whose centre of the self was a person's identity."

    Stuart Hall, David Held and Tony McGrew (1992) *Modernity and Its Futures*, Cambridge, Polity Press, p. 275.
81. M.K. Gandhi *India of My Dreams*, p. 8.
82. *Harijan*, 20–4–1934.
83. Raghavan N. Iyer op. cit., p. 394.
84. Ronald J. Terchek (2001) op. cit., Vol. 23, No. 1, p. 11.
85. Susanne H. Rudolph and Lloyd L. Rudolph (1987) *Gandhi: The Traditional Roots of Charisma*, Hyderabad, Orient Longman, p. viii.
86. M.K. Gandhi (2001) *An Autobiography: My Experiments with Truth*, Ahmedabad, Navajivan Publishing House, Introduction, p. XI.
87. Ronald J. Terchek (1992) "Contesting Civilization", *Gandhi Marg*, New Delhi, Gandhi Peace Foundation, Vol. 13, No. 4, pp. 419–431.
88. Nicholas F. Gier (1996) op. cit., Vol. 17, No. 3, pp. 261–281.
89. *Hind Swaraj*, 1942.
90. M.K. Gandhi (1941) *Constructive Programme*, Ahmedabad, Navajivan Publishing House.
91. Douglas Allen op. cit., p. 139.
92. Bhikhu Parekh (1989) *Gandhi's Political Philosophy: A Critical Examination*, London, Macmillan Press, p. 146.
93. "... method of satyagraha offered a way-out. It combined the patience and persuasive power of reason with the urgency and energy of violence. It represented and reconciled the integrity of the parties involved, tapped and mobilized their moral and spiritual energies, and paved the way for a better mutual understanding," *Harijan*, 18–8–1940.
94. Bhikhu Parekh op. cit., 122pp. 148–149.
95. R.K. Prabhu and U.R. Rao (1945) *The Mind of Mahatma Gandhi*, London, Oxford University Press, pp. 22–23.

96. "Ironically, although a different goal is reached, it appears that French postmodernism agrees with the idea of 'other' constitution. For the French deconstructionist, the self does not make her own life any more that the author writes his own book. The constructive postmodernist, following either Whitehead, Merleau-Ponty, or George Herbert Mead, combines self and other constitution and recreates a relational, social-self that revives the best aspects of the relational self found in Buddhism, Hebrew religion and confucianism."

    Nicholas F. Gier (1996) op. cit., pp. 261–281.
97. Arne Naess op. cit., p. 43.
98. M.K. Gandhi *India of My Dreams*, p. 100.
99. Douglas Allen op. cit., p. 160.
100. Nicholas F. Gier op cit., p. 11.

4

Truth and Non-Violence

A Foundation of a New World Order

The ultimate objective of any society is to produce essential goods and to distribute them by following a just and an egalitarian procedure. Various institutions of any society could use different means for this purpose. Culture of a society depends on the nature of these means. If these means are truthful, just and healthy, then the society emerged would surely be a constructive one. It reflects that only an ideal means would lead to an ideal society. Therefore, truth and non-violence are playing an utmost important role in Gandhian philosophy.

Based on the principles of truth and non-violence, what kind of a New World Order would emerge there? The chapter gives an extensive illustration on that. For that purpose it is divided into two parts while the first part deals with the basic principles of truth and non-violence, the second part describes nature of politics, economics, religion, education and position of women in this new world order.

I
Truth and Non-Violence in Gandhian Philosophy

Truth and non-violence have been two foundational stones of Gandhian philosophy. Truth is the end and non-violence is the means to achieve this end. These are the two guiding principles for Gandhi. His whole life was devoted to these two principles.

Truth

To analysis the principle of truth in Gandhian philosophy, we can have three perspectives:

- Etymological perspective,
- Religious perspective, and
- Moral perspective.

Let us start with the etymological perspective. It is concerned with the origin of the meaning of the term truth, i.e., *satya*. The word *'sat'* is employed in the sense of reality, goodness or praiseworthy action. Steadfastness in sacrifice, penance, and gift are also called *sat*, and so many actions for such purpose are called *sat*. Whatever offering or gift is made, whatever rite is observed, without faith, is called *asat*.[1] From the etymological perspective, what really is, what really can be said, and what really is to be done, in this worldly life, is called *satya*. Since, only truth is real, for Gandhi, it must be the ultimate objective of our life. Accordingly:

> Devotion to this truth is the sole justification for our existence. All our activities should be very breath of our being. When once this state in the pilgrims' process is reached, all other rules of correct living will come without effort and obedience to them will be instructive. There should be Truth in thought, Truth in speech and Truth in action. To a man who has realized this truth in its fullness, nothing else remains to be known because all knowledge is necessarily included in it.[2]

For Gandhi, essence of life lies in its simplicity and truth is the instrument, the medium to achieve it. An individual's all small or big efforts are directed by truth only. As this is the truth, which will make an individual truthful in real sense of the term. *Upanishads* also correspond closely to these ideas. According to *Mundaka Upanishad*, "Truth prevails and not untruth".[3] Similarly, *Taittiriya Upanishad* says, "Speak the truth, observe duty, do not swerve from truth".[4]

The Gandhian conception of truth was equally influenced by all these ancient Indian religious-cum-philosophical writings. Truthfulness is the only way which makes the seeker after truth a truthful person. Because truth is the ultimate knowledge, if we once learn how to apply this never-failing test of truth, we will at once be able to find out what is worth reading.[5]

Thus, etymologically only truth exists. To attain this truth is the ultimate objective of our life. The real essence of life resides in this truth only. One who realizes this truth, nothing remains to be known because truth is the ultimate ruling authority. But one may raise this question: what is the inherent meaning of this truth? In which form we should accept it and how to obtain it? The religious perspective will satisfy all these queries in its fullest sense.

All our religious texts, scriptures, institutions and teachers accept only one existence on this earth and that is of God. Thus, if truth means sense of being or to be existed, then obviously it means God. For Gandhi, "to realize God, to realize the self and to realize truth are three experiences for the same development."[6] In his earlier days, Gandhi used to say that God is truth. It means to know about truth, one has to know God first. For Gandhi:

> God is self existent all knowing living force, which inheres every other force known to the world. God is even more intangible then other. He is both imminent and transcendent.[7]

In Gandhian philosophy the idea of God is explained from scientific, moral and philosophic perspectives. Like a scientist, who usually propounds his thoughts on the basis of cause and effect relationship, Gandhi too explains if our beings are there along with our fathers and grandfathers then we are bound to accept this truth that there does also exist the father of the whole universe. He again illustrates that there is a system in this world through which the whole universe of living beings is regulated. This system cannot be an abstract and immortal because abstract laws would not be applicable on living beings. And this law and system is nothing but the God himself. He himself is the law and the regulator of those laws. According to Gandhi:

> I do dimly perceive that whilst everything around me is ever changing all that change a living power that is changeless, that hold all together that creates, dissolves and regrets. This informing power and spirit is God. And since nothing else I see merely alone is. And is this power benevolent or malevolent? See it as purely benevolent, for I can see in the midst of untruth, truth persists, in the midst of darkness, light persists. Hence, I gather that God is life, Truth and Light. He is love. He is the Supreme God.[8]

In this manner, as a scientist, Gandhi tries his best to define the concept of God within the criteria of universally accepted definition by keeping aside all community, religion, time and space based definitions.

But, it does not mean that universal-scientific-rational definition of God in Gandhian philosophy ignores the importance of individualistic perspective. Gandhian philosophy even sees the God from moral perspective. For Gandhi:

> There are innumerable definitions of God, because His manifestations are innumerable. They overwhelm me with wonder and are for a moment stun me. But I worship God as Truth only. I have not yet found him, but I am seeking after him.[9]

Accordingly, God can be seen from different perspectives. Even for theists its existence is there. "You may call yourself an atheist, but so long as you feel akin with mankind you accept God in practice."[10]

While defining God, sometimes, Gandhi also feels like opportunist thinkers. But Gandhi himself explains the reason in the following manner:

> God is the indefinable something that we shall follow but do not know. To me God is Truth and Love; God is ethics and morality; God is fearlessness. God is source of light and life and yet He is above and beyond all these. God is conscience. He is even the atheism of the atheist ... he embodies to those who need His touch. He is purest essence. He simply is to those who have faith. He is all things to all man. He is in us and yet above and beyond us ... He is long suffering. He is patient but He is also terrible ... with Him ignorance is no essence. And withal He is ever forgiving for He always given us the chances to repent. He is the greatest democrat the world knows, for He leaves us 'unfettered' to make our own choice between evil and good. He is the greatest tyrant ever known, for He often dashes the cup from our lips and under the cover of the freewill leaves us a margin so wholly inadequate as to provide only mirth to Himself ... Therefore, Hinduism calls it all His sport.[11]

Thus, like a spiritual thinker, Gandhi assumes God as knowledge, love, compassion, inner-consciousness, logic-reason etc. Not only this, but for him the reason and logical perception of atheists is also another form of God. And, ultimately, he said, "if it is possible for the human tongue to give the fullest description of God, I have come to the conclusion that for myself, God is Truth."[12] It shows that for Gandhi God can be defined from individualistic, pluralistic and in so many different universalistic perspectives.

Bhikhu Parekh, in his *Gandhi's Political Philosophy: A Critical Examination,* says that earlier Gandhi used the term *'Brahman'*. But he was somewhat uneasy with its historical association and preferred to use such terms as eternal principle, supreme consciousness or intelligence, mysterious force and cosmic power, spirit or *shakti*. Later, he preferred to call it *satya* or truth and thought that this was its only correct and fully significant description. Following Indian philosophical tradition, Gandhi used the term *'satya'* to mean the eternal and unchanging, what alone persists in the midst of change and holds the universe together. For a long time he said that "God is Truth", implying both that truth was one of God's many properties and that the concept of God was logically prior to that of truth. In 1926, he reversed the proposition and said that truth is God. He regarded this as one of his most important discoveries and thought that it crystallized his years of grouping. The new proposition implied that the concept of truth was prior to that of God, and that calling it God did not add anything new to it but only made it more concrete and comprehensible to the human mind.

By following the norms of the Indian thinkers, Gandhi intended to distinguish between the impersonal and personal God, and preferred to call the *Nirguna Brahman*. Since the term 'truth' is likely to create confusion I shall use the more familiar terms cosmic spirit or power.[13]

For Gandhi, the *Brahman*, truth or cosmic spirit was *nirguna*, i.e., beyond all qualities, including the moral. As he put it, "Fundamentally, God is indescribable in words ... . The qualities we attribute to God with the purest of motives are true for us but fundamentally false."[14] And again beyond the personal God there is formless essence which our reason cannot comprehend. The formless essence or cosmic spirit was not a 'personal being', and to think that it was represented a mistaken and 'inferior' conception of its nature. Although the cosmic power was without qualities, including personality, Gandhi argued that a limited being as man found it difficult to avoid attributing them to and personalizing it. First, the human mind was so used the world of qualities that it did not find it easy to think in non-qualitative terms. Second, man was not only thinking but also a feeling being and the 'head' and 'heart' had different requirements. The quality-free cosmic power satisfied the head but was too remote, abstract and detached to satisfy the heart. The heart required a being with heart, one who could understand and respond to the language of feeling.[15]

Even by accepting the various definitions and perceptions of truth discussed as above, Gandhian philosophy also present a universal notion of truth. Accordingly, "what is Truth?" "A difficult question, but I have solved it for myself by saying that it is what the voice within tells you. How then, you ask different people think of different and contrary truth? Well, seeing that the human mind works through innumerable media and that the evolution of the human mind is not the same for all, it follows that what may be truth for one may be untruth for another, and hence those who have made their experiments have come to the conclusion that there are certain condition to be observed in making those experiments ... . It is because we have at the present moment everybody claiming the right of conscience without going through any discipline what so-even that there is so much untruth being delivered to a bewildered world. All that I can do true humility present to you is that truth is not to be found by anybody who has not got an abundant sense of humility. If you would swim on the bosom of ocean of Truth you must reduce yourself to a zero."[16] It means, for Gandhi, there is no guarantee that we find the truth in any matter. But a continued selfless devotion in search of truth will make the seeker aware of errors and thus lead him further towards truth.[17]

What may appear as truth to one person will often appear untruth to another person. But that need not worry the seeker. Where there is honest effort, it will be realized that what appears to be different truth is like the countless and apparently different leaves of the same tree. Does not God Himself appear to difficult individuals in different aspects? But truth is the right designation of God. Hence, there is nothing wrong in everyone following truth according to his light. Indeed, it is a duty to do so.[18]

That is why, Gandhi, while presenting the solution, suggested that "the golden rule of conduct ... is mutual toleration, seeing that we will never all think alike and we shall see Truth in fragment and from different angles of vision. Conscience is not the something for all. Whilst, therefore, it is a good guide for individual conduct, imposition of that conduct upon all will be an insufferable interference with everybody's freedom of conscience."[19]

Thus, the etymological and ontological explanations reveal the physical and eternal meaning of truth. Now one may ask another question, how to achieve this truth which is both relative as well as absolute in nature.

For Gandhi, life is the name of dialectics. Life persists in continuous experiments and consequent development. Absolute truth is the ultimate truth to be achieved. It is the eternal reality but it is not easy to achieve because human mind has its own limitations. Relative truth is the way towards absolute truth. So long, according to Gandhi, "I must hold by the relative truth as I have conceived it. That relative truth must, meanwhile, be my beacon, my shield and buckler. Though this path is narrow and sharp as razor's edge, for me, it has been the quickest and easiest. Even my Himalayan blunders have seemed trifling to me because I have kept strictly to this path. For the path has saved me from coming to grief, and I have gone forward according to my light."[20]

Two things are coming in mind at the same time. Firstly, it is only the continuous practice through which this absolute truth would be achieved. And secondly, the extent to which an individual is relating this absolute truth with his/her relative truth to that extent s/he will orient towards absolute truth. That is why, this relative truth is different to different people. Therefore, Gandhi used to say that relative truth is the means to achieve the absolute truth. Thus, in Gandhian philosophy, we have both permanent and dynamic nature truth. Because, Gandhi never assumed that one's truth is the ultimate truth.

Now we have knowledge about different meanings of truth, yet it is not easy to realize or internalize this truth in real sense of the term. Realization of truth is a continuous process for which moral values are essentially required to inculcated. Because for Gandhi "to realize God" is another expression for "to become God" and "to face God".[21]

Gandhi used to say, "I am but a seeker after truth. I claim to have found a way to it. I claim to be making a ceaseless efforts to find it. But I admit that I have not yet found it. To find truth completely is to realize oneself and one's destiny, to become perfect. I am painfully conscious of my imperfections and therein lies all the strength I possess, because it is a rare thing for a man to know his own limitations. When the egotism-ego vanishes, something else grows that ingredient of the person that tends to identify itself with God, with humanity, all that lives. Therefore, once the reduction of one's egotism self is complete, one comes face to face with God, find truth, and realizes the universal-self, the Self. The way of humanity is essentially the way of reducing egotism.[22]

In Gandhian philosophy the concept of 'self' is considered from two perspectives: one is 'universal self' and second is 'individual self'. For Gandhian philosophy, the terms such as 'the universal self' can scarcely be given experimental meaning without resource of psychological and social processes of intense identification. They cannot only be facilitated by the practice of yoga, but also by various kinds of voluntary social work as these are now carried out by dedicated people in many countries. According to Arne Naess, the recent development in psychiatry and psychology favouring reciprocity in the therapist-patient relation helps to make the identification easier.

There is an intimate relation between a belief in the ultimate oneness of all that lives and the belief that one cannot reach one's own complete freedom without bringing about the freedom of others, or remove all feelings of pain without relieving the pain of others. Gandhi says:

> I do not believe ... that an individual may gain spiritually and those who surround him suffer. I believe in *advita* (non-duality), I believe in the essentially unity of man and, for that matter, of all that lies. Therefore, I believe that if one man gain spiritually, the whole world gains with him and, if one man fall, the whole world fall to that extent.[23]

Gandhi's tendency towards collectivism and egalitarianism is beautifully expressed in the following words:

> A drop torn from the ocean perishes without doing any good. If it remains a part of the ocean, it shares the glory of carrying on its bosom a fleet of mighty ships.[24]

And, an individual self, the seeker after truth, can become a universal self by putting himself last among his fellow creatures. Inculcated moral values will impoverish a being in this way of becoming a universal being.

Hence, it can be said that truth is the sovereign principle. It is ultimate reality. It is the fundamental principle of all thought and action. Though it is ultimate and absolute by nature, even then, each and every living being can achieve it. A partial knowledge of this truth will never allow us to be perfect.

Hence, the different perspectives of truth in Gandhian philosophy, such as etymological perspective, religious perspective and moral perspective, try to give a complete meaning of truth. If etymological perspective believes in the existence of truth being the only reality, the religious perspective teaches the lesson that God is truth. Whereas moral perspective, says that God, love, compassion, motherhood etc. are the different shades of truth. Truth is the only universal principle which is prevailing everywhere. Moral perspective of truth encompasses all those different aspects of truth. A seeker after truth will never assume his truth as ultimate truth and thus will have respect for other's truth also.

In this untruthful social order which is prevailing everywhere these days, Gandhi presents a very consistent, balanced, universally accepted definition of truth, which is the absolute reality and thus the ultimate goal of human life. It was the only purpose of all experiments which Gandhi did throughout his life. That is why, in his philosophy of ideal life, truth plays an important role.

Non-Violence (*Ahimsa*)

For Gandhi, "It is practically impossible to disentangle Truth and non-violence. They are like the two sides of a coin, or rather of a smooth, unstamped metallic disc "who can say", he asks "which is the observe, and which is the reverse."[25] Because of the fact, he says, "means and ends are convertible term in my philosophy of life. They say ends are after all everything. I would say, means are after all everything. As the means so the ends. There is no wall of separation between means and ends. Indeed, the creator has given us control (and that to very limited) over means none over the ends. Realization of the goal is in exact proportion to that means. This is a proportion that admits of no expectations."[26] For Gandhi, to get the truth, *ahimsa* is the only instrument. In his own words:

> *Ahimsa* is my God. And Truth is my God. When I look for *Ahimsa*, Truth says find it out through me, when I look for Truth, *Ahimsa* says find it out through me.[27]

In fact, all the human values of a humanitarian society are inspired by the principle of *ahimsa*. In every religion, whether it is Hinduism, Buddhism or Jainism, this principle of *ahimsa* has played a very important role. In Indian philosophical tradition, this has been surviving since times immemorial.

Chandopnishad, Patanjali Yoga Sutras, and in so many philosophical-intellectual traditions of India, *Ahimsa* has a very important place. Similarly, in the Jain philosophy, *Ahimsa* is assumed to be a big vow. In Trithankar Mahavir Swami's words, "*Ahimsa* is a highest religion which is regulated by tolerance and strict practice of self-discipline." According to Jainism, all religions are the different branches of the same tree. The ultimate objective of all religions is self-realization or self-actualization. For Mahavir Swami, if the principle of *ahimsa* is required for an individual to regulate his/her life, then socially it is required just to secure the social life. Accordingly, we are all part of an ultimate superpower. Whatever the sufferings, agonies and the problems we are facing in our life are also there in other's life. We should try to understand this reality and *ahimsa* will teach us the importance of life. That is why, *ahimsa* is also called as a very strict principle of life.[28]

Even in Buddhist tradition *ahimsa* plays important and centrifugal role. It is said in this tradition that *ahimsa* implies not to give injury to anyone by speech and action. The follower of this principle will never create problem for anyone and not even encourage anyone else to do so. Because to give injury or to encourage anyone for injury both are recorded as *himsa*.

Hence, in the philosophies of life, which were evolved with the evolution of human civilization in Indian society, *ahimsa* plays a very important and vibrant role. Its concept and norms are continuously changing according to the societal changes. The Gandhian philosophy has its own significance to establish the notion of *ahimsa* in the modern context. By keeping all these issues in mind, we can say that for Gandhi, *ahimsa* was the biggest *dharma* and highest form of morality. It is the purest means to attain the end, i.e., God and truth. Gandhi used to say:

> By instinct I have been truthful, but not non-violent ... I was capable of sacrificing non-violence for the sake of truth. In fact, it was in the course of my pursuit of Truth that I discovered non-violence.[29]

Gandhi accepted that truth is the end and *ahimsa* is the means. The concept of *ahimsa* in Gandhian philosophy can be explained from two perspectives:

- Negative *ahimsa*, and
- Positive *ahimsa*.

Negative Ahimsa

From the negative perspective *ahimsa* means 'a'+'*himsa*', which again means, absence of *himsa*. The word is correctively written: *hiñsa* or *hinsa*, meaning harming, hurting, injuring, from the root *hiñs*, harm, hurt, injure, slay ... . The word *hiñ* may in turn have been a form of the verbal root *han*, which has a large number of meanings: strike, smite, slay, kill, destroy, dispel (darkness) etc. These meanings seem on the whole to be more predominantly physical than those of *himsa*.

It reflects, in general conception, *ahimsa* means avoiding injury to anything on earth in thought, word or deed.[30] But in this absolute sense, the applicability of *ahimsa* is not possible at all.[31] Even Gandhi accepted this. He says:

> Perfect non-violence is impossible so long as we exist physically, for we would want some space at least to occupy. Perfect non-violence whilst you are inhabiting the body is only a theory like Euclid's point or straight line, but we have to endeavor every moment of our lives.[32]

If we turn our eyes to the time of which history has any record down to our own time, we shall find that man has been steadily progressing towards *ahimsa*. Our remote ancestors were cannibals. Then came a time when they were fed up with cannibalism and began to live on chase. Next came a stage when man was ashamed of leading the life of a wandering hunter. He, therefore, took to agriculture and depended principally on mother earth for his food. Thus, from being a nomad he settled down to civilized stable life, founded villages and towns and from member of a family he became member of a community and a nation. All these are signs of progressive *ahimsa* and diminishing *himsa*. Had it been otherwise, the human species should have been extinct by now, even as many of the lower species have disappeared. Prophets and *avatars* have also taught the lesson of *ahimsa* more or less. Not one should it be otherwise? *Himsa* does not need to be taught. Man as animal is violent, but, as spirit is non-violent. The moment he awakes to the spirit within, he cannot remain violent. Either he progresses towards *ahimsa* or rushes to his doom. That is why, the prophets and *avatars* have taught us the lessons of truth, harmony, brotherhood, justice, etc., which are all attributes of *ahimsa*.[33]

Thus, evidences of the history prove it very well that in our life some *himsa* is inevitably essential. It is not possible to lead a life without *himsa*. Therefore, Gandhi explained the difference between *himsa* and *ahimsa* in detail. Firstly, to sustain a life, some *himsa* is essentially required and that must be exempted. In Gandhi's words:

> Taking life may be a duty. We do destroy as much life as we think necessary for sustaining our body. Thus, for food we take life, vegetable and other, and for health we destroy mosquitoes and the like by the use of disinfectants etc. and we do not think that we are guilty of irreligious in doing so ... for the benefit of the species we kill carnivorous beasts ... .[34]

Secondly, to protect shelters if slaughter is required, then *himsa* can exempted. In Gandhi's own words:

> Even man slaughter may be necessary in certain cases. Suppose a man runs amuck and goes furiously about, sword in hand and killing anyone that comes in his way and no one dares to capture him alive. Anyone who dispatches this lunatic will earn the gratitude of the community and be regarded as a benevolent man.[35]

Thirdly, to take the life of a person, who is struggling for his life, is not *himsa*. For Gandhi:

> I see that there is an initiative horror of killing living beings under any circumstances whatever. For instance, an alternative has been suggested in the shape of confining ever rabid dogs in a certain place and allowing them to die a slow death. Now my idea of compassion makes this impossible for me. I cannot for a moment bear to see a dog or for that matter any other living being, helplessly, suffering the torture of a slow death. I do not kill a human being thus circumstanced because I have more helpful remedies. I should kill a dog similarly situated because in its case I am without a remedy.[36]

Further, he added:

> Should my child be attacked with rabies and there was no helpful remedy to relieve his agony, I should consider it my duty to take his life. Fatalism has its limits. We leave things to fate after exhausting all the remedies. One of the remedies and the final one to relieve the agony of a tortured child is to take his life.[37]

All these statements prove that life itself involves so many violence but we have to choose the path of least violence. And negative concept of *ahimsa* in Gandhian philosophy tells us how to lead a non-violence life.

Positive Ahimsa

"In its positive form, *ahimsa* means the largest love, greatest charity. If I am a follower of *ahimsa*, I must love my enemy. I must apply the same rules to the wrong-doer who is my enemy or a stranger to me, as I would do to my wrong-doing father or son. This active *ahimsa* necessarily includes truth and fearlessness. As man cannot deceive the loved one, he does not fear or frighten him or her. Gift of life is the greatest of all gift; a man who gives it in reality, disarms all hostility. He has paved the way for an honorable understanding. And none who is himself subject to fear can bestow that gift. He must therefore be himself fearless. A man cannot then practice *Ahimsa* and be a coward at the same time. The practice of *Ahimsa* calls forth the greatest courage ... ."[38]

For Gandhi, *ahimsa* really means that "you may not offend anybody; you may not harbour an uncharitable thought even in connection with one who may consider himself to be your enemy ..."[39]

Even all the scriptures of the world have registered emphatic and unequivocal testimony in favour of non-violence being practised by all, not merely singly but collectively as well. In all humanity, Gandhi had often felt that having no axes to grind and having by nature a detached mind, he gives a true interpretation of the Hindu, Islamic or other scriptures. For this humble claim, Gandhi anticipated the forgiveness of Sanatanists, Christians and Mussalmans.[40]

Defining the very concept of *ahimsa* in its positive form, Gandhi said: "Having flung aside the sword, there is nothing except the cup of love which I can offer to those who oppose me. It is by offering that cup that I expect to draw them close to me. I cannot think of permanent enmity between man and man and believing as I do in the theory of rebirth, I live in the hope that if not in this birth, in some other birth, I shall be able to hug all humanity in friendly embrace."[41]

It shows that by *ahimsa* Gandhi not only means avoiding injury to anything or anyone on earth in thought, words or deed, but it also implies active and creative love, charity, humanity etc. in order to create a peaceful, respectful and dignified world order.

Characteristics of the Devotee of Ahimsa

We have explained the term *'ahimsa'* above in a very wide spectrum from both negative and positive perspectives. But it is also essential to discuss about the characteristics of the devotee of *ahimsa,* as it will elaborate the meaning of the term in a more comprehensive manner.

The first characteristic of a true devotee of *ahimsa* is love. Love in the strongest force the world possesses and yet it is the humblest imaginable.[42]

Ahimsa, in the form of love, is also related to other characteristics. It is *ahimsa*, from where the senses of forgiveness, generosity, tolerance, love etc. have its important role to play. That is why, Gandhi used to say that without *ahimsa* it is difficult to achieve the end of truth. But this love does not mean to love only your friends and fellow-beings. In Gandhi's words, "It is no non-violence if we merely love those that love us. It is non-violence only when we love those that hate us. I know how difficult it is to follow this grand law of love. But are not all great and good things difficult to do? Love of hater is the most difficult of all. But by the grace of God even this most difficult thing becomes easy to accomplish if we want to do it."[43]

Gandhi assumes that God looks after us due to this love only. Hence, love is the first and foremost characteristic of the devotee of *ahimsa*. Gandhi says:

> He who seeks refuge in God ought to have a glimpse of the *Atma* that transcends the body; and the moment one has a glimpse of the imperishable *Atma,* one sheds the love of the imperishable body. Training in non-violence is thus diametrically opposed to training in violence. Violence is needed for the protection of things external; non-violence is needed for the protection of the *Atma*, for the protection of one's honour.[44]

In his manner, as a true devotee of the principle of *ahimsa*, Gandhi tried to flourish both the internal as well as external aspects of human personality. To inculcate this sense of *ahimsa* was his ultimate objective. Because, only a sensitive being will able to build a human society, which will be an ideal society in its own way.

Further, fearlessness and self-confidence are other qualities of a devotee of *ahimsa*. In Gandhi's words, "without fearlessness and self-confidence, *ahimsa* is not possible." [45] He further says:

> Non-violence and cowardice go ill together. I can imagine a fully armed man to be at heart a coward. Possession of arms implies an element of fear, if not cowardice. But true non-violence is impossibility without the possession of unadulterated fearlessness. My creed of non-violence is an extremely active force. It has no room for cowardice or even weakness. There is hope for a violent man to be some day non-violent, but there is none for a coward. I have therefore said more than once in these pages that if we do not know

> how to defend ourselves, our women and our places of worship by the force of suffering, i.e., non-violence, we must, if we are men, be at least able to defend all these by fighting.[46]

For Gandhi, cowards can never be moral because they are uncommitted to their own integrity or moral projects, unless it is safe or convenient.[47] Insisting that a person's autonomy is always paramount, Gandhi repeatedly argues that open, straightforward violence on behalf of one's own integrity is preferable to running away, but non-violence is superior to both. He says:

> Where there is only a choice between cowardice and violence I would advice violence. Thus, when my eldest son asked me what he should have done, had he been present when I was almost fatally assaulted in 1908, whether he should have run away and seen me killed or whether he should have used his physical force which he could and wanted to use, and defended me, I told him that it was his duty to defend me even by using violence.[48]

It shows, though Gandhi accepts the courage and bravery of soldiers, yet he finds the soldier's courage is defective, incomplete and inferior to that of the *Satyagrahi* because the possession of arms implies an element of fear. But, true non-violence is impossibility without the possession of unadulterated fearlessness.[49] Gandhi accepts fear but only in one condition and that is the fear of God. He says:

> The votary of *ahimsa* has only one fear that is of God. He who seeks refuge in God ought to have a glimpse of the *Atma* that transcends the body; and the moment one has a glimpse of the imperishable *Atma* one sheds the love of the perishable body.[50]

In this way, *ahimsa* is a quality of *Atma,* which consists of the further qualities of love, generosity, fearlessness or in its holistic sense God itself. It does not mean not to fight against injustice and cruelty, but it means all these have to be avoided by conducive and truthful means. And it would be possible if the follower of *ahimsa* has proper control over his action and thought. It means, the devotee of *ahimsa* has to be tolerant and suffering-being. Gandhi says:

> It is not that I am incapable of anger, for instance, but I succeed on almost all occasions to keep my feelings under control. Whatever may be the result, there is always in me conscious struggle for following the law of non-violence deliberately and ceaselessly. Such a struggle leaves one stronger for it. The more I work at this law, the more I feel the delight in my life the delight in the scheme of the

universe. It gives me a peace and a meaning of the mysteries of nature that I have no power to describe.[51]

Thus, for Gandhi, qualities of toleration and patience are the biggest qualities of a devotee of *ahimsa* because it will expand the heart of the devotee where the other qualities like love, compassion, fraternity will naturally flourish. Even in religious field Gandhi welcomed toleration and compassion. He writes:

> I do not want my house to be walled in on all sides and my windows to be stuffed. I want the cultures of all land to be blown about my house as freely as possible, but I refuse to be blown, of my feet by any of them. Mine is not a religion of the prison house, it has room for the least among God's creatures, but it is proof against the insolent bride of race, religion or colour.[52]

For Gandhi, *ahimsa* is the highest form of compassion and it is possible only if the seeker could remain himself humbler than the dust. The world crushes the dust under its feet, but the seeker after truth should so humble that even the dust could crush him. Thus compassion, tolerance and forgiveness are some essential qualities of the devotee of *ahimsa* and truth.

In Gandhian philosophy, the concepts of *ahimsa* and truth can be applicable not only in religious and moral fields, but also in political, economic and social fields. He defined the new concept of *ahimsa* not only for individual life, but also for social life. For Gandhi, "non-violence is not an individual virtue but a course of spiritual and political conduct for the individual and community."[53]

A devotee of *ahimsa* must know how to control his emotions and anger in social and individual life. It is the collective being, community or society from where we can get inspiration for *ahimsa*. To have a balance and comprehensive society, *ahimsa* is mandatory. Thus, a non-violent society would be a society where there would not be any discrimination on the basis of class, caste, sex, colour, creed, birthplace etc. If the individualistic concept of *ahimsa* means compassion, love, toleration and patience, then the socialistic concept of *ahimsa* means absence of exploitation and discrimination based domination, i.e., presence of a free society.

To conclude, *ahimsa* is a means not only to gain spirituality and salvation or *Moksha* for an individual, but also it is an instrument to preserve a comprehensive and balanced society. Consequently, *ahimsa* became first and foremost principle in the Gandhian philosophy and practice. To spread and disseminate it was the ultimate aim of his life for which he struggled throughout.

II
Other Aspects of a New World Order

In the previous section we have seen how truth and non-violence have been playing significant role as foundational values for a new world order. It is a unique world order in the sense that nature of politics, economics, religion as well as the system of educations are totally different in Gandhian plan of life. The section follows shall try to present a comprehensive picture of various tenets of this new world order one-by-one.

Politics

Politics of a new world order, which is essentially based on the principle of truth and non-violence, would be influenced by morality and spirituality. Gandhi's ultimate aim was to spiritualize the politics. Different experiences, which he got through the different experiments, revealed him that truth and non-violence are those principles which govern our life. That is way, his politics is directed by spiritual and moral laws. For him, even politics is a kind of social or religious work. Gandhi says, "For me politics bereft of religion are absolute dirt, even to be shunned. Politics concerns nation and that which must be one of the concerns of a man who is religiously inclined, in other words, a seeker after God and truth. For me, God and Truth are convertible terms, and if anyone told me that God is a God of untruth or a God of torture, I would decline to worship him. Therefore, in politics also we have to establish the kingdom of Heaven."[54] That is why, Ronald J. Terchek says that "for Gandhi political life must be an echo of public life and there cannot be any division between the two and each to be morally directed."[55] As religion and morality provide a kind of inspiration to individual's personal life, similarly, his public life is also influenced by religion. For Gandhi, politics is directly related with the development of nation and, it is possible, if we use truthful and non-violent means into political sphere. Politics, which is achieved through non-violent means and which is based on the religious values and moral norms in Gandhian philosophy, is explained in this section.

Non-Violent State

Gandhi opines:

> To me political power is not an end but one of the means of enabling people to better their condition in every department of life. Political power means capacity to regulate national life through national representatives. If national life becomes so perfect as to become self-regulated, no representation is necessary. There is then a state

> of enlightened anarchy. In such a state everyone is his own ruler. He rules himself in such a manner that he is never a hindrance to his neighbours. In the ideal state therefore there is no political power because there is no state. But the ideal is never realized in life. Hence, the classical statement of Thoreau that Government is best which governs the least must be accepted ...[56]

Though Gandhi's ultimate aim was to realize *Ramrajya*, yet *Swaraj* was his second best state. *Ramrajya* is an end, is an ideal, *Swaraj* is the way, *Swaraj* is the means, the reality. *Swaraj* is also based on the principles of *satya* and *ahimsa*. For Gandhi non-violence is the means to flourish the way of democratic life in real sense of the term. Because the aim of democracy is to provide liberty as much as possible and it can be flourished only in a proper non-violent society. Therefore, non-violence should be cherished as much as possible. By criticizing the western concept of democracy Gandhi said that either they should declare themselves as dictators or should try to evolve themselves as democrats in real sense of the term. For western philosophy the practice of non-violence is related with an individual's personal life. But Gandhi applied it even in public and political spheres and presented a new form of politics oriented towards a peaceful, truthful, non-violent, humanitarian society. By police force, he meant:

> The police of my conception will, however, be of a wholly different pattern from the present day force. Its rank will be composed of believers in non-violence. They will be servants, not masters, of the people. The people will instinctively render them every help, and through mutual cooperation they will easily deal with ever-decreasing disturbances. The police force will have some kind of arms, but they will be rarely used, if at all. In fact, the policeman will be reformers.[57]

Thus, in Gandhi's non-violent society police force will adopt evolutionary steps for the sinner, not the discriminatory measures. In fact, the policemen would be reformers. Their police work would be confided primarily to robbers and dacoits. Similarly, there will be no room for communal disturbance.[58] In this manner, Gandhi's state is the synonym of real democracy.

Discussing about the internal set-up of a non-violent society, Gandhi says that it will be based on the principle of decentralization. For him, centralization of power is the main cause of exploitation and violence. Therefore, power must be decentralized. Within a decentralized structure, each and every state, institution, village and individual will get an opportunity for development. In his own words:

> In this structure composed of innumerable villages there will be ever widening, never ascending circles. Life will not be a pyramid with the apex sustained by the bottom. But it will be an oceanic circle whose centre will be the individual always ready to perish for the circle of villages, till at last the whole becomes one life composed of individuals, never aggressive in their arrogance but ever humble, sharing the majority of the oceanic circle of which they are integral units.[59]

Accordingly, in such a scheme of non-violent society, villages will be ready to sacrifice themselves for the development of the state and similarly states will be ready to devote themselves for the development of the villages. In this society all the members will help each other and no one would be assumed as more dominant and powerful. The concept of equality will be prevailed there in real sense of the term. All the members of the society would be totally devoted for the egalitarian and just development of the society.

It acknowledges that in the Gandhian non-violent society, state and other institutions will be treated as servants of the people. And as much as this sense of duty will be increased, the state will be withering away because now all the members are so conscious and alert for their duties and responsibilities that any regulating authority will not be required at all. It will now be a perfect enlightened anarchy, which is the ultimate objective to be achieved.

Autonomy of Individual in Gandhian State

In Gandhian non-violent state every individual has to play his/her role in a right manner. By accepting the importance of an individual, Gandhi said:

> If the individual ceases to count, what is a society? Individual freedom alone can make man voluntarily surrender himself completely to the service of society. If it is wrested from him he becomes an automation and the society is ruined. No society can possibly be built on a denial of individual freedom.[60]

Gandhi used to say that an individual is the combination of negative and positive instincts. Positively, he is the combination of spirituality, morality and rationality. Negatively, he looks for many hedonistic pleasures. Individual's life is continuously struggling within all these positive and negative instincts. Thus, the state should try to flourish the positive instincts in individual. As much the state will be non-violent, individual will consume his/her liberty and lead a moral life. For Gandhi, non-violent state will always be against the centralization of power. He says:

> I look upon an increase in the power of the state with the greatest fear, because although while apparently doing good by minimizing exploitation, it does the greatest harm to mankind by destroying individuality which lies at the root of all progress.[61]

It shows that state represents violence in a concentrated and consolidated form. The individual has a soul, but as the state is a soulless machine, it can never be weaned from violence to which it owes its very existence. Gandhi proposes the concept of voluntary organization to be replaced by the state. It means that "... Real Swaraj will come not by the acquisition of authority by a few but by the acquisition of capacity by all to resist authority when it is abused. In other words, Swaraj is to be obtained by educating the masses to a sense of their capacity to regulate and control authority."[62] Thus, in Gandhi's non-violent state, moral individual is the ideal one.

Political Means: Satyagraha and Non-Violent Movement

As politics and its various branches are based on the principles of truth and non-violence, similarly various institutions of politics are also influenced by these principles. Thus, an ideal state, which is non-violent, will be directed only by the ideal instrument. And for Gandhi *satyagraha* is the main instrument in a non-violent ideal society.[63]

In fact, the philosophy, which works behind the action of *satya-graha*, is the philosophy of truth and non-violence itself. *Satya* is the end and *ahimsa* is the means. The term *satyagraha* stands for soul force. According to Gandhi, "Passive resistance is a method of securing right by personal suffering; it is the reverse of resistance by arms. When I refuse to do a thing that is repugnant to my conscience, I use soul force. For instance, the government of the day has passed a law which is applicable to me. I do not like it. If by using violence I force the government to repeal the law, I am employing what may be termed body force. If I do not obey the law and accept the penalty for its breach, I use soul force. It involves sacrifice of self."[64]

Actually, *satyagraha* stands for two terms – *satya* and *agraha*. *Satya* means truth and *agraha* means insisting on something without becoming obstinate or uncompromising. When the two terms are combined, there is a beautiful duality of meaning, implying both insistences on and for truth. A moral agent insists on truth as he sees it, but acknowledges that he might be wrong and invites his opponents to join him in a cooperative search for truth. That is why, sometimes, it is also called as sacrifice of self or active love for others. Gandhi writes:

> Passive resistance is an all sided sword, it can be used anyhow, it bless him who uses it and him against whom it is used. Without drawing a drop of blood it produces far reaching results. It never ruined and can not be stolen. Competition between passive resistors does not exhaust. The sword of passive resistance does not require a scabbard. It is strange indeed that you should consider such a weapon to be weapon merely of the weak.[65]

To become a passive resister is easy enough but it is also equally difficult. All satyagrahis are bound one and all to refrain at all hazard from violence, not to throw stones or in anyway whatever to injure anybody. *Satyagrahi,* in Gandhian formulation, would be a self-disciplined person. Truth, non-violence, *Brahmacharya*, *Aparigraha*, *Astaya*, fearlessness are some guiding principles for a *satyagrahi*. By following all these principles in her/his individual life, an individual may become a true *satyagrahi* individually as well as socially. A true *satyagrahi* must have faith in good human nature. A person, who himself is not free from all these whims, how he/she will handle the situations at individual or social spheres. Gandhi said after his great deal of experience that "those who want to become passive resister for the service of the country have to observe perfect chastity, adopt poverty, follow truth and cultivate fearlessness."[66] He further said:

> Chastity is one of the greatest disciples without which the mind cannot attain requisite firmness. A man who is unchaste loses stamina, becomes emasculated and cowardly.[67]

By following all these rules and regulations a *satyagrahi* can be a good and balanced person and can use all these practices in public and political affairs. Gandhi assumes that only self-disciplined, fearless and non-violent can become a true *satyagrahi*. And it is not difficult to be a *satyagrahi* because all these qualities are inherent in human nature.

As a political instrument, *satyagraha* can be exercised in the following ways:

Non-Violent Movement

Gandhi believes that it is citizen only who allows the state to do exploitation. If people will not accept the bad laws, the state automatically will not be able to pass bad legislation. Accordingly, "that we should obey laws whether good or bad is a new fangled notion. There was no such thing in former days. The people disregarded those laws they did not like and suffered the penalties for their breach. It is contrary to our manhood if we obey laws repugnant to our conscience. Such teaching is opposed to a religion and means slavery."[68]

Law-abiding citizen means the *satyagrahi* citizen and a true *satyagrahi* will always protest against injustice and exploitation. But, the way to protest will always be unique in its terms. Following are some non-violent programmes which Gandhi used during 1920s:

- To resign from each and every kind of government services, honours and posts.
- Non-participation, directly or indirectly, in any public/government functioning.
- To close all the educational institutions funded by government.
- To protest against government laws, lawyers and conflicts rising by government and try to organized their own *panchayat* institutions.
- To boycott all the foreign-based services protected by government.
- To popularize *swadeshi* and boycott of the foreign goods.

Satyagraha would be different in different context. If a *satyagrahi* is protesting against his opponent and he can do his work without any disturbance, then it will be called self-purification process in a very strict sense because apparently your opponent is not coming in the way. In other aspect, *satyagraha* may be very radical in nature. Because here your opponent would not be able to do any work without your presence, without your help and cooperation. Hence, here lots of considerations are required before going through the path of *satyagraha*. If really an atmosphere becomes so stressful and unbearable then only one should adopt this type of protest for the sake of *dharma*, humanity and morality.

Civil Disobedience Movement

Like non-cooperation, civil disobedience is another branch of the same tree i.e., *satyagraha*. According to Gandhi, it is the duty of every *satyagrahi* to resist and disobey all those laws, which he considers to be unjust and immoral. But he insisted that such disobedience must be civil in the sense of being polite, dutiful and non-violent.[69]

Gandhi believes that if you are disobeying inhuman laws, there is not any harm. Actually, most people not understand the complicated machinery of the government. They do not realize that every citizen silently but nonetheless certainly sustains the government of the day in the way of which he has no knowledge. Every citizen therefore renders himself responsible for every act of his government. And it is quite proper to support it so long as the actions of the government are bearable. But when they hurt his nation, it becomes his duty to withdraw his support.[70]

With this conception in his mind, Gandhi insists that no government exists independently of its people. Citizens may accede to their government because they generally support it. Or, they may disagree with the state's conduct but nevertheless acquiesce because the costs of dissent are high, because they are felicitous, or because they are preoccupied with their own individual concerns. Whatever the reasons, Gandhi argues, government rests on their sufferance, even though the state or individuals might deny the relationship. By making power visible and by teaching people that they are the basis of power, he thinks he can domesticate it and make it accountable to clear-righted citizens.

Gandhi credits individuals with power appears in his call for the individual to stand alone, if necessary, to reclaim power. On his account, lonely assertion of power can have a powerful demonstration effect as others come to see their complicity in their own domination and understand that they can recover the power they ceded to others.[71]

By explaining the inherent meaning of civil disobedience, Gandhi tells if there is a democratic institution, government is very much cooperative to their citizens, and citizens are ready to do work with government and if its different agencies are very satisfactory, then there is no need to go for civil disobedience. Because for small cause one cannot launch civil disobedience movement. It does not mean that small cause is not important. It is important and can be solved by small gathering instead of going for a movement. Tolerance and patience are playing an important role in civil disobedience. The person who is more tolerant and more patient will prove himself as a good follower of the principle of civil disobedience. By locating 'civil disobedience', Gandhi says:

> If civil disobedience movement is taking a form/shape where innocent people are losing their life and if *Satyagraha* is realizing the

fact that it is going to be uncontrollable, then it would be better to take the movement back.[72]

In this manner, one can infer that the disobedience of law will be called disobedience only if it is non-violent in real sense of the term. The ultimate objective of civil disobedience movement, which is non-violent, is to win the opponent by facing all the kinds of inhuman atrocities.

Strikes

Strikes are also taken by Gandhi as a non-violent political action. For Gandhi, "I do not deny that such strikes can serve political ends. But they do not fall within the plan of non-violent non-cooperation. It does not require much effort of the intellect to perceive that it is most dangerous thing to make political use of labour until labours understand the political conditions of the country and are prepared to work for the common good. This is hardly to be expected of them all of a sudden and until they have bettered their own conditions so as to enable them to keep body and soul together in a decent manner.

The greatest political contribution that labourer can make is to improve their own condition, to become better informed, to insist on their rights, and even to demand proper use by their employers of the manufactured goods in which they have had such an important hand. The proper evolution, therefore, would be for the labourers to raise themselves to the status of part proprietors.

Strikes, therefore, for the present situation should only take place for the direct betterment of labourers' lot, and when they have acquired the spirit of patriotism, for the regulation of prices of the manufactured goods.

The basic conditions of a successful strike are as follows:

- The cause of the strike must be just.
- There should be practical unanimity among the strikers.
- There should be no violence used against non-strikers.
- Strikes should be able to maintain themselves during the strike period without falling back upon union funds and such therefore occupy themselves in some useful and productive temporary occupation.
- A strike is no remedy when there is enough other labour to replace strikers. In that case, in the event of unjust treatment or inadequate wages or the like, resignation is the remedy.

- Successful strikes have taken place even when the above conditions have not been fulfilled, but that merely proves that the employers were weak and had a guilty conscience.

Thus, it is clear that there should be no strike which is not justifiable on merits. No unjust strike should succeed. All public sympathy must be withheld from such strikes. The public have no means of judging the merits of a strike, unless they are backed by impartial persons enjoying public confidence. Interested men cannot judge the merit of their own case. Hence, there must be an arbitrator accepted by the parties or a judicial adjudication.[73]

Fasting

Fasting is a potent weapon for the *satyagrahi*. Like another means of non-violent resolution, fasting is also an instrument of self-purification and that of your opponent. It cannot be taken by everyone. According to Gandhi, "Mere physical capacity to take it is no qualification for it ... it should never be mechanical effort or a mere imitation. It must come from the depth of one's soul. It is, therefore, rare."[74] He further says:

> A *Satyagrahi* should fast only as a last resort when all other avenues of redress have failed. There is no room for imitation in fasts. He, who has no inner strength, should not dream of it, and never with attachment to success ... Ridiculous fasts spread like plague and are harmful."[75] For Gandhi, "there can be no room for selfishness, anger, lack of faith, or impatience in a pure fast .... Infinite patience, firm resolve, single mindedness of purpose, perfect clam and no anger must of necessity be there. But since it is impossible for a person to develop these entire qualities al at once, no one who has not devoted himself to following the laws of *ahimsa* should undertake a *Satyagrahi* fast.[76]

It shows how Gandhi has made fast as a public/political instrument, which was earlier treated only as an individual effort. Public fasting increases the confidence of laymen and also alert them for previous mistakes. It is the strongest instrument to change the heart of your opponent.

Hizrat

Hizrat is another very significant instrument of non-violent movement. *Hizrat* means to leave your place by your own consent or to leave the place of exploitation to protest against exploitation. For Gandhi, *Hizrat* is an important instrument in the hands of *satyagrahi*. To preserve their self-respect and self-esteem, the exploited people are bound to leave the place. To leave the place where imperialist or dominating rule is prevailing. *Satyagrahi* has to face all these physical, emotional and mental sufferings alone. Others will not be invited.

Thus, Gandhi tried his best to present new tools to protest. Actually, he intended to attach *'Neeti'* with *'Rajya'*. His concept of politics revolved around the concept of morality or humanity. Politics is an instrument in one's hand to establish a new world order which would be more humane and conducive.

Economics

What Gandhi means by real progress is not merely material progress but integral human progress where moral progress is of high priority. He suspects that material advancement has a strong tendency to lead moral decay.[77] For Gandhi, "I must confess that I do not draw a sharp or any distinction between economics and ethics-economics that hurt the well-being of an individual or a nation are immoral and, therefore, sinful. Thus, the economics that permit one country to prey upon another are immoral. It is sinful to buy and use articles made by sweated labour."[78]

Accordingly, true economics never militates against the highest ethical standard, just as all true ethics to be worth its name must at the same time be also good economics. An economics that inculcates Mammon worship, and enables the strong to amass wealth at the expense of the weak, is a false and dismal science. It spells death. True economics, on the other hand, stands for social justice; it promotes the good of all equally including the weakest, and is indispensable for decent life.[79]

Gandhi said, that the economic constitution of India and for the matter of that of the world should be such that no one under it should suffer from want of food and clothing. In other words, everybody should be able to get sufficient work to enable him to make the two ends meet. And this ideal can be universally utilized only if the means of production of the elementary necessities of life remain in the control of the masses. These should be freely available to all as God's air and water are or ought to be; they should not be made a vehicle for the exploitation of others. Their monopolization by any country, nation or group of persons would be unjust. The neglect of this simple principle is the cause of the destitution that we witness today not only in this land but in other parts of the world too.[80]

Actually, Gandhi wants to propound such an economic order where each and everyone will be treated equally. Quarrel between capital and labour will be stopped for ever. In his own words:

> "I want to bring about an equalization of status. The working classes have all these centuries been isolated and relegated to a lower status. They have been *shoodras*, and the word has been interpreted to mean an inferior status. I want to allow no differentiation between the son of a weaver, of an agriculturalist and of a school-master.[81]

For Gandhi, economic equality is the master to non-violent independence. Working for economic equality means abolishing the eternal conflict between capital and labour. It means the levelling down of the few rich in whose hands is concentrated the bulk of the nation's wealth on the one hand, and a levelling up of the semi-starved naked millions, on the other. A non-violent system of government is clearly an impossibility so long as the wider gulf between the rich and the hungry millions persists. The contrast between the palaces of New Delhi and the miserable hovels of the poor, labouring class cannot last one day in a free India in which the poor will enjoy the same power as the richest in the land.[82]

But one may put this question: how to propound an economic order on the basis of equality? According to Gandhi, the first step in this direction would be the principle of controlling self or in other words the principle of trusteeship. He says:

> A violent and bloody revolution is a certainty one day unless there is a voluntary abdication of riches and the power which riches give and sharing them for the common good. I adhere to my doctrine of trusteeship in spite of the ridicule that has been poured upon it. It is true that it is difficult to reach. So is non-violence difficult to attain. But we made up our mind in 1920 to negotiate that steep ascent.[83]

According to the doctrine of trusteeship, one may not possess a rupee more than their neighbours. How is this to be brought about? Non-violently? Or should the wealthy be dispossessed of their possessions? To do this, we would naturally have to resort to violence. This violent action cannot benefit society. Society will be the person, for it will lose the gifts of a man who knows how to accumulate wealth. Therefore, the non-violent way is eventually superior. The rich man will be left in possession of his wealth, of which he will use what he reasonably requires for his personal needs and will act as a trustee for the remainder to be used for society. In this argument honesty on the part of the trustee is assumed. According to Gandhi:

> As soon as a man looks upon himself as a servant of society, earns for its sake, spends for its benefit, then purity enters into earrings and there is *Ahimsa* in his venture. Moreover, if man's mind turn towards this way of life, there will come about a peaceful revolution in society, and that without any bitterness.[84]

Further, Gandhi's concept of economics is centred not only up to individual. Explaining his concept of economics at societal level, Gandhi criticized the western notion of economics where matter is at the centre. Contrary to this, in Gandhian philosophy, an individual is a supreme consideration. For Gandhi, man himself is a big asset. That is why Gandhi used to say, whatever we are doing our supreme consideration must be for human cause. But, in modern economic set-up, we have ignored all the moral and human aspects of the society. Gandhi has criticized all the symbols of modern economy one by one. At the first step he has condemned machines. In *Hind Swaraj*, He writes:

> Today machinery merely helps a few to ride on the backs of millions. The impetus behind it all is not the philanthropy to save labour, but greed. It is against this constitution of things that I am fighting with all my might … . The supreme consideration is man. The machine should not tend to atrophy the limbs of man.[85]

The machinery which is developing today is becoming the means of exploitation and further domination by rich countries and rich people. Today's machine-based industrialization of economy is centred on profit-making tendency. Gandhi criticizes the machine being responsible for creating the panic situation of unemployment. Imagine a nation working only five hours per day on an average, and this not by choice but by force of circumstances, and you have a realistic picture of India. He also explains the reason why our average life rate is deplorably low, and why we are getting more and more impoverishment is that we have neglected our 7,00,000 villages. We have indeed thought of them, but only to the extent of exploiting them. We read thrilling accounts of the "glory that was India and of the land that was flowing with milk and honey; but today it is a land of starving millions. We are sitting in this time *pandal* under a blaze of electronic lights, but we do not know that we are burning these lights at the expense of the poor. We have no right to use these lights if we forget that we owe these to them."[86]

Gandhi was not against machines. He himself said, "How can I be when I know that even this body is a most delicate piece of machinery? The spinning wheel is a machine; a little toothpick is a machine. What I object to is the craze for machinery, not machinery as such. The craze is for what they call labour-saving machinery. Men go on 'saving labour' till thousands are without work and thrown on the open streets to die of starvation. I want to save time and labour not for a fraction of mankind but for all. I want the concentration of wealth, not in the hands of a few, but in the hands of all."[87] He looks for localized production as it is required there in the society. According to Gandhi:

> When production and consumption both become localized, the temptation to speed up production, indefinitely and at price, disappears. All the endless difficulties and problems that our present day economic system presents, too, would then come to an end.[88]

Gandhi believed that industrialization on a mass scale will necessarily lead to passive or active exploitation of the villages as the problems of competition and marketing come in. Therefore, we have to concentrate on the village being self-contained, manufacturing mainly for use. Provided this character of the industry is maintained, there would be no objection to villages using even the modern machines and tools that they can make afford to use. Only they should not be used as a means of exploitation of others.[89]

Gandhi's industrialization will be established by industrious people. His industrialization will be non-violent in nature. As the non-violent nation will be self-dependent. And, our self-dependency will definitely reduce our dependence on machines. Gandhi propounds the philosophy of 'village republic'. He was very much confident about the fact that *Swaraj* will be established by village industry (then only economic will be inspired by morality). He says:

> My idea of village Swaraj is that it is a complete republic, independent of its neighbours for its own vital wants and yet independent for many others in which dependence is necessary. Thus, every village's first concern will be to grow its own food crops, and cotton for its cloth. It should have a reserve for its cattle, recreation and playground for adults and children. Then if there is more land available, it will grow useful money crops, thus excluding *ganja*, tobacco, opium and the like.[90]

Thus, the economic world order based on truth and non-violence will totally be ethical in nature. It is possible only if each and every unit of the society will be self-sufficient and self-dependent. Therefore, in Gandhian philosophy, each and every aspects of life would be ethical and moral principles. In Gandhian philosophy economics is a part of moral life as its ultimate aim is to propound an ideal and moral world order.

Religion

In the new world order religion will play an important and vibrant role. In fact, God has always been the centre of Gandhian thought. In his philosophy the meaning of religion has its unique understanding. In his own words:

> Let me explain what I mean by religion. It is not the Hindu religion, which I certainly prize above all religion, but the religion which transcends Hinduism, which changes one's very nature, which binds one indissolubly to the truth within and which ever purifies. It is a permanent element in human nature which ... leaves the soul restless until it has found itself.[91]

Religion does not mean any particular religion or community. Religion is one which can flourish an individual's moral and ethical nature. According to Gandhi, the essence of religion lies in morality and humanity. For a true morality religion plays a similar role as water plays for seed within clay.

For Gandhi, religion is not only limited up to the concept and essence of God but it is a day-to-day practice. Our entire daily works, whether it is economics, politics, religion or all our deeds, are supposed to achieve the same distinctions. They are intermingled. They are interlinked or interdepended. Separately, they do not have any importance and relevance. Ultimately, we want to know our own nature with different experiences gained in life as self-realization is the absolute end.

Actually, Gandhian philosophy of religion propounds the concept of fraternity and brotherhood via different religions. Even then he finds the idea of religious convention profoundly irreligious and offensive.

For Gandhi, every man is born into a particular religion. Since no religion is wholly false, he should be able to work out his destiny in and through it. And if he feels attracted to some aspects of another religion, he should be at liberty to borrow them. Gandhi cannot see why a man should even need to give up his religion.

Gandhi acknowledges that men might find sufficient similarities between their conceptions of God to induce them to belong to a common religion. However, since men are naturally different, their conception and way of relating to God can never be completely identical. Every organized religion must therefore remain a loose fellowship of believers, and accommodate, even encourage, individual diversity. Insistence on total creedal conformity derives their individuality, violates their spiritual integrity and leads to untruth.

In fact, every major religion articulates a unique vision of God and emphasizes different features of the human condition. The idea of God as a loving father is most fully developed in Christianity, and the emphasis on love and suffering is also unique to it. I cannot say that it is singular, or that it is not to be found in other religions. But the presentation is unique. Rigorous monotheism and the spirit of equality are most beautifully articulated in and particular to Islam. The distinction between the impersonal and personal conceptions of God, the principle of the unity of all life and the doctrine of *ahimsa* are distinctive to Hinduism. Every religion has a distinct moral and spiritual ethos and represents a wonderful and irreplaceable 'spiritual composition'. To a truly religious man all religions should be equally dear.[92]

Gandhi argues that since the cosmic power is infinite and the limited human mind can grasp only a 'fragment' of it, and that too inadequately, every religion is necessarily limited and partial.[93] Even then we cannot say them as untruth. But again they won't be called as perfect or absolute one. Those claiming to be directly revealed by God are revealed to men with their fair share of inescapable human limitations and communicated to others in necessarily inadequate human languages.[94] To claim that a particular religion offers an exhaustive or even definitive account of the nature of the cosmic spirit is to imply both that some men are free from inescapable human limitations and that God is partial and thus to be guilty of both spiritual arrogance and blasphemy. Since no religion is final and perfect, each can greatly benefit from a dialogue with other religion.[95]

In fact, for Gandhi, every human being has a unique psychological and spiritual constitution. He cannot leap out of it anymore than he can jump out of his body. Every God is therefore someone's God, that is, his or her way of understanding the cosmic spirit. No individual can avoid looking at the cosmic power through his own eyes and conceptualizing it in terms of his uniquely personal dispositions, tendencies and needs. Since the very idea of a personal God has its origin to man's moral and emotional needs, and the latter vary from individual to individual, Gandhi insists that one cannot consistently accept the legitimacy of a personal God and deny each individual's right to form his own distinctive conception of Him.[96] According to him, "Religion represents the way man conceives and relates himself to God".[97] At another place, he writes, "The formal, customary, organized or historical religions center on the personal, and the pure or eternal religion around the impersonal God. For Gandhi Hinduism, Christianity, Judaism, Islam and the other religion all based on specific conceptions of a personal God. They involve distinct forms of prayer, worship, rituals and beliefs about His nature and relation to the world, and are sectarian."[98]

The true or pure religion lies beyond them, and has nothing more and nothing less than recognizing that the universe is pervaded and governed by a cosmic and organizing one's entire life accordingly. It is basically living in the contrast, intimate and unmediated presence of the cosmic spirit, and represents the purest form of spirituality. Thus, the true religion 'transcends [but] does not supersede' organized religions and constitutes their common 'basis' and connecting 'link'.

Education

In the new world order, which will be based on the foundations of truth and non-violence, education will also play a very healthy and positive role. For Gandhi, to establish a new society, a new approach to education will be required. That is why, he did a very serious and continuous effort with his fellow-beings.[99]

For Gandhi, the ultimate aim of each and every type of education is to flourish inherent qualities of an individual. An education system, where an individual's intellectual, spiritual and physical aspects are adhered, will be called as true education.[100]

It can be assumed that an individual's personality has three aspects, viz., intelligence, emotion and appetite. Theoretically, these may be termed by different terminologies but in actual practice they are not different from each other. In psychology, these is called as intelligence, emotions and appetite, whereas in daily life as wisdom (*Gyan*), devotion (*Bhakti*) and service (*Karma*). All these three elements are there within an individual's inherent personality. Now how to make a comprehensive, consistent and balanced development of these aspects of human personality would be the ultimate aim of education in Gandhian philosophy.[101]

Through the proper constructive programme, Gandhi outlined the system of education in his own and unique way, in the following manner:

Basic Education

The objective of the basic education is that of intellectual, physical and moral development of the children through the medium of a handicraft. But I hold that any scheme, which is sound from the educative point of view and effectively managed, is bound to be sound economically.[102] Basic education links the children, whether of the cities or the villages, to all that is best and lasting in India. It develops both the body and mind, and keeps the child rooted to the soil with a glorious vision of the future in the realization of which he or she begins to take his or her share from the very commencement of him or her career in school.[103]

Let us now have a cursory glance at the fundamentals of basic education:

- All education to be true must be self-supporting, that is to say, in the end it will pay its expenses excepting the capital which will remain intact.
- In it the cunning of the hand will be utilized even up to the final stage, that is to say, hands of the pupils will be skillfully working at some industry for some period during the day.
- All education must be imparted through the medium of the provincial language.
- In this scheme of education there is no room for giving sectional religious training. Fundamental universal ethics will have full scope.
- This education, whether it is confined to children or adults, male or female, will find its way to the home of the pupils.
- Since millions of students receiving this education will consider themselves as of the whole of India, they must learn an inter-provincial language. This common inter-provincial speech can only be Hindustani written in *Nagari* or *Urdu* scripts. Therefore, pupils have to master both the scripts.[104]

The introduction of manual training, as an important part of basic education, will serve a double purpose in a poor country like ours. It will pay for the education of our children and teach them an occupation on which they can fall back in after-life, if they choose, for earning a living. Such a system must make our children self-reliant. Nothing will demoralize the nation so much as that we should learn to despise labour.[105]

Higher Education

While discussing about higher education Gandhi said, "I would revolutionize college education and relate it to national necessities. There would be degrees for mechanical and other engineers. They would be attached to the different industries which should pay for the training of the graduates they need. Thus, the Tatas would be expected to run a college for training engineers under the supervision of the state, the mill associations would run among them a college for training graduates whom they need."

Similarly, Gandhi said, for the other industries that may be named. Commerce will have its college. There remain arts, medicine and agriculture. Several private arts colleges are today self-supporting. The state would, therefore, cease to run its own. Medical colleges would be attached to certified hospitals. As they are popular among moneyed men, they may be expected by voluntary contributions to support medical colleges. And agricultural colleges to be worthy of the name must be self-supporting. Gandhi said that he had a painful experience of some agricultural graduates. Their knowledge is superficial. They lack practical experience. But if they had their apprenticeship on farms, which are self-restrained and answer the requirements of the country, they would not have to gain experience after getting their degrees and at the expense of their employers.[106]

The suggestion has often being made that in order to make education compulsory, or even available to every boy and girl wishing to receive education, our schools and colleges should become almost, if not wholly, self-supporting not through donation or state aid or fees extracted from students, but through remuneration work done by the students themselves. This can only be done by making industrial training compulsory. And it is possible only when our students begin to recognize the dignity of labour. Gandhi was totally against the concept of scholarship. In his own words:

> Is it not far better that we find work for poor students than that we pauperize them by providing free studentship? It is impossible to exaggerate the harm we do to Indian youth by filling their minds with the false notion that it is ungentlemanly to labour with one's hands and feet for one's livelihood or schooling. The harm done is moral and material, indeed much more moral than material. A free ship lies and should lie like a load upon a conscientious lad's mind throughout his whole life. No one likes to be reminded in after life that he had to depend upon charity for his education. Contrarily

> where is the person who will not recall with pride those days if he had the good fortune to have had them when he worked in a carpentry shop or the like for the sake of education himself – mind, body, and soul?[107]

Further, Gandhi presents a very unique concept of university education. He said:

> Universities will look after the whole of the field of education and will prepare and approve courses of studies in the various departments of education. No private school should be run without the previous sanction of the respective Universities. University charters should be given liberally to any body of persons of proved worth and integrity, it being always understood that the Universities will not cost the state anything except that it will bear the cost of running a Central Education Department.[108]

About adult education, Gandhi said that if I had charge of adult education, I should begin with opening the minds of the adult pupils to the greatness and vastness of their country. The villager's India is contained in his village. If he goes to another village, he talks of his own village as his home. Hindustan is for him a geographical term. We have no notion of the ignorance prevailing in the villages. The villages know nothing of foreign rule and its evils ... they do not know that the foreigner's presence is due to their own weakness and their ignorance of the power they possess to rid themselves of the foreign rule. Gandhi continues "My adult education means, therefore, first, true political education of the adult by word of mouth ... side by side with the education by mouth will be the literary education. This is itself a specially. Many methods are tried in order to shorten the period of education."[109]

Gandhi believes that mass illiteracy is India's sin and shame and must be liquidated ... . Of course, the literacy campaign must not begin and end with knowledge of the spread of useful knowledge. The dry knowledge of the three R's is not even now, it can never be, a permanent part of the village's life. They must have knowledge given to them which they must use daily. It must not be thrust upon them. They should have the appetite for it. What they today is something they neither want nor appreciate. Give the villagers village arithmetic, village geography, village history and the literary knowledge that they must use daily, i.e., reading and writing letters, etc. They will treasure such knowledge and pass on to the other stages. They have no use for books which give them nothing of daily use.[110]

About religious education, Gandhian philosophy is very much clear. Gandhi does not believe that state can concern itself or cope with religious education. He believes that religious education must be the sole concern of religious associations. He is against the mixing up of religion and ethics. In his own words:

> I believe that fundamental ethics is common to all religions. Teaching of fundamental ethics is undoubtedly a function of the state. By religion I have not in mind fundamental ethics but what goes by the name of denominationalism. We have suffered enough from State-aided religion and a State Church. A society or a group, which depends partly or wholly on State aid for the existence of its religion, does not deserve, or, better still, does not have any religion worth the name.[111]

By explaining the curriculum of religious education, Gandhi said that it should include a study of the tenets of faith other than one's. For this purpose the students should be trained to cultivate the habit of understanding and appreciating the doctrines of various great religions of the world in a spirit of reverence and broad-minded tolerance. This, if properly done, would help to give them a spiritual assurance and a better appreciation of their own religion ... there is one rule, however, which should always be kept in mind while studying all great religion and, that is, that one should study them only through the writings of known votaries of the respective religions.[112]

As for women's education, Gandhi was not very much sure whether it should be different from men's and when it should begin. But he was a firm supporter that women should have the same facilities as men and even special facilities where necessary.[113]

The most important aspect of the Gandhian philosophy of education is the role played by teachers. For Gandhi, all teachers should essentially be men of character.[114] Even if teacher is not an expert in his subject, he must be a man of character. The teacher who is concerned only with syllabus to be taught, not with the character of his student, he would not be called as true teacher at all. Thus, education of character is much more important than the literary education.

Apart from a man of character, a teacher must also be very much aware about the new development in his field. A teacher should always be ready for new initiative. In Gandhi's own words:

> ... every teacher, if he is to do full justice to his pupils, will have to prepare the daily lesson from the material available to him. This, too

> he will have to suit to the special requirements of his class. Real education has to draw out the best from the boys and girls to be educated. This can never be done by packing ill-assorted and unwarranted information into the heads of the pupils.[115]

It means, a teacher should lead a more scholastic life than a student. A good teacher should always try to evolve new and more better ways of teaching so that the students can raise questions and the teacher should try to solve them in a more gentle and intelligent way.

Like teacher's responsibility, Gandhi also stresses on student's sense of duty. He tells that students should keep their faith in their teachers. A good and healthy teacher-student relationship would be there in Gandhian scheme of education.

The above scheme of education in Gandhian thought shows that education system, which is very much unique here, will play vibrant role for societal reconstruction. As Gandhi said that the aim of education should be to reconstruct the whole society and not only a student. New society will be created by a new education system. This system will definitely be not partial or individual in nature but it would be totally comprehensive and balanced one. It will produce such a kind of curious students who are really devoted for the development of their society.

Position of Women

In the plan of life based on non-violence, women have as much right to shape their own destiny as men. But as every right in a non-violent society proceeds from the previous performance of a duty, it follows that rules of social conduct must be framed by mutual cooperation and constitution. The non-violent society would be based on the following principle:

> Woman is the companion of man gifted with equal mental capacities, she has the right to participate in every minute detail in the activities of man and she has an equal right of freedom and liberty with him. She is entitled to a supreme place in her own sphere of activity as man is in his. This ought to be the natural condition of things and not as a result only of learning to read and write. By sheer force of a vicious custom, even the most ignorant and worthless men have been enjoying a superiority over women which they do not deserve and ought not to have. Many of our movements stop half way because of the conditions of our women. Much of our work alone does not yield appropriate results; our lot is like that of the

penny-wise and pound foolish trader who does not employ enough capital in his business.[116]

Gandhi tried to see the difference between the sexes in wider perspective and kept his faith in fundamental unity. He was of the opinion that both of them are the creation of God. In Gandhi's words:

> My own opinion is that, just as fundamentally man and woman are one, their problem must be one in essence. The two live the same lives have the same feelings. Each is a complement of the other. The one cannot live without the other's active help. Nevertheless there is no doubt that at some point there is bifurcation. Whilst both are fundamentally one, it is also equally true that in the form there is a vital difference between the two. Hence, the vocation of the two also must be different. The duty of motherhood, which the vast majority of women will always undertake, requires qualities which man need not possess. She is passive, he is active. She is essentially mistress of the house. He is the breadwinner; she is the keeper and distributor of the bread. She is the caretaker in every sense of the term. The art of bringing up the infants of the race is her special and sole prerogative. Without her care the race would become extinct.[117]

For Gandhi, equality of sexes does not mean equality of occupations. Nature has created sexes as complements of each other. Their functions are defined as their forms.[118] Gandhi was never in favour of the modern conception of equality of occupations. There may be no legal bar against a woman hunting or wielding a lance. But she instinctively recoils from a function that belongs to man.[119]

It shows that in Gandhian philosophy man and woman are of equal rank but they are not identical. They are a peerless pair being supplementary to one another. Each helps the other, so that without the one the existence of the other cannot be expected, and therefore it follows as a necessary corollary from these facts that anything that impairs the status of either will involve the equal ruination of both.

Actually, Gandhi was of the view that man and woman are different in their physical construction, thus their nature and qualities are different. That is why, their education and workplace will automatically be different from each other. Gandhi says:

> In framing any scheme of women's education this cordial truth must be constantly kept in mind. Man is supreme in the outward activities of a married pair and, therefore, it is the fitness of things that he should have a greater knowledge thereof.[120]

For Gandhi, home life is entirely the sphere of women and, therefore, in domestic affairs, in the upbringing and education of children, women ought to have more knowledge. Not that knowledge should be divided into watertight compartments, or that some branches of knowledge should be closed to any one, but unless courses of instruction are based on a discriminating appreciation of these basic principles, the fullest life of man and woman cannot be developed.[121]

Gandhi thought that it was the irrational social norms and practices which have degraded women's position in the society. Accordingly, the legal and customary status of women is bad enough throughout and demands radical alteration.[122] Gandhi says:

> Legislation has been mostly the handiwork of man; and man has not always been fair and discriminating in performing that self-appointed task. The largest part of our effort, in promoting the regeneration of women, should be directed towards remaining those blemishes which are represented in our *Shastras* as the necessary and ingrained characteristics of women. Who will attempt this and how?[123]

Gandhi further added,

> In my humble opinion, in order to make the attempt we will have to produce women, pure, firm and self-controlled as *Sita, Damayanti and Draupadi*. If we do produce them, such modern sisters will have the same authority as the *Shastras*. We will feel ashamed of the stray reflections on them in our *Smritis*, and will soon forget them. Such revolutions have occurred in Hinduism in the past, and will still take place in future, leading to the stability of our faith.[124]

In this way, in a unique non-violent and truthful world order, women will play a important role. By flourishing their feminine qualities women will contribute their essential role in the development of the society. Gandhi said that when a woman whom we all call *abala* becomes *sabala*, all those who are helpless will become powerful.[125] Thus, women are more responsible for the societal development.

Hence, Gandhi presented a very comprehensive and balanced model of a new world order, which is morally oriented and spiritually directed. All the aspects of this society, whether it is politics, economics, education, religion etc., are aimed at flourishing human values. For Gandhi all our social behaviour is oriented towards the implementation of truthful and non-violent society. Thus, politics, economics, education etc. will be assumed as instruments to achieve this aim. Therefore, all these different aspects of society are interlinked. There is fundamental unity among these institutions and all of them are looking towards the development of truthful and non-violent society. Only a comprehensive physical, moral and spiritual enhancement of society will make it a just and all-encompassing society.

The above analytical discussion reveals that truth and non-violence, which may seem meta-narratives in its nature, are the basis of Gandhian philosophy. Gandhi believes that only truth and non-violence are the ultimate reality and therefore the last objective of life to be achieved. But, postmodernist thinkers are contrary to any conception of meta-narratives whether it is truth, culture or discourse on identity.

Notes

1. *Bhagavad Gita*, 17.26–17.28.
2. *Young India* (1921) Ahmedabad, Navajivan Publications.
3. *Mundaka Upanishad*, 111,1.6.
4. *Taittiriya Upanishad*, 1,11,1.
5. Raghavan N. Iyer op. cit., p. 163.
6. Arne Naess, op. cit.
7. M.K. Gandhi (1947) *Ramanama*, Karachi, p. 76.
8. M.K. Gandhi (1961) V.B. Kher (Comp. and Ed.) *In Search of Supreme*, Ahmedabad, Navajivan Publication, Vol. I, pp. 5-6.
9. M.K. Gandhi op. cit., p. 8.
10. Arne Naess, op. cit., p. 24.
11. Ibid.
12. *Young India*, 31–12–1931, p. 428.
13. Bhikhu Parekh, op. cit., p. 70.
14. Collective Works of Mahatma Gandhi (CWMG), Vol. 50, p. 200.
15. *Hind Swaraj*, 12 July 1947.
16. R.K. Prabhu and U.R. Rao (1945) *The Mind of Mahatma Gandhi*, London, Oxford University, p. 17.
17. Arne Naess, op. cit., p. 28.
18. Ibid., p. 30
19. Ibid., p. 28.
20. M.K. Gandhi, op. cit., p. IX.
21. *Young India*, 17–11–1921.
22. Arne Naess, op. cit., pp. 38–39.
23. *Young India*, 4–12–1924, p. 398.
24. *Harijan*, 23–3–1947, p. 78.
25. M.K. Gandhi, *Yervada Mandir*, pp. 8–9.

26. Ibid., p. 37.
27. *Young India*, 4–6–1925.
28. Dashvakalik, Chapter 1. Also see, Dashvakalik, Chapter 4, Gatha-9.
29. *Harijan*, 28–3–1936.
30. *Harijan*, 7–9–1735, p. 234.
31. *Young India*, 2–4–1937.
32. *Harijan*, 27–7–1940.
33. Krishna Kripalani (1960) (comp. and ed.) *All Men are Brothers*, Ahmedabad, Navajivan Publications, p. 114.
34. Ibid., p. 121.
35. Ibid., p. 122.
36. N.K. Bose (1948) *Selections from Gandhi*, Ahmedabad, Navajivan Publications, p. 147.
37. Ibid.
38. Krishna Kripalani (1960) (comp. and ed.) *All Men are Brothers*, Ahmedabad, Navajivan Publications, p. 122.
39. *Speeches and Writings of Mahatma Gandhi*, 4rth Publication, Madras, p. 346.
40. Arne Naess op. cit., pp. 49–50.
41. Ibid., p. 152.
42. N.K. Bose op. cit., p. 147.
43. Ibid., p. 18.
44. Ibid., p. 16.
45. *Young India*, 21–11–1926.
46. N.K. Bose op. cit., p. 154.
47. *Young India*, 21–11–1926.
48. Ibid., 15–07–1939.
49. *Harijan*, 15–7–1939.
50. N.K. Bose op. cit., p. 16.
51. Ibid., p. 154.
52. *Harijan*, May 14, 1938.
53. *Harijan*, September, 22–1940, p. 299.
54. R.K. Prabhu and U.R. Rao (comp.) (1945) *The Mind of Mahatma Gandhi*, London, Oxford University Press.
55. Ronald J. Terchek (1998) *Gandhi Struggling for Autonomy*, New Delhi, Vistaar Publication, p. 161.
56. Manmohan Choudhuri (1989) *Exploring Gandhi*, New Delhi, Gandhi Peace Foundation, p. 157.
57. *Collected Works of Mahatma Gandhi*, Vol. 72, pp. 403–04.
58. *Harijan*, 1–9–1940
59. *India of My Dreams*, p. 100.

60. Manmohan Choudhuri (1989) *Exploring Gandhi*, New Delhi, Gandhi Peace Foundation, p. 105.
61. *The Modern Review*, 1935, p. 142.
62. Thomas Vettickal (2002) *Gandhian Sarvodaya Realizing A Realistic Utopia*, New Delhi, Gyan Publishing House, p. 23.
63. "The means may be likened to a seed, the end to a tree; and there is just the same inviolable connection between the means and the ends as there is between the seed and the tree. I am not likely to obtain the result flowing from the worship of God by laying myself prostrate before Satan".
    Krishna Kripalani (comp. and ed.) (1958) *All Men are Brothers*, Ahmedabad, Navajivan Publishing House, p. 108.
64. *Hind Swaraj*, p. 71.
65. *Hind Swaraj*, p. 74.
66. Ibid., p. 75.
67. Ibid.
68. Ibid., pp. 71–72.
69. M.P. Mathai *Mahatma Gandhi's World View*, p. 251.
70. *Young India*, July 28, 1920.
71. *Harijan*, June 19, 1940.
72. As Gandhi himself did it in the year 1922 at Chauri Chura Movement.
73. *India of My Dreams*, pp. 36–38.
74. *Harijan*, 18–3–1939.
75. Ibid., 21–4–1946.
76. Ibid., 13–10–1940.
77. Thomas Vettickal (2002) *Gandhian Sarvodaya: Realizing A Realistic Utopia*, New Delhi, Gyan Publishing House, pp. 85–86.
78. *Young India*, 13–10–1921.
79. *Harijan*, 9–10–1937.
80. *Young India*, 15–11–1928.
81. *Harijan*, 15–1–1938.
82. *Constructive Programme*, pp. 20–21.
83. Ibid.
84. *India of My Dreams*, pp. 73–74.
85. *Hind Swaraj*, p. 8.
86. *India of My Dreams*, pp. 47–48.
87. *Hind Swaraj*, pp. 7–8.
88. *Harijan*, 2–11–1934.
89. Ibid., 29–8–1936.
90. *India of My Dreams*, p. 96.
91. *Young India*, 27 November, 1924.
92. Raghavan N. Iyer, op. cit., Vol. I, p. 542.

93. *Young India*, September 22, 1927.
94. Raghavan N. Iyer, op. cit., Vol. 11, p. 539.
95. *Young India*, January 19, 1928.
96. See, Bhikhu Parekh (1989) *Gandhi's Politcal Philosopy*, London, Macmillan Press.
97. *Collective Works of Mahatma Gandhi*, Vol. 50, p. 188.
98. *Young India*, 11–8–1920.
99. *Harijan*, 11–9–1937.
100. V.T. Patil (ed.) (1983) *Studies on Gandhi*, New Delhi, Sterling Publishers, p. 177.
101. Dr Ramjee Singh (1989) *Gandhi Darsan Mimansa*, Patna, Bihar Hindi Grantha Academy, p. 249.
102. *Harijan*, 6–4–1940.
103. *Constructive Programme*, pp. 15–16.
104. *Harijan*, 2–11–1947.
105. *Young India*, 1–9–1921.
106. *Harijan*, 31–7–1937.
107. *Young India*, 2–8–1928.
108. *Harijan*, 2–10–1937.
109. *Constructive Programme*, pp. 16–17.
110. *Harijan*, 22–6–1940.
111. Ibid., 23–3–1947.
112. *Young India*, 6–12–1928.
113. *India of My Dreams*, p. 201.
114. *India of My Dreams*, p. 201.
115. *Harijan*, 1–12–1933.
116. *India of My Dreams*, pp. 223–226.
117. *Collected Works of Mahatma Gandhi*, pp. 208–9.
118. *Harijan*, 2–12–1939.
119. *Harijan*, 2–12–1939.
120. *India of My Dream*, p. 231.
121. Ibid.
122. *Constructive Programme*, pp. 17–18.
123. *Speeches and Writings of Mahatma Gandhi*, p. 4242.
124. *India of My Dreams*, p. 225.
125. Message to All India Women's Conference, December 23, 1936.

5

A Critical Evaluation

The extensive studies referred to in previous chapters thus suggest that postmodernism and Gandhism are two different philosophies. Even though they look to be identical, yet when studied deeply they are different from each other. Gandhian philosophy is such an all-encampassing and comprehensive one that it would not be justified to categorize under any particular category whether it is premodern, modern or postmodern. The discussion follows shall try to throw lights on this assumption.

Let us start our critical evaluation by keeping both these philosophies, i.e., postmodernist and Gandhism, parallel to each other. The first facet of the postmodern philosophy is localism. As we all know, postmodernists are away from any conception of meta-narrative or grand-narrative. They reject the idea that there are essential, universal concepts such as class, history or mode of production in the world. Instead, they argue that truth, knowledge and understanding are located within particular contexts. Completeness and consistency in a system of phenomenon and of its representations is impossible. Analysis never ends. As a result, postmodernists are robust critics of unity whenever it is claimed to appear, the unity of the world, of knowledge, of society, of self, of the meaning, of the word.[1] Actually, postmodernist thinkers have no tolerance for the values of Enlightenment. Reason, universality, morality and progress – all these Enlightenment features mean nothing to them. They see the world as a dance of the demonstratively creative and creatively destructed God.

They proclaim not only the 'death of God' but also the 'death of morality and metaphysics'. When truth and reason are dead, what becomes of knowledge? Postmodernism considers all types as well as sources of knowledge with equal skepticism. There is hardly any difference between science and magic. For postmodernists, knowledge is acquired not through inquiry but by imagination. As such, fiction rather than philosophy, and narratives rather than theory, provide a better perspective on human behaviour. Wittgenstein argued that all we have is language, even though its re-presentation of the reality is, at best, approximate and faulty. Rorty asserts that we should drop even the idea of language as representation, and the postmodern project should consist only of attempts 'to de-divinize the world'.[2] Irony, ridicule and parody are the basic tools with which this postmodernist goal is to be achieved.[3]

Jean-Francois Lyotard, one of the propounders of the postmodernist philosophy, writes: "I define postmodern as incredulity towards meta-narratives."[4] Lyotard rejects the idea of grand direction, meaning and moral path of human 'development'. Lyotard has in mind the teleology of Marxism, the certainty of science and the morality of Christianity.[5] Lyotard and Rorty share with Michel Foucault the idea that knowledge is not metaphysical, transcendental or universal. Foucault characterized his theory of localism through the unique relationship between 'power' and 'knowledge'. Accordingly, knowledge, discourse and power are the keywords through which the postmodernist society develops. Foucault instructs us to develop action, thought and desires by proliferation, juxtaposition and disjunction and to prefer what is positive and multiple, difference over uniformity, flows over units and mobile arrangements over system. Believe that what is productive is not sedentary but nomadic. All the action in the postmodernist society is moving towards instability rather than stability. By explaining the nature of knowledge, Foucault says: "Knowledge is not metaphysical, transcendental or universal. Rather, it is specific to particular times and spaces."[6]

Similarly, Jean Jacques Derrida also accepts localism as the basic feature of the postmodernist society. He develops his unique principle of deconstruction. Deconstruction is associated with 'undoing' of the binaries of Western philosophy and its extension into the field of literature and postcolonial theory. To deconstruct is to take apart, to undo, in order to seek out and display the assumption of a text. In particular, deconstruction involves the dismantling of the hierarchical conceptual opposition such as man/woman, black/white, reality/appearance, nature/culture, reason/madness etc., which serve to guarantee truth by excluding and devaluing the 'inferior' part of the binary.

Hence, all the postmodernist philosophers move towards truth and knowledge with the deconstructive (Derrida), fragmentative (Foucault) and linguistic (Lyotard) approach. They are insisting that truth is not something we will discover but it is something which will be created within a continuous process.

Interestingly, truth seems to play a significant role in the postmodernist philosophy just like in the Gandhian philosophy. Gandhi was critical of any fixed definition of truth. Once it was asked to Gandhi: "What is truth?" He replied: "A difficult question; but I have solved it for myself by saying that it is what the voice within tell you."[7] Just like the postmodernists' rejection of foundationalism Gandhi's attempt was to justify realist knowledge through recourse to 'basic', 'fundamental' or 'incorrigible cognition'. According to Gandhi, one of the greatest evils of modern political and other human relations has been our tendency to absolutise what is necessarily relative. Gandhi's insistence on the relativity of all political, religious and other human perspectives is a justification for toleration and respect for others' relative perspectives to truth and reality. That is why, Douglas Allen wrote:

> ... emphasis in Gandhi's political thinking on relativity of truth and the tolerance of and respect for multiple voices, diversity and an enriching pluralism of significant difference are similarities what one finds in various postmodernist political orientations.[8]

Accordingly, Gandhi accepts that in the way of struggle after truth we should try to provide due respect for the other's truth. Gandhi's own dynamic, open-ended, relative, experimentative approach with truth may be analysed here in the postmodernist philosophy of localism where the nature of truth is temporal, a-historical and contextual. For so many times, like postmodernists, Gandhi says: "What may appear truth to one person will often appear untruth to another person. But that need not worry the seeker."[9] But it does not mean that Gandhi's concept of truth is identical to the postmodernist truth. Though in Gandhian philosophy the relativity of truth is there, this relativity of truth has an ultimate aim, that is, to achieve the absolute truth. Gandhi himself said about this time and again:

> But for me, truth is the sovereign principle, which includes numerous other principles. This truth is not only truthfulness in word, but truthfulness in thought also, and not only the relative truth of our conception, but the *Absolute Truth*, the eternal Principle that is God. (Emphasis is mine)[10]

Here is a very important point to be noted in Gandhian philosophy, relative truth is a means to achieve the end, that is, absolute truth, which the postmodernist thinkers have failed to note, acknowledge and discuss. Their localism is an end in itself. Local culture, local traditions are important in their philosophy. Why? To give voice to the marginalized people so that they can also feel as a member of the society. A fragmented, ambiguous and uncertain quality of the world, marked by a higher level of reflexivity, is said to be a characteristic of the postmodern culture. This goes hand in hand with the stress on contingency, irony and the blurring of cultural boundaries. Texts are typified by the self-conscious, and intertexuality. For some thinkers, postmodern culture heralds the collapse of the modern distribution between the real and simulations. That is why, some thinkers assume that postmodernism celebrates egoism in the name of localism. What world and whose world they will achieve with this concept of fragmentation are not clear in their philosophical approach. But Gandhian philosophy is very much clear on this sphere. He gave us the idea of unity within diversity. In his words:

> A drop torn from the ocean perishes without doing any good. If it remains a part of the ocean, it shares the glory of carrying on its bosom a fleet of mighty ships.[11]

Besides truth, non-violence is another grand-narrative in Gandhian philosophy. *Ahimsa* (non-violence) means avoiding injury to anybody on earth in thought, word or deed.[12] Moreover, this is possible only if we are ready to vanish our ego. We have to reduce ourselves up to zero.[13] In order to understand non-violence, as suggested by Gandhi and others, it is imperative to understand how selfless action is compatible with complete self-realization of the individual person. Gandhi says, to make oneself a zero is to realize oneself completely. When the egotism/ego vanishes, something else grows – that ingredient of the person that tends to identify itself with God, with humanity, all that lives. Therefore, according to Gandhi, once the reduction of one's egotism takes place, the self is complete, one comes face to face with God, finds truth, and realises the Universal Self.[14] It shows that there is an intimate relationship between a belief in the ultimate oneness of all that lives and the belief that one cannot reach one's own complete freedom without bringing about the freedom of others, or remove all feelings of pain by relieving the pain of others. He expressed this concept of *advaita* (non-duality) in the following words:

> I do not believe ... that an individual may gain spiritually and those who around him suffer. I believe in advaita (non-duality), I believe in the essential unity of man and, for that matter, of all that lives. Therefore I believe that if one man gains spiritually, the whole world gains with him and, if one man falls, the whole world falls to that extent.[15]

Gandhi's thought, when approaching the philosophical question, is close to that of *Advaita Vedanta*. In this system, the word closest to the meaning of 'self' (individual self) is '*jiva*' to that of 'Self' (universal self) is 'Atman', and 'God' in the writings of Gandhi, 'Brahman'.[16] With this interesting power of discrimination between 'self' and 'Self', the universality of the self is discerned. This leads to the conception of the essential oneness of all humanity. That is why, Gandhi believed in the essential unity of man and for that matter of all that lives.[17] One's own self-realization must therefore somehow include that of others. The requirement of helping the self-realization of others, and hurting nobody, follows without further assumptions. This approach towards universal unity and spiritual oneness is found totally missing in postmodernist thinking. Thus, Gandhian thought cannot be categorized as postmodernist philosophy.

Further, according to the anti-essentialist postmodernists, the speaking subject is dependent on the prior existence of the discursive position. Truth is not so much found as made and identities are discursive constructions. Instead of the scientific certainty of structuralism, they offer us irony, an awareness of the contingent understanding which lacks firm universal foundations. Thinkers like Michel Foucault, Chandra Talpade Mohanty, Gayatri Spivak and others are some of the pioneers in this direction. For postmodernist anti-essentialist thinkers, we are constituted as individuals in a social process using socially shared materials. This is commonly understood as socialization or articulation. Without articulation, we should not be persons, as we have understood that notion in our everyday lives. Without language, the concepts of personhood and identity would be unintelligible to us. There are no transcendental or a-historical elements to what is to be a person. Identity is very social and cultural.[18] If we feel that we have a unified identity from birth to death, it is only because we construct a controlling story or narrative of the self about ourselves.[19] " ... the inner core of the subject was not autonomous and self-sufficient, but was formed in relation to significant others', who mediated to the subject, the values, meaning and symbols – the culture – of the world he/she inhabited." Foucault explains it in the following manner:

> Subjects are not the producers of discourse but rather 'positions' in discourse which can be occupied by [any] individuals. The subject is not the 'speaking consciousness', nor 'the author' of the formulation [of discourse] but a position which may be filled in certain conditions by various individuals. The subject is shaped by power through his/her body rather than through his/her consciousness. [Therefore], we should try to grasp subjection in its material instance as a constitution of subjects.[20]

It shows that Foucault concentrates on issues of discourse, discipline and power. Subjects are understood as discursive constructions and the products of power, which the discourse regulates.

Contrary to that, Gandhian philosophy assumes the importance of the individual instead of talking about their death! In his philosophy, the individual is not only a speaking-conscious being, but also a creator or formulator of social values and social norms. He himself says:

> If the individual ceases to count, what is left of society? Individual freedom alone can make man voluntarily surrender himself completely to the service of society. If it is wrested from him, he becomes an automation and society is ruined. No society can possibly be built on a denial of individual freedom.[21]

Actually, Gandhi's autonomous individual who governs himself resists any source of domination, whether it is a controlled/limited ancient society or the modern liberal world order. Gandhi holds that no text and no economic process can claim to possess a truth that displaces the autonomy of individuals. He says:

> Man is the maker of his own destiny in the sense that he has freedom of choice as to the manner in which he uses that freedom. But he is no controller of the results. The moment he thinks he is, he comes to grief.[22]

He repeatedly makes it clear by saying,

> Man's happiness really lies in contentment. He who is discontented, however much he possessed, becomes a slave to his desires. All the sages have declared from the housetops that man can be his own worst enemy as well as his best friend. To be free or to be a slave lies in his own hands. And what is true for the individual is true for society.[23]

Thus, Gandhi's individual is a very conscious being. Unlike the postmodernists' subject, Gandhi's subject is not only the maker of his own destiny, but also a choice-maker. He can hear his own inner voice and takes decisions accordingly. Gandhi enlists his theory of conscience in his arguments on behalf of *satyagraha* or civil disobedience. He expects the *satyagrahi* to be honest to her/his deepest convictions and ready to suffer on behalf of her/his commitments. Gandhi goes on to argue that those who witness this suffering will be prompted by their conscience and be converted.[24] Thus, in Gandhian thought, there is not any 'death of men' and 'end of metaphysics' as it is there in postmodernist philosophy. It once again follows that he is not a postmodernist thinker.

Further, some of the postmodern anti-essentialist scholars are discussing in favour of different kinds of marginalized and subaltern movements to make them free from domination and exploitation. Similarly, Gandhian thought is also concerned with different downtrodden movements. That is why, for Ronald J. Terchek, "the postmodern Gandhi is also talking about so many revolutions and movements for marginalized and subaltern sections of the society who are exploited and dominated by centralized powerful elite classes".[25] Like Spivak and Foucault, Gandhi never takes religious texts as sacrosanct and pure, but he studies those texts as a seeker after truth. Terchek notes: "His archaeological approach does not look at traditional texts or practises sacrosanct expression of unchangeable knowledge. Rather, he wants to move beyond standard readings of traditional practices and expose those that spawn domination".[26]

Similarly, in the context of women or gender relations, Gandhian philosophy seems to be completely identical with the postmodernist philosophy. Gandhi spoke out against the arbitrary rules of society, which our female folk are forced to follow. In this context, Gandhi says:

> ... the ancient laws were made by seers who were men. The woman's experience, therefore, is not represented in them. Strictly speaking, as between man and woman, neither should be regarded as superior or inferior.[27]

According to Gandhi, the woman has been suppressed under custom and law for which man was responsible and in the shaping of which she had no hand. Since postmodernist feminists like Cathrien Mackinnon and Carol Gilligon also talk about the deconstruction of all the historical, structural and hierarchical notions in the society, several thinkers insist that the Gandhian philosophy can be categorized as a postmodernist philosophy.

But this is just an illusion. Unlike postmodernist thinkers, Gandhi in his *Hind Swaraj* writes: "The *Swaraj* of my ... our ... dream recognizes no race or religious monopoly neither of the limited persons nor for all ..."[28] *Swaraj* is a society where every individual, whether man or woman, is a self-sufficient, self-disciplined and self-conscious being. It is a self-governed society. It will not be governed by any extended power at all.

Further, in the context of decentralization and dispersion of powers, the Gandhian approach was different from others. Gandhi says:

> In this structure composed of innumerable villages there will be ever widening, never ascending circles. Life will not be a pyramid with the apex sustained by the bottom. But it will be an oceanic circle whose centre will be the individual always ready to perish for the circle of villages, till at last the whole becomes one life composed of individuals, never aggressive in their arrogance but ever humble, sharing the majority of the oceanic circles of which they are integral units.[29]

The above lines well affirm that Gandhi's theory of *Swaraj* and decentralization is very different from that of the Derridian theory of deconstruction and the Foucauldian discourse of fragmentation of power. Postmodernist thinkers emphasize differences but negate any possibility of coherence. Contrary to that, Gandhian philosophy emphasizes certain grand or universal values, viz., absolute truth, non-violence and *dharma*. Its objective is to create a more moral and humane socio-political-economic system. It is interesting to find that all the postmodernist thinkers talk about differences with equal stress. This also shows that there is a kind of unity that lies beneath their approach to differences. It further proves that there are some universal values in the universe about which Gandhian philosophy discusses at length. It also proves that unity is natural and differences are artificially created. Gandhian philosophy can never see individual or relative truth in the absence of universal or absolute truth. Both are parallel to each other. In his famous book *India of My Dreams*, Gandhi, while presenting the theory of Oceanic Circle, has accepted the fact that the individual's recognition and societal existence are complementary to each other. Thus, he cannot be categorized as a postmodernist thinker.

The third feature of the postmodernist philosophy is anti-rationalism. Philosophers like Foucault reject the Enlightenment's rational discourses. Foucault casts doubt on the Enlightenment understanding of progress. Knowledge as discourse does not unfold as historical evolution but is rather discontinuous. That is why, Foucault identifies significant epistemological breaks in knowledge across time and rejects any notion of *telo* or the inevitable direction of human society. He makes it obvious that there is a clear, distinctive and fine break between Enlightenment and post-Enlightenment thoughts. Foucault's thinking, along with the others', split with the premises of 'classical' Enlightenment thought. They assumed that knowledge is perspective in character. There cannot be one totalizing knowledge, which is able to grasp the 'objective' character of the world. Rather, we both have and require multiple viewpoints or truths by which to interpret a complex heterogeneous human existence. Postmodernist thinkers argue that the Enlightenment has created a rational and logical society, which is instrumental in nature. This instrumental rationality creates a kind of rational imperialism.

One can find the same line of thinking even in Gandhian philosophy which rejects the domination of rationality. Gandhi was of the opinion that experience, emotion, intuition etc. are the other aspects of an individual's personality, and these are as important as reason. In his words, "we resist the tyranny and domination of the modernity idols of science, rationalism and objectivity". The Enlightenment gave us narrow, oppressive, hierarchical, reductionist projects of rationalistic and scientific hegemony. However, the rational scientific discourse is only one of the many possible ways that human beings construct their stories about political reality. The scientific narrative does not have exclusive privileged access to political truth. Metaphysical spiritual narratives are other ways of constructing accounts that shed light on political truth and reality, and should not be reduced to scientific, rational, historical and other non-ethical and non-spiritual discourses.[30] This shows that Gandhi also approached the same postmodernist philosophy of rejection of reason. But, there is a difference. Just have a cursory glance at the following statement of Gandhi:

> I have come to the fundamental conclusion that if you want something really important to be done you must not merely satisfy the reason, you must move the head also. The appeal to reason is more to the head.[31]

For Gandhi, it is impossible to make a watertight compartmentalizing between head and heart, rationality and spirituality. According to him, rational ideas are the instrument not only to find out what is not right or untruth but also to know about truth in the real sense of the term. One is bound to go to the heart or sometimes irrational discussions! Both head and heart have their importance in Gandhian philosophy. Any discourse where only one, that is, either heart or head, works was not acceptable to Gandhi.

Once he wrote:

> [the] belief in God has to be based on faith which transcends reason. Indeed, even the so-called realisation has at bottom the elimination of faith without which it cannot be sustained.[32]

Gandhi was of the opinion that faith is more important than reason. Faith and belief are the medium through which one may achieve divinity but its existence cannot be proved merely by rationality. Further, what is truth? This will not only be decided by reason or head. To give a rational definition of truth in the absence of the cultural, institutional and historical background means to bow before the imperial-capitalist rationality.

Actually, all the postmodernist thinkers try to redefine the nature of truth not because they are striving to know about the essence of the truth like Gandhi, but they just want to avoid the domination or shackles of intellectual or rational power. That is why, Foucault argues in favour of dispersal of power, Derrida for deconstruction and Lyotard of a new grammatology.

However, for Gandhi, the issue is not that rationality has nothing to offer; he rejects traditional practices and ideas that he sees as 'irrational', such as child marriage or untouchability. For him, however, reason can overstep what he takes to be its appropriate boundaries; it cannot always be the sole arbiter to the claims of truth. He repeatedly insists that morality must meet some minimal rational standard.[33] He said:

> Rationalism is a hideous monster when it claims for itself omnipotence. Attribution of omnipotence to reason is as bad a piece of idolatry as is worship of stock and stone believing it to be God. I plead not for the suppression of reason, but [an appreciation of its inherent limits].[34]

In Gandhi's account, there are some things we know apart from reason. Our love, trust, forgiveness and generosity do not flow primarily from reason. Indeed, for some rationalists, their feelings may be misplaced; but not for Gandhi. He sees their disposition and the actions that flow from them embodying the best in human beings.

He also knows that the opposite of these dispositions is not always reason. When love or trust is involved, the choice is not invariably between them and reason, but between love and hate or trust and suspicion. To assume that reason should always be the arbiter is to misunderstand both its strengths and limitations. Reason can speak to an impulse to love, for example, but after a while, reason is exhausted and has nothing more to say. Gandhi wants to unite love, trust and forgiveness from calculation and join them to the development capacities of everyone. Actually, Gandhi does not deny the importance of reason in understanding oneself and the broader world. However, he holds it is only one way of organizing ideas and, in some cases, not the important one.[35]

In a nutshell, Gandhi was looking for a comprehensive and balanced approach. To define a society with its single determinants would be a patient attempt. In ancient times we tried to do it with the help of religion, in the modern era we did the same mental exercise with the help of reason and now in this postmodern era we are doing it with the help of language. However, a balanced and comprehensive approach is yet to be achieved. This is possible if religion, reason and morality all play their active, vibrant and comprehensive roles in their own spheres of action. A unique blend of both of these philosophies, that is, postmodernism and Gandhism, may go a long way towards unveiling a new horizon.

Notes

1. Lawrance Cahoone (ed.) (2003) *From Modernism to Postmodernism*, Oxford, Blackwell Publishers, p. 10.
2. Richard Rorty (1989) *Contingency, Irony and Solidarity*, Cambridge, Cambridge University Press.
3. See, Ziauddin Sardar (1998) *Postmodernism and the Other: The New Imperialism of Western Culture*, London, Pluto Press.
4. See Jean-Francois Lyotard (1984) *The Postmodern Condition*, Minneapolis, University of Minnesota Press.
5. Chris Baker (2000) *Cultural Studies: Theory and Practice*, London, Sage Publications, p. 21.
6. Michel Foucault (1984) "What is Enlightenment?" in Rabinow (ed.) *The Foucault Reader*, New York, Pantheon, p. 249.
7. Krishna Kripalani (1958) *All Men are Brothers*, Ahmedabad, Navajivan Publishing House, p. 94.

8. Douglas Allen (2000) "Gandhi, Contemporary Political Thinking and Self-other Relations", in B.N. Ray (ed.) *Contemporary Political Thinking*, New Delhi, Kanishka Publications, p. 139.
9. M.K. Gandhi (2001) *An Autobiography: The Story of My Experiments with Truth*, (Introduction), Ahmedabad, Navajivan Publishing House, p. xi.
10. Ibid. (Emphasis is the author's).
11. *Harijan*, 23rd March 1947.
12. Ibid., 7th September 1935.
13. "The seeker after truth should be humbler than the dust. The world crushes the dust under its feet, but the seeker after truth should so humble himself that even the dust could crush him. Only then, and not till then, will he have a glimpse of the truth." M.K. Gandhi, *The Story of My Experiments with Truth*, (Introduction), p. xii.
14. Arne Naess (1974) *Gandhi and Group Conflict: An Exploration of Satyagraha*, Oslo, Universitetsoflaget, p. 39.
15. *Young India*, 4th December 1924.
16. See, Mahadev Desai (1946) *The Gospel of Selfless Action for the Gita according to Gandhi*, Ahmedabad, Navajivan Publishing House.
17. *Young India*, 4th December 1924, p. 398.
18. S. Hall (1992) "The Question of Cultural Identity", in S. Hall, David Held and Toney McGrew (eds) *Modernity and its Future*, Cambridge, Polity Press, p. 277.
19. Ibid., p. 275.
20. Michel Foucault (1977) *The Archaeology of Knowledge*, London, Tavistock Publication, p. 97.
21. *Harijan*, 1st February 1942.
22. Ibid., 23rd March 1940.
23. Ibid., 1st February 1942.
24. *Young India*, 21 August 1921.
25. Ronald J. Terchek (2001) "Problematizing Modernity: Gandhi's Decentering Impulse", *Gandhi Marg*, Vol. 23, No. 1, p. 9.
26. Ibid., p. 11.
27. Raghavan N. Iyer (ed.) (1986) *The Moral and Political Writings of Mahatma Gandhi*, Vol. 3, Oxford, Clarendon Press, p. 394.
28. *Young India*, 26th March 1931.
29. *Harijan*, 28th July 1946.
30. Douglas Allen (2000) op. cit., p. 139.
31. See, Bhikhu Parekh (1998) *Gandhi's Political Philosophy: A Critical Examination*, London, Macmillan Press, p. 146.
32. R.K. Prabhu and U.R. Rao (1945) *The Mind of Mahatma Gandhi*, London, Oxford University Press, pp. 22–23.

33. Thomas Pantham (1998) "On Modernity, Rationality and Morality, Habermas and Gandhi", *Indian Journal of Social Sciences*, No. 2, pp. 187–208. Also see, Bhikhu Parekh op. cit., p. 74.
34. *Young India*, 27th June 1939.
35. See, V.R. Mehta (1992) *Foundations of Indian Political Thought*, New Delhi, Manohar, Chapter 2.

Bibliography

Bibliography on Gandhi

Primary Sources on Gandhi

Books

All are in the Eyes of God, Delhi, Publication Division, Ministry of Information and Broadcasting, Government of India, 1964.

An Autobiography or the Story of My Experiments with Truth, Ahmedabad, Navajivan Publishing House, 1927.

Ashram Observation in Action, Ahmedabad, Navajivan Publishing House, 1955.

Basic Education, Ahmedabad, Navajivan Publishing House, 1961.

Bread Labor: Gospel of Works, Ahmedabad, Navajivan Publishing House, 1960.

Communal Unity, Ahmedabad, Navajivan Publishing House, 1949.

Conquest of Self (comp. by R.K. Prabhu and U.R. Rao), Bombay, Thacker Co, 1946.

Constructive Programme: Its Meaning and Place, Ahmedabad, Navajivan Publishing House, 1961.

Delhi Diary, Ahmedabad, Navajivan Publishing House, 1948.

Democracy, Ahmedabad, Navajivan Publishing House, 1948.

Discourses on the Gita (trans. by B. Rama Iyer), Madras, S. Ganesan, 1930.

Fasting in Satyagraha: Its Use and Abuse, Ahmedabad, Navajivan Publishing House, 1965.

From Yervada Mandir (trans. by V.C. Desai), Ahmedabad, Navjivan Publishing House, 1957.

Gandhian Correspondences with the Government, 1942–1947, (comp. by Pyare Lal), Ahmedabad, Navajivan Publishing House, 1959 and 1965.

Gita According to Gandhi, Ahmedabad, Navajivan Publishing House, 1969.

Gita My Mother (edited by A.T. Hingorani), Bombay, Bhartiya Vidya Bhavan, 1965.

God is Truth (edited by A.T. Higorani), Bombay, Bharatiya Vidya Bhavan, 1962.

Hind Swaraj or Indian Home Rule, Ahmedabad, Navajivan Publishing House, 1938.

Hindu Dharma (edited by Bharatan Kumarappa), Ahmedabad, Navajivan Publishing House, 1938.

In Search of the Supreme (comp. and edited by V.B. Kher), 3 Vols., Ahmedabad, Navajivan Publishing House, 1961–62.

India of My Dream, Ahmedabad, Navajivan Publishing House, 1947.

My God (comp. by R.K. Prabhu), Ahmedabad, Navajivan Publishing House, 1962.

My Non-Violence (comp. and edited by S.K. Bandopadhyaya), Ahmedabad, Navajivan Publishing House, 1960.

My Philosophy of Life, Bombay, Pearl Publication Ltd, 1961.

My Religion (comp. and edited by Bhartan Kumarapa), Ahmedabad, Navajivan Publishing House, 1955.

My Socialism (comp. by R.K. Prabhu), Ahmedabad, Navajivan Publishing House, 1959.

My Varnashrama Dharma (edited by A.T. Hingorani), Bombay, Bharatiya Vidya Bhavan, 1965.

Non-Violence in Peace and War (edited by Mahadev Desai), Ahmedabad, Navajivan Publishing House, 1942.

Panchayat Raj (comp. by R.K. Prabhu), Ahmedabad, Navajivan Publishing House, 1959.

Political and National Life and Affairs (comp. and edited by V.B. Kher), Ahmedabad, Navajivan Publishing House, 1967.

Practical Non-Violence, Ahmedabad, Navajivan Publishing House, 1938.

Prohibition at Any Cost (comp. by R.K. Prabhu), Ahmedabad, Navajivan Publishing House, 1960.

Removal of Untouchability, Ahmedabad, Navajivan Publishing House, 1954.

Sarvodaya: Its Principles and Programme, Ahmedabad, Navajivan Publishing House, 1962.

Satyagraha in South Africa (trans. by V.G. Desai), Madras, S. Ganesan, 1928.

Selected Letters (comp. and trans. by V.G. Desai), I Series Ahmedabad, Navajivan Publishing House, 1949, II Series, 1962.

Selected Writing of Mahatma Gandhi, London, Faber and Faber Ltd, 1951.

Selection from Gandhi (comp. by N.K. Bose), Ahmedabad, Navajivan Publishing House, 1972.

Speeches and Writings of M.K. Gandhi (comp. by G.A. Natesan) Madras, G.A. Natesan & Co. 1937.

The Collected Works of Mahatma Gandhi, Delhi, The Publication Division, Ministry of Information and Broadcasting, Government of India, 1958–1971.

The Hindu Muslim Unity (edited by A.T. Hingorani), Bombay, Bhartiya Vidya Bhavan, 1965.

The Law of Love (edited by A.T. Hingorani), Bombay, Bhartiya Vidya Bhavan, 1962.

The Message of Mahatma Gandhi (comp. and edited by U.S. Mohan Rao), New Delhi, Publication Division, Ministry of Information and Broadcasting, Government of India, 1968.

The Selected Works of Mahatma Gandhi (edited by Shriman Narayan), Ahmedabad, Navajivan Publishing House, 1968.

The Supreme Power (edited by A.T. Hingorani), Bombay, Bhartiya Vidya Bhavan, 1963.

The Way to Communal Harmony (comp. and edited by U.R. Rao), Ahmedabad, Navajivan Publishing House, 1963.

Trusteeship (comp. by Ravindra Kelekar), Ahmedabad, Navajivan Publishing House, 1960.

Truth is God (comp. by R.K. Prabhu), Ahmedabad, Navajivan Publishing House, 1955.

Unto the Last: A Paraphrase, Ahmedabad, Navajivan Publishing House, 1956.

Untouchability, Ahmedabad, Navajivan Publishing House, 1959.

Voluntary Poverty (comp. by Ravindra Kelekar), Ahmedabad, Navajivan Publishing House, 1961.

Women and Social Injustice, Ahmedabad, Navajivan Publishing House, 1954.

Women's Role in Society (comp. by R.K. Prabhu), Ahmedabad, Navajivan Publishing House, 1959.

Journals

Harijan, Ahmedabad, Navajivan Publishing House, 1933–1948.

Indian Opinion, Natal, South Africa, 1903–1914.

Young India, Ahmedabad, Navajivan Publishing House, 1919–1932.

Correspondence

Bapu's Letter to Mira (edited by Mira), Ahmedabad, Navajivan Publishing House, 1949.

Letter From and To Gandhi at the Office of the Collected Works of Gandhi, New Delhi, Ministry of Information, Government of India.

Letters From and To Gandhi at the Gandhi Smarak Nidhi, New Delhi.

Letters From and To Gandhi at the Sabarmati Sangrahalaya, Ahmedabad.

Miscellaneous

Encyclopaedia Britannica, Chicago, Willion Benton Publisher, 1969, Vol. 9.

Encyclopaedia of Philosophy, New York, Macmillan Company, Free Press, Vol. IV.

Encyclopaedia of Social Sciences, New York, Macmillan Company, Vol. VII and VIII, 1953.

Mohandas Karamchand Gandhi: A Bibliography, (A project of the Indian Council of Social Science Research), New Delhi, ICSSR, Published by Orient Longman, 1974.

The Encyclopaedia of Gandhian Thought, New Delhi, T. Anand Hingorani and A. Ganga Hingorani, All India Congress Committee (I), 1985.

The New Encyclopaedia Britannica, Chicago, 1985, Vol. 20.

Secondary Sources

Books

Afaque, Khan Mohammad (1986) *Gandhian Approach to Communal Harmony: A Critical Study,* Delhi, Ajanta Publication.

Ahluwalia, B.K. (ed.) (1968) *Facts of Gandhi,* New Delhi, Lakshmi Book Store.

Alexander, Horace (1949) *Social and Political Ideas of Mahatma Gandhi,* New Delhi, Indian Council of World Affairs.

——. (1984) *Gandhi through Western Eyes,* Philadelphia, New Society Publishers.

Anand, Mulk Raj (1990) *The Humanism of M.K. Gandhi,* Chandigarh, The Registrar, University of Punjab.

Arnold, David (2001) *Gandhi,* London, Longman, An imprint of Pearson Education.

Asha Rani (1981) *Gandhian Non-violence and India's Freedom Struggle,* Delhi, Shree Publishing House.

Bakshi, S.R. (1987) *Gandhi and Hindu Muslim Unity,* New Delhi, Deep and Deep Publications.

Bandyopadhyay, J. (1969) *Social and Political Thought of Gandhi,* New Delhi, Allied Publishers.

Bedi, B.P.L. (ed.) (1948) *Saint of Human Rights: Gandhi,* Delhi, Unity Book Club of India.

Benays, Robert (1931) *Naked Fakir,* London, Victor Gollancz Ltd.

Bharathi, K.S. (1990) *Satyagraha of Mahatma Gandhi,* New Delhi, Indus Publishing Company.

——. (1991) *Socio-Religious Thought of Mahatma Gandhi,* New Delhi, Concept Publishing Company.

Bhattacharya, Buddhadeva (1969) *Evolution of the Political Philosophy of Mahatma Gandhi,* Calcutta, Calcutta Book House.

Biswas, S.C. (ed.) (1990) *Gandhi: Theory and Practice, Social Impact and Contemporary Relevance,* Shimla, Indian Institute of Advanced Study.

Bondurant, John V. (1959) *Conquest of Violence: The Gandhian Philosophy of Conflict,* Bombay, Oxford University Press.

Bose, N.K. (1966) *Gandhiji: The Man and His Mission,* Bombay, Bhartiya Vidya Bhawan.

Chakrabarti, Mohit (1922) *Gandhian Humanism,* New Delhi, Concept Publishing Company.

——. (1994) *Mahatma Gandhi: A Revaluation,* New Delhi, Ashish Publishing House.

Chakravarty, Amiya (1945) *Mahatma Gandhi and the Modern World,* Calcutta, Book House.

Choudhuri, Manmohan (1989) *Exploring Gandhi,* New Delhi, Gandhi Peace Foundation.

Dadhich, Naresh (1993) *Gandhi and Existentialism,* Jaipur, Rawat Publications.

——. (2003) *Non-Violence Peace and Politics: Understanding Gandhi,* Jaipur, Aavishkar Publishers.

Dalton, Dennis (1999) *Gandhi's Love: Nonviolence in Action,* New York, Oxford University Press.

Dandavate, Madhu (1977) *Marx and Gandhi,* Bombay, Popular Prakashan.

Desai, Mahadev (1929) *The Story of Bardoli,* Ahmedabad, Navajivan Publishing House.

——. (1951) *Righteous Struggle,* Ahmedabad, Navajivan Publishing House.

Desai, V.G. (1953) *Diary of Mahadev Desai,* Ahmedabad, Navajivan Publishing House.

Dhavan, Gopi Nath (1962) *The Political Philosophy of Mahatma Gandhi,* Ahmedabad, Navajivan Publishing House.

Dhebar, U.N. (1964) *Gandhiji: A Practical Idealist,* Bombay, Bhartiya Vidya Bhavan.

Dhiman, O.P. (1971) *Gandhian Philosophy: A Critical and Comprehensive Study,* Ambala Cant., Indian Publications.

Dope, J.J. (1909) *M.K. Gandhi: An Indian Patriot in South Africa,* Madras, G.A. Natesan & Co.

Dutta, D.K. (1980) *Social, Moral and Religious Philosophy of Mahatma Gandhi: A Critical Analysis,* New Delhi, Intellectual Book Corner.

Elst, Koenraad (2001) *Gandhi and Godse: A Review and A Critique,* New Delhi, Voice of India.

Erikson, Erik H. (1969) *Gandhi's Truth: On the Origins of Militant Non-violence,* New York, W.W. Norton & Company.

Fisher, Louis (1950) *The Life of Mahatma Gandhi,* New York, Harper & Bros Publications.

Fox, Richard (1989) *Gandhian Utopia: Experiments with Culture,* Boston, Beacon Press.

Gandhi, Arun (ed.) (1994) *World without Violence,* New Delhi, Wiley Eastern Ltd..

Gangal, S.C. (1960) *The Gandhian Way to World Peace,* Bombay, Vora & Co..

Gora (1951) *An Atheist with Gandhi,* Ahmedabad, Navajivan Publishing House.

Hick, John (ed.) (1989) *Gandhi's Significance for Today,* London, Macmillan Press.

Hunt, James D. (1986) *Gandhi and the Nonconformists Encounters in South Africa,* New Delhi, Promilla & Co. Publishers.

Hussain, S. Abid (1959) *The Way to Gandhi and Nehru,* Bombay, Asia Publishing House.

Iyer, Raghavan N. (ed.) (1973) *The Moral and Political Thought of Mahatma Gandhi,* London, Oxford University Press.

——. (1986) *The Moral and Political Writings of Mahatma Gandhi,* 3 Vols., Oxford, Clarendon Press.

Iyer, Raghavan N.(ed.) (1991) *The Essential Writings of Mahatma Gandhi,* Delhi, Oxford University Press.

Jones, E. Stanley (1963) *Mahatma Gandhi: An Interpretation,* Lucknow, Lucknow Publishing House.

Joshi, Pushpa (comp.) (1988) *Gandhi on Women,* Ahmedabad, Navajivan Publishing House.

Kalelkar, Kakasaheb (ed.) (1952) *To Ashram Sisters,* (from 6–12–1926 to 30–12–1929), (trans. by Arvindlal L. Mazmudar), Ahmedabad, Navajivan Publishing House.

Kapoor, A.N. and V.P. Gupta (eds) (1995) *A Dictionary of Gandhian Thought,* Delhi, Ambe Books.

Karna, K.K.L. (1981) *Mahatma Gandhi: Contribution to Hinduism,* New Delhi, Classical Publishing Company.

Kothari, M.M. (1996) *Critique of Gandhi,* Jodhpur, Critique Publications.

Kripalani, J.B. (1970) *Gandhi: His Life and Thought,* New Delhi, Publication Division, Ministry of Information and Broadcasting, Government of India.

Kripalani, Krishna (comp. and edited) (1958) *All Men are Brothers,* Ahmedabad, Navajivan Publishing House.

Kripalani, R.R. (1947) *Gandhi, Tagore and Nehru,* Bombay, Hind Kitabs.

Kumarappa, J.C. (1948) *Gandhian Economy and Other Essays,* Wardha, J.C. Kumarappa.

Lohia, Ram Manohar (1963) *Marx, Gandhi and Socialism,* Hyderabad, Navahind.

Mahadevan, T.K. (ed.) (1970) *Truth and Non-Violence,* New Delhi, Gandhi Peace Foundations.

Mathai, M.P., M.S. John and Siby K. Joseph (eds) (2002) *Meditations on Gandhi,* New Delhi, Concept Publishing Company.

Mathur, J.S. (1990) *Peace, Non- Violence and World Order,* (Gandhian Perspective), 2 Vols., Allahabad, Vora Publishers & Distributors.

Mazumdar, B.B. (ed.) (1957) *Gandhian Concept of State,* Calcutta, M.C. Sarkar and Sons Private Ltd.

Mishra, Anil Dutta (1995) *Fundamentals of Gandhism,* New Delhi, Mittal Publications.

Mukerjee, Hiren (1979) *Gandhi: A Study,* New Delhi, Peoples Publishing House.

Mukherjee, Subrata (1991) *Gandhian Thought: Marxist Interpretation,* New Delhi, Deep and Deep Publications.

Naess, Arne (1947) *Gandhi and Group Conflict: An Exploration of Satyagraha, Theoretical Background,* Oslo, Universitetsforlaget.

Nair, C.S. (1922) *Gandhi and Anarchy,* Madras, Tata Printing Works.

Nanda, B.R. (2002) *In Search of Gandhi: Essays and Reflections,* New York, Oxford University Press.

Nanda, B.R. (ed.) (1995) *Mahatma Gandhi: 125 Years,* New Delhi, Wiley Eastern Ltd.

Nateshan, G.A. (ed.) (1930) *Mahatma Gandhi: The Man and His Mission,* Madras, G.A. Natesan & Co.

Paranjape, Makarand (1993) *Decolonization and Development: Hind Svaraj Revisioned,* New Delhi, Sage Publications.

Parekh, Bhikhu (1989) *Colonialism, Tradition and Reform: An Analysis of Gandhi's Political Discourse,* New Delhi, Sage Publications.

——. (1989) *Gandhi's Political Philosophy: A Critical Examination,* London, Macmillan Press.

Patil, V.T. (ed.) (1983) *Studies on Gandhi,* Bangalore, Sterling Publishers Pvt. Ltd.

Powel, Paul F. (1960) *Gandhi on World Affairs,* Washington, Public Affairs Place.

Powel, Paul F. (ed.) (1971) *The Meanings of Gandhi,* Hawaii, The University Press of Hawaii.

Prabhu, R.K. and U.R. Rao (comp. and edited) (1967) *The Mind of Mahatma Gandhi,* Ahmedabad, Navajivan Publishing House.

Prasad, Mahadev (1958) *Social Philosophy of Mahatma Gandhi,* Gorakhpur, Vishwavidyalaya Prakashan.

——. (ed.) (1985) *Hind Swaraj: A Fresh Look,* New Delhi, Gandhi Peace Foundation.

Prasad, Nageshwar (ed.) (1990) *Gandhi: Historical and Contemporary Perspectives,* New Delhi, Segment Book Distributors.

Pyare Lal, (1950) *A Pilgrimage for Peace,* Ahmedabad, Navajivan Publishing House.

Radhakrishanan, S. (ed.) (1968) *Mahatma Gandhi: 100 years,* New Delhi, Gandhi Peace Foundations.

Raman, T.A. (1943) *What Does Gandhi Want?* New York, Oxford University Press.

Ramchandran, C. and T.K. Mahadevan (ed.) (1970) *Quest for Gandhi,* New Delhi, Gandhi Peace Foundation.

Rao, U.R. (1969) *Let Us Know Gandhiji,* New Delhi, Publication Division, Government of India.

Rathnam, Chetty K.M. (1991) *Sarvodaya and Freedom: A Gandhian Appraisal,* New Delhi, Discovery Publishing House.

Renolds, R. (1952) *A Quest for Gandhi,* New York, Double day and co.

Rolla, Romain (1926) *Mahatma Gandhi: The Man Who Become One with the Universal Being,* (trans. by C.P. Groth), The Swarthomore Press Ltd.

Rothermund, Dietmar (1992) *Mahatma Gandhi: An Essay in Political Biography,* New Delhi, Manohar Publishers.

Roy, Himansu (2001) *Poverty of Gandhian Philosophy,* New Delhi, Concept Publishing Company.

Roy, Ramashray (1984) *Gandhi: Soundings in Political Philosophy,* Delhi, Chanakya Publications.

——. (1985) *Self and Society: A Study in Gandhian Thought,* New Delhi, Sage Publications.

Roy, Ramashray (ed.) (1986) *Contemporary Crisis and Gandhi,* Delhi, Discovery Publishing House.

Sharma, B.S. (1956) *Gandhi as a Political Thinker,* Allahabad, The Indian Press.

Sharma, Sri Ram (1985) *Gandhi: The Man and the Mahatma,* Chandigarh, Rajan.

Singh, K.N. (1979) *Gandhi and Marx: An Ethic-Philosophical Study,* Patna, Associated Book Agency.

Singh, M. Kirti (1994) *Philosophical Import of Gandhism,* Delhi, South Asia Publications.

Singh, Ramjee (1993) *Gandhi and the Twenty First Century,* New Delhi, Peace Publishers.

Singh, Ramjee (ed.) (1997) *Gandhi and the Future of Humanity,* Varanasi, Manak Publications Pvt. Ltd.

Tagore, R.N. (1932) *Mahatmaji and Depressed Humanity,* Calcutta, Vishwabharati.

Tahtinen, Unto (1979) *The Core of Gandhian Philosophy,* New Delhi, Abhinav Publications.

Tendulkar, D.G. (1951–54) *Mahatma: Life of Mohandas Karamchand Gandhi,* Bombay, V.K. Jhaveri and D.G. Tendulkar.

Terchek, Ronald J. (1998) *Gandhi: Struggling for Autonomy,* New Delhi, Vistaar Publications.

Unnithan, T.K.N. (1956) *Gandhi and Free India: A Socio-Economic Study,* Bombay, Vora & Co.

——. (1979) *Gandhi and Social Change,* Jaipur, Rawat Publications.

Verma, V.P. (1959) *The Political Philosophy of Mahatma Gandhi and Sarvodaya,* Delhi, Lakshmi Narayan Agrawal.

Vettickal, Thomas (2002) *Gandhian Sarvodaya: Realizing a Realistic Utopia,* New Delhi, Gyan Publishing House.

Articles

Bhan, Susheela, "Diversity of Religions: The Indian Context", *Gandhi Marg,* Gandhi Peace Foundation, New Delhi, Vol. 25, No. 3, October-December 2003, pp. 299–318.

Bilgrami, Akeel, "Gandhi, the Philosopher", *Economic and Political Weekly,* Mumbai, September 27, 2003, pp. 4159–4165.

Bose, Atindranath, "Gandhi Man of the Past or the Future", in *Modern Review,* Calcutta, 1957, Vol. 1, No. I, pp. 21–22.

Chaudhuri, Ranjit, "Religion of Mahatma Gandhi", *Gandhi Marg,* Gandhi Peace Foundation, New Delhi, Vol. 23, No. 2, July-September 2001, pp. 167–177.

Desai, M.P., "End and Means in Politics", *Gandhi Marg,* Gandhi Peace Foundation, New Delhi, 1957, Vol. 1, No. 2, pp. 153–157.

Diwaker, R.R., "Gandhi's Spiritual Quest", in *Gandhi Marg,* Gandhi Peace Foundation, New Delhi, 1963, Vol. VII, No. 2, pp. 107–112.

Dube, M.P., "Gandhi and His Style of Leadership", Gandhi and Peace Studies, *Journal of Jaipur Peace Foundation,* January-June, 2001, pp. 3–8.

Dutta, Samar, "Mahatma Gandhi and Suffering Humanity", in *Modern Review,* Vol. 1, 26–27, May, 1970, pp. 374–377.

Gier, Nicholas F., "Gandhi and Mahayans Buddhism", *Gandhi Marg,* Gandhi Peace Foundation, New Delhi, Vol. 25, No. 2, July-September 2003, pp. 155–177.

Gier, Nicholas F., "Gandhi and The Virtue of Non-violence", *Gandhi Marg,* Gandhi Peace Foundation, New Delhi, Vol. 23, No. 3, October-December 2001, pp. 261–286.

——. "Gandhi's Philosophy: Pre-modern, Modern, or Postmodern?" *Gandhi Marg,* Gandhi Peace Foundation, New Delhi, Vol. 17, No. 3, October-December 1996, pp. 261–281.

Gokhale, B.G., "Gandhism and Socialism", *Gandhi Marg,* Gandhi Peace Foundation, New Delhi, July, 1958, pp. 258–265.

Gopinathan, K., "Gandhi and Marixism in an Era of Postmodernism", *Gandhi Marg,* Gandhi Peace Foundation, New Delhi, Vol. 23, No. 3, October-December 2001, pp. 359–363.

Gordon, Leonard A., "Mahatma Gandhi's Dialogues with Americans", *Economic and Political Weekly,* Mumbai, January 26, 2002, pp. 337–352.

Jain, Nilanjana, "The Idea of Justice in Gandhi's Socio-Political Thought", *Gandhi Marg,* Gandhi Peace Foundation, New Delhi, Vol. 23, No. 2, July-September 2001, pp. 178–187.

Jha, Sadan, "Charkha, Dear Forgotten Friend of Widows: Reading the Erasures of a Symbol", *Economic and Political Weekly,* Mumbai, July 10, 2004, pp. 3113–3120.

Jodhka, Surinder, "Nation and Village: Images of Rural India in Gandhi, Nehru and Ambedkar", *Economic and Political Weekly,* Mumbai, August 10, 2002, pp. 3343–3353.

John, M.S., "Gandhian Concept of World Order", in *Gandhian Perspective: Journal of Gandhian Studies,* Vol. V, 1992, pp. 1–22.

Kripalni, J.B., "Civil Disobedience", *Gandhi Marg*, Gandhi Peace Foundation, New Delhi, 1959, Vol. III, No. 4, pp. 251–260.

Mishra, K.P., "Gandhi and Rousseosu as Critics of Modern Civilization: A Comparative Perspective", *Gandhi Marg,* Gandhi Peace Foundation, New Delhi, Vol. 24, No. 2, July-September 2002, pp. 161–172.

Naidu, C.M., "Noakhali Riots and Mahatma Gandhi's Mission for Hindu Muslim Unity", *Gandhi and Peace Studies,* Peace Foundation Jaipur, No. 1, January-June, 2001, pp. 17–21.

Narayan, Jaya Prakash, "Gandhi and Social Revolution", *Gandhi Marg,* Gandhi Peace Foundation, New Delhi, October 1969, pp. 184–197.

Nayak, V. Tellis, "Gandhi on the Dignity of the Human Person", in *Quest for Gandhi,* pp. 371–387.

Padia, Chandrakala and Nalini Pant, "Indigenizing Political Theory: A Discourse on Gandhi", *Gandhian Perspective*, Journal of the Gandhian Institute of Studies, Varanasi, Vol. IX, No. 1, Spring, 1996, pp. 17–28.

Pandey, Upasana, "Concept of Global Non-Violence and Gandhi's Religion", *Gandhi Marg,* Gandhi Peace Foundation, New Delhi, Vol. 28, No. 4, January-March, 2007.

——. "Globalisation and Gandhi", *Mainstream*, Perspective Publications Private Ltd., September 30–October 6, 2005.

——. "Ramrajya and Moral Values", *Mulya Vimarsh,* Center for Value Education, Banaras Hindu University, Varanasi, July-December 2006.

Pandey, Upasana, "Rastra Nirman Aur Mahatma Gandhi", *Mulya Vimarsh,* Center for Value Education, Banaras Hindu University, Varanasi, Jan-June, 2007.

——. "Science, Society and Spirituality", in Gandhian Philosophy, *Mainstream,* September 30–October 6, 2006.

——. *Problem with Postmodern Gandhi, Mainstream,* September 29–October 4, 2007.

Parekh, Bhikhu, "Gandhian Vision of Life and Peace", *Bulletin of Peace Proposals,* Vol. 18, No. 3, 1987, pp. 469–476.

Patil, V.T. and A.S. Anikivi, "An Enquiry into the Gandhian Model of Democracy", *Gandhi Marg,* New Delhi, Vol. 5, No. 6, September 1983, pp. 338–346.

Patil, V.T., "Gandhi's Concept of Decentralisation: An Analysis", *Gandhi Marg,* New Delhi, Vol. 3, No. 7, October 1981, pp. 384–403.

Prasad, A., "The Gandhian Model of Democratic Socialism", *Gandhi Marg,* Gandhi Peace Foundation, New Delhi, Vol. 4, No. 9, December, 1982, pp. 786–795.

Prasad, Nageshwar, "J.P's Philosophical Quest", *Gandhi, Marg,* Gandhi Peace Foundation, New Delhi, Vol. 24, No. 3, October-December 2002.

Prasad, Rajendra, "Gandhi, Globalisation, and Quality of Life: A Study in the Ethics of Development", *Gandhi Marg,* Gandhi Peace Foundation, New Delhi, Vol. 23, No. 2, July-September 2001, pp. 154–166.

Prasad, Shambhu, "Towards an Understanding of Gandhi's Views on Science", *Economic and Political Weekly,* Mumbai, September 29, 2001, pp. 3721–3732.

Radha Krishnan, N., "Re-interpreting Gandhi in the New Millennium", *Journal of Jaipur Peace Foundation,* No. 2, July-December 2001, pp. 16–18.

Rao, B. Shiva, Mahatma Gandhi: "A Champion of Human Rights", *Khadi Gramodyog,* June, 1968, pp. 643–648.

Sahni, Geetanjali, "Gandhi and the Birth of Modern India", *Gandhi Marg,* Gandhi Peace Foundation, New Delhi, Vol. 24, No. 3, October-December 2002, pp. 335–338.

Sarangi, Parkash, "Protection of Human Rights as Precondition of Peace: An Analysis of the Ideas of Kant and Gandhi", *Journal of Jaipur Peace Foundation,* No. 1, January-June. 2001, pp. 9–16.

Sattar, Abdul, "Gandhi's Humanism and Contemporary Society", *Gandhi Marg,* New Delhi, 1991, Vol. 12, No. 4, pp. 444–453.

Saxena, S.K. and Chandrakala Padia, "Gandhi on Women and Liberty", *Gandhi Marg,* Gandhi Peace Foundation, New Delhi, Vol. 22, No. 3, October-December 2000, pp. 291–299.

Sergo, Mikoyan, "Gandhi's Contribution to Humanist India", *Link,* Vol. 12, August-October, 1996, p. 42.

Sharma, M.L., "Human Rights: A Gandhian Perspective", *Gandhi Marg,*Gandhi Peace Foundation, New Delhi, Vol. 23, No. 1, April-June, 2001, pp. 81–97.

Sinha, V.C., "Gandhi: An Approach to Rural Industrialisation", *Journal of Gandhian Studies,* Vol. 7, No. 2, July 1980, pp. 187–200.

Subrahmanya, M.H. Bala, "Small Industry and Globalisation: Implications, Performance and Prospects", *Economic and Political Weekly,* Mumbai, May 1, 2004, pp. 1826–1834.

Terchek, Ronald J., "Problematizing Modernity: Gandhi's Decentering Impulse", *Gandhi Marg,* Gandhi Peace Foundation, New Delhi, Vol. 23, No. 1, April-June, 2001, pp. 5–20.

Tiwari, A.P., "Gandhian Approach to Property Relations and Class Conflict", *Journal of Gandhian Studies,* Vol. 3, No. 10, January, 1975, pp. 197–207.

Tripathi, A., "Gandhi's Social Philosophy", *Journal of Gandhian Studies,* Vol. 7, No. 28, pp. 139–152.

Walker, "Gandhi's Message to the World", *Vishwabharati Quarterly,* Gandhi Memorial Peace, October, 1949, pp. 53–59.

Bibliography on Postmodernism

Primary Sources

Books

Baudrillard, Jean (1988) *Selected Writings,* (ed.) Mark Poster, Stanford, Stanford University Press.

——. (1993) *From Symbolic Exchange and Death,* (trans. by Lain H. Grant), London, Sage Publications.

Bell, Bernard Iddings (1939) *Religion for Living: A Book for Postmodernist,* London, The Religious Book Club.

Bell, Daniel (1976) *The Coming of Postindustrial Society,* New York, Basic Books.

Bentham, Jeremy (1879) *An Introduction to The Principles of Morals and Legislations,* Cambridge, Oxford Press,

Butler, Judith (1990) *Gender Trouble,* New York, Routledge.

——. (1993) *Bodies that Matter,* New York, Routledge.

Dahrendorf, Ralf (1979) *Life Chances,* Chicago, University of Chicago Press.

de Onis, Federico (1934) *Antologia De La Poesia Espanola A Hispanoamericana,* Madrid.

de Saussure, Ferdinand (1966) *Course in General Linguistics* (trans. By Wade Baskin), New York, McGrew Hill.

Derrida, Jacques (1980) *De Carte Postal,* Chicago, University of Chicago Press.

——. (1976) *Of Grammatology,* Baltimore, Johns Hopkins University Press.

——. (1981) *Writing and Deference,* London, Routledge Publishers.

——. (1995) *The Gift of Death* (translated by David Wills), Chicago, The University of Chicago Press.

Descartes, Rene (1931) *Discourse in Method,* (trans. by Haldon and Ross), Cambridge, Cambridge University Press.

Eagleton, Terry (1996) *The Illusions of Postmodernism,* Oxford, Blackwell Publishers.

Foucault, Michel (1984) *What is Enlightenment?,* Pantheon, New York.

——. (1967) *Madness and Civilization,* London, Tavistock.

——. (1972) *The Archaeology of Knowledge,* (translated by A.M. Sheridan Smith), London, Tavistock Publications.

Foucault, Michel (1973) *The Birth of the Clinic,* London, Tavistock.

——. (1980) *Power/Knowledge,* (translated and edited Colin Gordon, Leo Marshall, John Mepham and Kate Soper), New York, Pantheon Books.

Freud, Sigmund (1961) *Civilization and its Discontents,* (trans. by James Strachey), New York, Norton Press.

Giddens, Anthony (1990) *The Consequences of Modernity,* Cambridge, Polity Press.

——. (1991) *Modernity and Self-Identify,* Cambridge, Polity Press.

——. (1993) *New Role of Sociological Methods,* Cambridge, Polity Press.

Gott, Richard (1986) *Modernism and Postmodernism: The Crisis of Contemporary Culture,* Guardian.

Gramsci, Antonio (1978) *Some Aspects of the Southern Question,* (trans. Quintin Hoare), New York, International Publishers.

Guha, Ranjit (ed.) (1982) *Subaltern Studies I: Writing on South Asian History and Society,* Delhi, Oxford University Press.

Habermas, Jurgen (1976) *Legitimation Crisis*, Cambridge, Polity Press.

——. (1979) *Communication and the Evolution of Society,* (trans. by Thomas McCarthy), London, Heinemann.

——. (1985) *Modernity: An Incomplete Project,* Cambridge, Pluto Press.

Hall, David (1991) *Culture and Modernity: East-West Philosophic Perspectives,* (eds) Eliot Deutsch, Honolulu, University of Hawaii Press.

Harvey, David (1996) *The Condition of Postmodernity,* Cambridge, Blackwell Publishers.

Hassan, Ihab (1968) *The Literature of Silence,* New York, Knopf Publishers.

——. (1975) *Paracriticisms: Seven Speculations of the Times,* Urbana, University of Illinois Press.

——. (1987) *The Postmodern Turn: Essays in Postmodern Theory and Culture,* Columbus, Ohio State University Press.

Hobbes, Thomas (1947) *Leviathan,* (trans. by New York, Oxford University Press.

Horkheimer, Max and Theodor Adorno (1972) *Dialectic of Enlightenment,* (trans. by John Cumming), New York, Seabury.

Jameson, Fredric (1992) *Postmodernism or the Cultural Logic of Late Capitalism,* London, Verso.

——. (2000) *The Cultural Turn: Selected Writings on the Postmodern, 1983–1998,* London, Verso Publications.

Jenkins, Keith (1991) *Re-thinking History,* London, Routledge.

——. (ed.) (1997) *The Postmodern History,* Reader, London, Routledge.

Jenks, Charles (1995) *The Architecture of the Lumping Universe,* London, Academy Editions.

——. (1995) *The Language of Postmodern Architecture,* London, Academy Editions.

Kuhn, Thomas (1962) *The Structure of Scientific Revolutions,* Chicago, University of Chicago Press.

Laclau, E. and C. Mouffe (1985) *Hegemony and Socialist Strategy,* London, Verso Publications.

Locke, John (1946) *The Second Treaties of Civil Government*, edited by J.W. Cough, New York, Oxford.

Lyotard, Jean Francois (1997) *The Postmodern Condition: A Report on Knowledge*, (trans. by Geoff Bennington and Brian Massumi), Manchester, Manchester University Press.

Machiavelli, Niccolo (1903) *The Prince* (translated Luigi Ricci) London, Oxford University Press.

——. (1950) *The Prince and the Discourses*, New York, Random House.

MacIntyre, Alsdair (1981) *After Virtue*, Notre Dame, University of Notre Dame Press.

Marcuse, Herbert (1964) *One Dimensional Man*, London, Routledge Publishers.

McDougall, William (1908) *Introduction to Social Psychology*, London, Cambridge.

——. (1920) *The Group Mind*, New York.

——. (1936) *Psychoanalysis and Social Psychology*, London.

McGuigan, Jim (1992) *Cultural Pluralism*, London, Routledge Publishers.

——. (1996) *Culture and the Public Sphere*, London, Routledge Publishers.

——. (1997) *Cultural Methodologies*, London, Sage Publications.

Nicholson, L. (ed.) (1990) *Feminism/Post modernism*, New York, Routledge.

Nicholson, L. and S. Seidman (eds) (1995) *Social Postmodernism*, Cambridge, Cambridge University Press.

Nietzsche, F.W. (1968) *The Will to Power*, New York, Vintage Books.

Pannwitz, Rudolf (1917) *Die Krisis der Europaeischen Kultur*, Nuremberg, Hans Carl.

Parson, Talcott (1951) *The Social System*, London, Routledge & Kegan Paul.

Popper, Karl (1952) *The Logic of Scientific Discovery*, London, Hutchinson Publication.

——. (1971) *The Open Society and its Enemies*, Vol. I, Princeton, Princeton University Press.

Rengger, N.J. (1995) *Political Theory, Modernity and Post-modernity*, Oxford, Blackwell.

Rorty, Richard (1985) *Solidarity or Objectivity?* New York, Columbia University Press.

Rousseau, J.J. (1968) *The Social Contract*, Penguin, Harmondsworth.

Sabine, G.H. (1973) *A History of Political Theory*, Oxford, Oxford Publishers.

Spencer, Herbert (1884) *Man versus the State*, New York, Oxford,

Taylor, Charles (1990) *Sources of Self*, Cambridge, Cambridge University Press.

Toynbee, Arnold (1939) *A Study of History*, London, Oxford University Press.

Venturi, Robert (1966) *Complexity and Contradiction in Architecture*, New York, Museum of Modern Art.

Wayper, C.L. (1969) *Political Thought*, London, St. Paul's House Warwick, Lane.

Weber, Max (1946) *Essays in Sociology*, (trans. and edited by H.H. Gerth and C. Wright Mills), New York, Oxford University Press.

Weber, Max (1964) *The Theory of Social and Economic Organization,* London, McMillion Press.

Wise, John (1861) *Vindication of the Government of New England,* Boston, Boston Publishers.

Wittgenstein, Ludwig (1961) *Tractatu Logico-Philosophicus,* (trans. by D.F. Pears and B.F. McGuinness), London, Routledge and Kegan Paul.

Woodworth, R.S. (1948) *Contemporary School of Psychology,* New York, Ronald Press.

Young, Iris Marion (1990) *Justice and the Politics of Difference,* Princeton, Princeton University Press.

Secondary Sources

Avnon, Dan and Avner de-Shalit (1999) *Liberalism and its Practice,* London, Routledge.

Baert, Patrick (1998) *Social Theory in the Twentieth Century,* Cambridge, Polity Press.

Barker, Chris (2000) *Cultural Studies: Theory and Practice,* New Delhi, Sage Publications.

Barker, Philip (1998) *Michel Foucault: An Introduction,* Edinburgh, Edinburgh University Press.

Becker, Carl (1932) *The Heavenly City of the Eighteenth Century Philosophers,* New Heaven, Yale University Press.

Beetham, David (1991) *The Legitimation of Power,* London, Macmillan Press.

Berry, Jeffrey M. (1999) *The New Liberalism: The Rising Power of Citizen Groups,* Washington D.C., Brookings Institution Press.

Bertens, Hans and Joseph Natoli (eds) (2002) *Postmodernism: The Key Figures,* Oxford, Blackwell Publishers.

Best, S. and D. Kellner (1991) *Postmodern Theory: Critical Interrogations,* London, Macmillan Publishers.

Bradshaw, David (ed.) (2003) *A Concise Companion to Modernism,* Oxford, Blackwell Publishers.

Britt, David (ed.) (1989) *Modern Art: Imperialism to Post-Modernism,* London, Thames and Hudson.

Brooks, Ann (1997) *Postfeminism: Feminism, Cultural Theory and Cultural Forms,* London, Routledge.

Cahoone, Lawrence (ed.) (2003) *From Modernism to Postmodernism: An Anthology,* Oxford, Blackwell Publishers.

Callinicos, Alex (1989) *Against Postmodernism: A Marxist Critique,* Cambridge, Polity Press.

Carty, Anthony (ed.) (1990) *Postmodern Law: Enlightenment, Revolution and the Death of Man,* Edinburgh, Edinburgh University Press.

Clifford, James (1988) *The Predicament of Culture,* Cambridge MA, Harvard University Press.

Crespigny, Anthony De and Kenneth Minoguel (eds) (1975) *Contemporary Political Philosophers,* New York, Dodd, Mead & Company.

Descombes, Vincent (1980) *Modern French Philosophy,* (trans.by L. Schott-Fox and J.M. Harding), New York, Cambridge University Press.

Docherty, Thomas (ed.) (1993) *Postmodernism: A Reader,* Brighton, Harvester Wheatsheaf.

Docker, Joh (1994) *Postmodernism and Popular Culture: A Cultural History,* Cambridge, Cambridge University Press.

Doherty, Jeo, Elspeth Graham and Mo Malek (eds) (1992) *Postmodernism and the Social Sciences,* Basingstoke, Macmillan Press.

Doney, Willis (ed.) (1970) *Descartes: A Collection of Critical Essays,* London, Macmillan Press.

Edwin R.A. Seligman and Alvin Johnson (eds) (1937) *Encyclopaedia of Social Sciences,* Vol. IX-X, New York, Macmillan Publications.

Falzon, Christopher (1998) *Foucault and Social Dialogue: Beyond Fragmentation,* New York, Routledge.

Featherstone, Mike (1992) *Consumer Culture and Postmodernism,* London, Sage Publications.

Flax, Jane (1990) *Thinking Fragments: Psychoanalysis Feminism and Postmodernism in the Contemporary West,* London, Routledge.

Ghirardo, Diane (1994) *Architecture after Modernism,* London, Thames & Hudson.

Gordon, Colin (ed.) (1980) *Power/Knowledge: Selected Interviews and Other Writings 1972–1977* Micheal Foucault (trans. by Colin Gordon, Leo Marshall, John Mepham and Kate Soper), New York, Pantheon Books.

Gray, Chris Hables (1997) *Postmodern War: The New Politics of Conflict,* London, Routledge.

Hall, Stuart and Bram Gieben (eds) (2001) *Formations of Modernity,* Cambridge, Polity Press.

Hall, Stuart, David Held and Tony McGrew (eds) (1992) *Modernity and its Futures,* Cambridge, Polity Press.

Hallowell, J.H. (1950) *Main Currents in Modern Political Thought,* Durham, North Carolina.

Howar, Dick (1988) *The Politics of Critique,* London, Macmillan Press.

Johnson, John (ed.) (1936) *Oxford English Dictionary,* New York, Oxford University Press.

Kumar, Krishna (1988) *The Rise of Modern Society, Aspect of the Social and Political Development of the West,* London, Blackwell Publishers.

Kymlicka, Will (1991) *Contemporary Political Philosophy: An Introduction,* Oxford, Clarendon Press.

Larrian, Jorge (1985) *Ideology and Cultural Identity: Modernity and the Third World Presence,* Cambridge, Pluto Press.

Lee, Alison (1990) *Realism and Power: Postmodern British Fiction,* London, Routledge.

Lessnoff, Michael H. (1999) *Political Philosophers of the Twentieth Century,* Oxford, Blackwell Publishers.

Lewis, Reina and Sara Mills (eds) (2003) *Feminist Postcolonial Theory: A Reader,* Edinburgh, Edinburgh University Press.

Lyon, David (1994) *Postmodernity*, Buckingham, Open University Press.

——. (2002) *Concepts in Social Thought: Postmodernity,* New Delhi, Viva Books Private Ltd.

Marsh, R.M. (1967) *Comparative Sociology,* New York, Harcourt.

McGowan, John (1991) *Postmodernism and its Critics,* New York, Cornell University Press.

McIlwain, C.H. (1932) *The Growth of Political Thought in the West,* New York, Macmillan.

Mulhall, Stephen and Adam Swift (1996) *Liberals and Communitarians,* Cambridge, Blackwell Publishers.

Mulhern, Francis (ed.) (1992) *Contemporary Marxist Literary Criticism,* London, Polity Press.

Nelson, Cary and Lawrence Grossberg (eds) (1988) *Marxism and the Interpretation of Culture,* Champaign, University of Illinois Press.

Norris, Christopher (1993) *The Truth about Postmodernism,* Oxford, Blackwell Publishers.

——. (1994) *Truth and Ethics of Criticism, Knowledge and Human Interests,* Manchester, Manchester University Press.

Owen, David (ed. (1997) *Sociology after Postmodernism,* London, Sage Publishers.

Pandey, Rajendra (1988) *Modernization and Social Change,* New Delhi, Criterion Publication.

Parekh, Bhikhu (1982) *Contemporary Political Thinkers,* Oxford, Martin Robertson.

——. (2000) *Rethinking Multiculturalism: Cultural Diversity and Political Theory,* London, Macmillian Press Ltd.

Patterson, Dennis (ed.) (1994) *Postmodernism and Law,* Aldershot, Darmouth Publishing.

Powell, Jim (2001) *Postmodernism for Beginners,* Hyderabad, Orient Longman Ltd.

Ray, B.N. (ed.) (2000) *Contemporary Political Thinking,* New Delhi, Kanishka Publishers.

Roberts, John (1990) *Postmodernism, Politics and Art,* Manchester, Manchester University Press.

Rose, Margaret (1991) *The Postmodern and the Postindustrial: A Critical Analysis,* Cambridge, Cambridge University Press.

Ross, Andrew (ed.) (1988) *Universal Abandon: The Politics of Postmodernism,* Minneapolis, University of Minnesota Press.

Ross, Andrew and Tricia Rose (eds) (1994) *Microphone Friends: Youth Music and Youth Culture,* New York and London, Routledge.

Roy, Ramashray (2002) *Politics and Society: A New Interpretation,* Delhi, Shipra Publishers.

Sardar, Ziauddin (1998) *Postmodernism and the Other: The New Imperialism of Western Culture,* London, Pluto Press.

Seidman, Stevan (ed.) (1994) *The Postmodern Turn: New Perspectives on Social Theory,* Cambridge, Cambridge University Press.

Shapiro, Ron (1998) *Surviving Postmodernism: Some Ethical and not so Ethical Debates in the Media and Universities,* Delhi, Prestige Publishers.

Sheridan, Alan (1984) *Michael Foucault: The Will to Truth,* London, Routledge Publishers.

Simpson, David (1995) *The Academic Postmodern and the Rule of Literature: A Report on Half Knowledge,* Chicago, University of Chicago Press.

Smart, Barry (1991) *Modern Conditions and Postmodern Controversies,* London, Routledge.

Smelser, Neil J. and Paul B. Baltes (eds) (2001) *International Encyclopaedia of the Social and Behavioral Sciences,* Cambridge, Cambridge University Press.

Smith, Steve, Ken Booth and Marysia Zalewski (eds) (1996) *International Theory: Positivism and Beyond,* Cambridge, Cambridge University Press.

Swingewood, Alan (1998) *Cultural Theory and the Problem of Modernity,* London, Macmillan Press.

Troeltsch, Ernest (1931) *The Social Teaching of the Christian Churches,* London, Macmillan Press.

Turner, Bryan S. (ed.) (1990) *Theories of Modernity and Postmodernity,* New Delhi, Sage Publications.

Waugh, Patrica (1992) *Practising Postmodernism Reading Modernism,* London, University of Durham.

Williams, James (1998) *Lyotard: Towards A Postmodern Philosophy,* Oxford, Polity Press.

Williams, James (2000) *Lyotard and the Political,* London, Routledge.

Woods, Tim (1999) *Beginning Postmodernism*, Manchester, Manchester University Press.

Woodworth, R.S. (1948) *Contemporary School of Psychology,* New York, Ronald Press.

Articles

Charkaborty, Chandrima, "Subaltern Studies, Bollywood and Lagan", *Economic and Political Weekly,* Mumbai, May 10, 2003, pp. 1879–1884.

Cooper, Laurence D., "Human Nature and the Love of Wisdom: Rousseau's Hidden and Modified Platonism", *The Journal of Politics,* Blackwell Publishers, Vol. 64, No. 1, February 2002, pp. 108–125.

D.N., "Localisation as an Alternative to Globalisation", *Economic and Political Weekly,* Mumbai, June 7, 2003, pp. 2246–2247.

De, Barun, "Geopolitics and Regional Identity: South Asia's North-West Frontiers", *Economic and Political Weekly,* September, 14, 2002, pp. 3812–3817.

Dubhashi, R.R., "People's Movement against Global Capitalism", *Economic and Political Weekly,* Mumbai, February 9, 2002, pp. 537–543.

Essays Review, "What is Living and What is Dead?", in The Interpretation of Hegel, *Political Theory: An International Journal of Political Philosophy,* Sage Publications, Vol. 29, No. 2, April 2001.

Gibson, James L. and Amanda Gouws, "Making Tolerance Judgements: Effects of Contents, Local and National", *The Journal of Politics,* Blackwell Publishers, Vol. 63, No. 4, November 2001, pp. 1067–1090.

Halberstam, Michael, "Totalitarianism and the Modern Conception of Politics", *Political Theory: An International Journal of Political Philosophy,* Sage Publications, Vol. 29, No. 4, August, 2001, pp. 595–601.

Huckfeldt, Robert, Paul E. Johnson and John Sprague, "Political Environments, Political Dynamics and the Survival of Disagreement", *The Journal of Politics,* Blackwell Publishing, Vol. 64, No. 1, February 2002, pp. 1–21.

Laborde, Cecile, "The Culture(s) of the Republic: Nationalism and Multi-culturalism in French Republican Thought", *Political Theory: An International Journal of Political Philosophy,* Sage Publications, Vol. 29, No. 5, October 2001, pp. 716–735.

Mayer, Robert, "Michael Walzer, Industrial Democracy and Complex Equality", *Political Theory: An International Journal of Political Philosophy,* Sage Publications, Vol. 29, No. 2, April, 2001, pp. 237–261.

Menon, Nivedita, "Citizenship and Passive Revolution: Interpreting the First Amendment", *Economic and Political Weekly,* May 1, 2004, pp. 1812–1819.

Mishra, K.P., "Gandhi and Rousseau as Critics of Modern Civilization: A Comparative Perspective", *Gandhi Marg,* Vol. 24, No. 2, July-September 2002, pp. 161–172.

Pandian, M.S.S., "One Step Outside Modernity: Caste, Identity Politics and Public Sphere", *Economic and Political Weekly,* May 4, 2002, pp. 1735–1741.

Patten, Alan, "Political Theory and Language Policy", *Political Theory: An International Journal of Political Philosophy,* Sage Publications, Vol. 29, No. 5, October 2001, pp. 691–715.

Puri, Bharati, "Deconstructing the Dalai Lama on Tibet", *Economic and Political Weekly,* August 24, 2002, pp. 3500–3503.

Index